Horizons of Hope

Reality in disability

Brian H Edwards

DayOne

© Day One Publications 2000

Scripture quotations are from The New King James Version.
Copyright © 1990, 1985, 1983 by Thomas Nelson, Inc.
and The New International Version © 1973, 1978, 1984, International Bible Society.
Published by Hodder and Stoughton, unless otherwise stated.

British Library Cataloguing in Publication Data available
1 903 087 023

Published by Day One Publications
3 Epsom Business Park, Kiln Lane, Epsom, Surrey KT17 1JF.
01372 728 300 FAX 01372 722 400
e-mail address: sales@dayone.co.uk
web site: www.dayone.co.uk

Designed by Steve Devane and printed by Clifford Frost Ltd, Wimbledon SW19 2SE

Dedication

This book is dedicated to the memory of Barbara, a wonderful wife and mother whose patient endurance, deep love for the Lord and longing to serve him, was an example to all who knew her. Thank you Lord, for Barbara.

Contents

God often permits the things that he hates to accomplish what he loves. The thing he loves most is to see his people finding salvation and hope in the gospel. *Horizons of hope* draws together the experiences of people who have known serious disability, but who have found that God meets all their needs. It is a book of hope and inspiration.

Joni Eareckson Tada
January 2000

The value of meanwhile

The side room Barbara occupied when she arrived at Frimley Park Hospital in Surrey overlooked a small quadrangle that was well stocked with shrubs. Each evening a flock of two dozen pied wagtails would gather to roost for the night in the buddleia bushes. It was a secure place surrounded on all sides by the strong walls of the hospital. On the fourth day, machinery moved in and within a few hours shrubs and bushes were ripped out and the ground was levelled. Frimley Park NHS Trust had new plans for that peaceful corner of the hospital complex. I stood by the window as the wagtails arrived for their usual night's rest. It was a pathetic sight to watch the disorientated birds as they flew down to the wasteland in search of their familiar security. After fluttering help-lessly above the churned earth and the torn and twisted bushes they lined up on the surrounding roof. Their security had gone; life would never be the same again. By the time Barbara left hospital the calm quadrangle was enclosed in steel and concrete. The experience of those little birds is a close parable of the life of most who live with an incurable and progressive disability.

Perhaps when we are young and healthy, we are ready with slick answers to hard questions. Because of God's kindness to us in giving us so much work to do, a busy life to live and some achievements to gain, Barbara and I never found it too difficult to find meaning and purpose in life. Like those pied wagtails in Frimley Park, our lives may have been surrounded by hospitals, but generally we could be secure in our plans for each day. For the entire thirty-five years of our marriage the tedium of regular queuing in outpatients was broken periodically by the challenge of hospitalization, but even then we always had plans for life after the bedpan. Finally, like those poor little birds, our ordered life fell apart. It was hard to come to terms with the fact that at times the chief objective each day was reduced to survival.

Our western life style doesn't equip us for a time when the daily purpose is simply to reach sundown safely. We are expected to think of job satis-faction and personal fulfilment. Even Christians are taught to secure this in a lifetime of service to others. But that is only one side of the teaching of the Bible. What if a life cannot consciously serve, and simply struggling through to the next day becomes the chief goal before nightfall? Barbara and I gained a strong empathy with the starving mother whose sole purpose is to find sufficient food to keep her family alive. Where then are our high ideals of service and fulfilment? It may be hard to spend weeks and months simply consulting with medical personnel in order to maintain life a little longer. But any alternative is to de-humanize human life altogether.

Our own stories

This is a very personal book for all who have contributed to it. In our own way, each of us has found parts of the story hard to tell. Recalling some events has at times been a painful experience. All the stories are about living with permanent disability; and all, except my own, are ongoing stories of grappling with the experiences described. For my part, I live with the memory but no longer the reality of that struggle, and I am still undecided which is worse. For most of us, this is the first time we have laid ourselves open to the gaze of others; the first time we have revealed our private lives of thought and reaction in years of debilitating illness, either in ourselves or in those we care for.

There are no heroes described here. As each shared their story with me, I was impressed by the openness and honesty of those who outwardly appear to cope so adequately with the challenges that confront their life. When I probed beneath that smile and the 'we're coping fine' gloss, I discovered what I knew must be there: times of intense frustration and fear, disappointment and discouragement, panic and impatience. I was secretly glad to find this, because it confirmed after all that Barbara and I were not so unusual or such great failures!

No two stories are the same. Some have disabilities that can only get worse, others have a static condition that is threatened by the side effects of immobility and the ever-present danger of an accident. Some live with physical pain, others with the constant frustrations of their inability to do ordinary things for themselves. However, all have a condition for which there is at present no human cure and which in some degree limits their involvement in life as they may like to have it. But then, as Tessa wisely observes, 'everyone has some disability – not everyone can climb a mountain, even though they may like to.' Most have disabilities that they were born with, though Claud has been disabled by disease and Edison through military action. Some have physical disabilities, whilst others contend with the disadvantage of severe learning disabilities.

As we express ourselves in our own way, the style of writing in each chapter is individual. We each reveal ourselves, perhaps more than we intended. I admit that mine has been written from a deeply personal and moving point of view, which is unusual for me; someone has described it as 'a love story' – and I would not argue with that. Though they take life seriously, Paul and Helle reveal their ability to laugh at themselves – even while they are rebuking society for its failures. Claire is a warm and outgoing young woman who is fully involved in life as she struggles to understand herself in response to her illness. Claud was a teenager two generations before Claire was born, and learnt to accept the hard knocks of life with a firm resolution that often finds it hard to express those deeper emotions. Edison would never be able to portray adequately in print his strong confidence in God and the sunny personality that shines through his face. An hour in the home of Graham and Tessa would convince anyone of their genuine enjoyment of life even in the face of obstacles that only resolute determination could overcome. Andrew and Helen reveal, with a frankness that must encourage us all, their parental love and anxiety and their fears and failures. Peter introduces us to Paul and his friends whose story is here because many might feel sorry for them; in reality their 'disability' may have introduced them to a quality of life that few of us can claim to have achieved. The significance of the stories is not what is wrong, but how each turned an apparent disadvantage to a positive end. Here are lives that in many ways, and to many people, count for good.

The focus of these stories has often been on those who are disabled, but we are not intending to overlook the experience of those who love them. To watch helplessly one you love battling with pain or disability is one of the most distressing emotions of life – whether it is little Charlotte crying with the discomfort of a summer's heat, Claire fighting yet another life-draining infection, or Claud struggling to communicate without a voice box. In Andrew and Helen's story, Charlotte is happily unaware of the trauma suffered by her parents who love her so much.

Even Claire admits that, as a child, she had little understanding of the seriousness of her illness or the deep anxiety of her parents. Those whose stories are told by Peter are generally gloriously happy with their lives and do not appreciate the frustration, even annoyance, that they may cause to others.

However, those who love as well as care – in the technical sense of that word 'care' meaning 'looking after' – do not want to talk or think of their task as a burden, but as a privilege. There is always so much to be gained in the mutual experiences of those who are disabled and those who share their disability. At times Barbara would tell me how sorry she was that she caused me so much worry and brought me so much trouble. Perhaps my poor handling of a situation sometimes gave her cause to think like this. But at that point we were both wrong, and I knew it. I understood how she felt, and I would have been saying the same in her position, but I frequently stressed, 'We're in this together. Our life and experience is shared. Everything is we, not you.' It is for this reason that I was with Barbara for every interview with consultants and surgeons. The operating theatre was about the only place I didn't go!

It is our prayer that these stories will be read not simply for entertainment, but thoughtfully. We want readers to discover what each of us is saying about such concepts as faith, value, meaning, fulfilment, relevance, purpose, hope and our determination to serve God. When society makes judgements on the quality and significance of life, it is often very wide of the mark.

When the unthinkable becomes tolerable

We have to admit to another agenda in writing our stories. Society is confronted today by the creeping influence of the advocates of euthanasia. Like the abortion lobby of the fifties and sixties, it presents itself as the caring face of society. And like the results of that lobby, our nation will realise too late that it has cheapened the value of life, hurt thousands and destroyed so many lives. In recent years we have witnessed a quiet acceptance by society of the right to take life under the pretence of caring. This book is not a theological polemic against the 'right to die' lobby, but it is most definitely a pastoral plea.

The notorious work of Dr Jack Kevorkian (Dr Death) in America has been with us for many years. He offered patients physician-assisted suicide. But when Tony Bland, the tragic victim of the Hillsborough Stadium disaster who was left unconscious and in a Persistent Vegetative State (PVS), was literally starved and dehydrated to death by a court order, a sinister chapter in British medical history was opened. A few years later, society silently agreed to what many Christians consider to be the murder by Dr Phillip Bennett of one of the twins in a mother's womb – simply because the mother said she could not look after two babies. But this is not new; many young mothers know the pressure that is put on them to have a baby aborted because a scan has revealed some deficiency that will affect the child's quality of life. If they were conceived today, more than half of those whose story is told in this book would not be allowed a story to tell.

A prevailing view in the current debate over moral judgements is that the goodness of an act is determined by the intention of those who perform it. That is another way of saying that the end justifies the means. This is precisely what gives the chilling actions of Dr Kevorkian and his supporters an air of respectability. He claims to want to alleviate suffering, so his methods must be all right. But on that ground, there is no limit to the number of crimes that could be committed in the name of mercy! In our nation there are thousands of would-be mothers who deeply regret their decision to abort their living child in the womb; but they did so because they were told that it was in everyone's best interests. We are already confronted with relatives who live with the guilt and regret of encouraging their loved one to take the fast exit from life. In every case, the decision is irreversible. Action is not legitimised by intention.

Encouraged by society's indifference to the value of life, the British Medical Association Ethics Committee has decreed that artificial nutrition and hydration (food and water) should be withdrawn from terminal patients on the word of doctors alone. Pre-empting the BMA, the Royal College of Paediatrics published guidelines to help doctors to decide which babies should be allowed to live. They included assisted death when 'survival is possible only with such severe mental or physical disability that the child will never be capable of choice.' As one editorial commented, 'Here, the Royal College has quietly tiptoed across the line between saying that the treatment is worthless, and saying that the patient is worthless' (*Daily Telegraph*, September 26th 1997). We may ask who will define the meaning of 'never capable of choice' or 'unbearable pain', or even, in the light of some remarkable recoveries, Persistent Vegetative State.

Eugenics (which means 'born well') and euthanasia (which means 'die well') are two ends of the same philosophy. Whatever their advocates claim, history proves that ultimately eugenics and euthanasia give society the right to determine who should live and who should die. Society slowly becomes more and more tolerant of the unthinkable. In a profound description of this, Joni Eareckson Tada wrote, 'Gradually, though no one remembers exactly how it happened, the unthinkable becomes tolerable. And then acceptable. And then legal. And then applaudable' (Joni Eareckson Tada, *When is it Right to Die?* Marshall Pickering, 1993, p53).

When a calf is born lame or its mother breaks a leg, the animal is simply 'put down'; it has no more value in this world. No one pretends that the vet and the farmer will be better people for caring for them. They may learn a few things about cow's legs, but that's all. We are in danger of drifting into this same mind-set regarding human life—drifting into the morality of the farmyard. The euthanasia lobby says, 'When you have had enough and cannot face the future any more, we won't learn better ways of treating you and working with you to discover new horizons; we won't make you feel wanted and cared for and valuable. On the contrary, like you, we too will just give up.' That lobby has made its decision, perhaps unintentionally, that you have no quality left, nothing to live for, and that your fight simply to survive is all a big waste of time, space, and – not to put too fine a point on it – of resources also.

Some years ago a particularly thoughtless consultant commented to a medical observer, in front of Barbara, 'Do you realise that it has cost us £25,000 to get this lady this far.' She was wrong on two counts. First, it was easily twice that figure. But far more significantly, she should never have been thinking, still less talking, in those terms. When, towards the end, Barbara cried, 'I am a pain to myself and I must be a nuisance to everybody', that particular consultant would probably have agreed. I recall sitting by Barbara's bed in an intensive care unit and I found myself reading the labels on some of the items in a locker. The sterile packs had prices on them. 'Nurse', they were designed to say, 'before you break this seal, is it really necessary? Remember, it costs £15.' I felt that Barbara had a price tag attached.

All of us who have written chapters in this book are aware of the arguments about limited budgets and prioritising, but it is the steady erosion of the nation's mind-set that concerns us. Those whose stories are told here are extremely expensive for the nation to support, and consequently they are vulnerable people. Vulnerable to a society that assumes it has the right to decide whether or not they have quality or value. As a matter of fact they themselves have all come to the conclusion that there is value and purpose in all human life. One of Tessa's grumbles is that carers often assume they know best, and it is frustrating when they insist on placing items beyond her reach in the kitchen. But that same mind-set may one day take upon itself the right to decide whether or not Tessa and Graham, Charlotte, Paul, Hughie, Anthony, Peter, Jane and the rest, have sufficient 'quality of life' to make it worthwhile for society to care for them. Or whether the significant outlay on drugs, nursing care and surgery required by Claud, Claire and Barbara is economically viable. Or whether a blown-up soldier from an African state, or a disabled man who can only type with his mouth, are really 'earning' their disability pensions.

All this may be shockingly frank, but over the past three decades we have seen the child in the womb downgraded to a 'foetus' – a word that simply doesn't exist in the Bible and therefore in Christian vocabulary. History teaches us that it was the eugenics crusade, so enthusiastically endorsed by Britain and America and virtually every major European country before the Second World War, that gave Adolf Hitler his philosophy to destroy tens of thousands of the physically and mentally disabled under the Third Reich. Those 1930s German posters that depicted the healthy Arian shouldering the burden of the imbecile are chilling reminders of what lay ahead. Even before the Jews were so fatally targeted, the infirm and insane were 'cleansed' from German society. Is that really what our society wants?

Britain can be justly proud of having two hundred and thirty-six hospices plus four hundred hospice home-care teams. The hospice movement was born out of the Christian ethic that all human life has value and meaning and that society becomes more human as it becomes more caring. The Christian approach to severe suffering and disability is to provide for the easing of pain and anxiety (palliative care) and support for spiritual and social healing, in a caring environment where patients are reassured of their value and quality.

We have come a long way from the days when disabled children were hidden away from the gaze of society, and yet paradoxically, as a form of Sunday afternoon entertainment the public went to stare at the bizarre antics of the tragic inmates of Bethlehem Hospital ('Bedlam') in London. But we are in danger of losing what we have gained, by making the infirm, the chronically ill and the disabled feel that they are a burden on society. If Claire, as a young person, says that the implications of legalised euthanasia scare her, what must it do to the elderly? Graham and Tessa know that the general mind-set of the medical profession and of society would ensure that people like them are no longer born. They would have been candidates for the eugenic cleansing of abortion. What does that tell Graham and Tessa about how the medical profession and society view them today?

Without a doubt, disabled people do feel vulnerable when confronted by the significant shifts among many in the medical profession. We have only to scan the correspondence columns of our national press after the latest pronouncement by the BMA or the Royal College of Paediatrics. One reader, herself disabled, wrote to the *Daily Telegraph* in September 1997, 'Doctors should wake up to the message they are sending out to disabled people. Recognising that the principle that futile treatment should be withdrawn is good medical practice, letting children die who could be saved, solely because they will be disabled, is a fatal form of discrimination against all people with disabilities.'

Euthanasia assumes that the right to 'physician assisted suicide' is the best guarantee that we die with dignity. The facts hardly support that. Oregon State in America legalised physician assisted suicide in November 1994, and since then many have wrestled painfully with this choice and others have left behind relatives deeply regretting their support for this irreversible decision. That is not dying with dignity. Nor is it dying with dignity to feel under pressure from a watching society – or even worse, waiting relatives – to do the decent thing. Still less is 'dying well' to be found in the involuntary 'granny-culling' reported from the

Netherlands. It is never dignified to grab at a quick exit to life. Dignity is found when a caring society skilfully supports those in greatest need, and ensures that everyone, whatever their disability, is persuaded of their value to society.

The Christian believes in the value of 'death with dignity', but is convinced that there is a far more dignified way of dying than the fast-fix solution of a shot of potassium chloride; this denies everyone the rich experience of caring and being cared for. The hospice movement encourages the Christian view that life is valuable and meaningful, however painful. It may be tempting to find a way out, but it is far more valuable to find a way through. In reality, those who need to be cared for, whether because of their learning or physical disabilities, actually contribute more to society than most people, and especially they themselves, will ever understand. I would never have chosen my path as a full-time carer, but I know that I am a better person for having been made to walk it.

To my knowledge, the euthanasia lobby has never followed their philosophy to its logical conclusion. In the experience of Barbara and myself, there were times when, if God had given us the option, we would have elected for us both to go to heaven together – right then! On the one hand I could not bear to see her constant suffering and I longed for her to find relief, and yet I did not want to live without her. Fortunately God has never put that option into our hands, and he never will. On that decision, as with every decision, he is far wiser than we are. But my feelings of pending loss and despair without Barbara raised an issue that the euthanasia lobby carefully avoids. If it is right for someone in physical suffering to request an end to their own life, then an equal case can be made that those who cannot bear to live without them should be allowed to take the same exit. After all, who is to say whether physical pain is worse than loneliness and a broken heart? It is a short step from legalising a living will to legalising a pair of living wills. That logical spiral of self-destruction knows no end.

This book is not a theological or medical treatise against the anti-Christian mind-set of the pro-euthanasia lobby, but it is a comment pastorally. Many in the following stories have struggled with the meaning and quality of life in severe disability or continual pain. Defenders of euthanasia may argue as much as they like, but the whole world should know that once euthanasia and the living will are legalised, the pressures upon the severely disabled and the feeble elderly would be immense. It is only the strong Christian ethic that will consistently resist the morality of the farmyard that says, 'When the animal is too sick to be viable, put it down.' Society's standards of viability are shifting constantly. When my life ceases to be of obvious value to society, I would prefer to be treated by a caring doctor rather than by the local vet!

Healing today?

I suppose that all Christians with a chronic disability, and those who care for them, have prayed for healing. In the early years of Barbara's disability we certainly did; and we politely listened to the kind advice of people who knew a special remedy or a gifted healer. But we came to a point, many years ago, when we knew that to pray for healing was no longer faith but distrust. Job was not the only person who had to prove that it is possible to love God not just for what you get out of it. Stories of healing are fine – when they are true. But they didn't help us, or our many disabled friends who had little expectation of being healed this side of heaven.

Those who boldly offer certain healing and then lightly off-load the failures onto the fault of 'negative thinking', have rarely sat in the school of long-term suffering. I have read and listened to the views of the health and happiness con men and have no hesitation in identifying them as Job's false friends – like them, they will be answerable to Job's God. Barbara and I found that Job and Jeremiah became very great friends of ours. When every joint in her body was ravaged by arthritis and each finger, one by one, was disabled into a floppy appendage as the disease snapped tendons, with artificial hips and knees, and some brilliant metalwork clamping her head to her neck, there were not too many people promising Barbara a full recovery in this life! However, we had a better kind of faith to see us through. All of us who have contributed to this book believe unquestionably in a God who can and does heal, but that is certainly not our preoccupation. Like the friends of Daniel who were threatened with the fiery furnace we are able to say, 'The God we serve is able to save us… but even if he does not…' we will never deny him (Daniel 3:17).

It was always a matter of interest to me that those who write and speak so winsomely of healing today are not queuing up to pray for the categories of disability described in this book. In reply to my question whether anyone had ever offered to pray for her healing, Tessa assured me that no one had. When I enquired why she thought this was, Tessa simply responded, 'Because people are realistic.' Less generously, I am tempted to suggest that they realised they had met their match!

Sense out of suffering?

In this book I have started with our own story because that is where it all began. Although Barbara and I lived together for thirty-five years with the steady erosion of her health and mobility by rheumatoid arthritis, we had never spoken publicly or written about our experiences. One of my earlier books was subtitled *making sense out of suffering*, but even then I managed to make no mention of our own experience. In fact one critic complained, 'He has probably never lived with pain.' Those who knew us best, knew that Barbara and I were very private people and were reluctant to share our needs. In more than thirty years of preaching I cannot recall ever referring specifically from the pulpit to our personal struggle with ill-health and disability, until once or twice during the final year of our life together. For her part, Barbara resolutely refused to speak or to be interviewed on the subject of suffering, and only once wrote a short article on 'Living with Disability' – that editor deserves an award for persistence! We were often urged to write our story, if only to help others, but we declined; mainly because we never considered that we had much to tell. We coped, but not as capably or as victoriously as some might have imagined from their observation of us.

So, what changed our mind? During the eighteen months prior to Barbara's death, we began to acknowledge that perhaps there was some value in our story. The frank admission of our weakness might encourage others who are similarly challenged to discover that they are coping better than they thought! If nothing else, we could set the record straight and allow people to judge for themselves whether we handled life well or not. We planned, therefore, to open the window and let others see what was going on inside. That would be a new and uncomfortable experience for us.

However, it did not take much thought to conclude that no one would want to read a whole book about us! We have been nowhere, achieved little, and are unknown beyond a relatively small circle. Besides, I have always assumed that anyone who writes an autobiography has to be either conceited or crazy. But we had met so many others whose stories are more interesting, and whose lives can teach us all valuable lessons. So, we decided to include some of their stories as well.

People often assumed that our acquaintance with disability would make us very understanding of those who suffered. Well, it did and it didn't. We could enter fully into the life of those who suffered and yet who still pressed on to the best of their ability; they had our support, admiration and love. Unfortunately we had little patience with those comparatively healthy people who did nothing but whine about their lot, pulled out of active service too soon, or felt too tired even to get out to the prayer meeting. I know that some people considered that we were hard on others, and they were probably right. It took us a long time to learn that we all have different pain and workload thresholds; in expecting others to push themselves as hard as we pushed ourselves, we probably forgot that some of them actually were, but that their tolerance broke sooner. I suppose it was typical of our life together that we were working on the revision of our marriage preparation book *No Longer Two* only forty-eight hours before the Lord called Barbara home. Personal suffering can make part of you warmly thoughtful, but another part coldly intolerant.

In a similar way, Barbara could never accept the oft-quoted assumption that suffering draws you nearer to God. She responded that this might be true in the stories of the great Christians, but she did not accept that it was true for her. She always maintained, and we can never know whether she was right, that her walk with God was in spite of and not because of her constant pain and disability. This is how Barbara's wry humour phrased it in some of her notes that I discovered, 'You often hear well-meaning preachers say, "suffering is a time of refining". All very true, but some long-term sufferers must by now be perfect.' For my part, when people assume that suffering makes for holiness, I often wonder whether their time alone with God is really enhanced when they have raging toothache or a blinding migraine. Surely, part of the purpose of suffering is discipline, and according to the apostle Paul who knew about these things, 'No discipline seems pleasant at the time, but painful' (Hebrews 12:11).

When he went on to write of the 'harvest of righteousness and peace', he was careful not to tell us when that harvest will be. Perhaps, after all, it is not always in this life. Sowing, yes, but not yet reaping.

Even when she felt at her lowest, Barbara always had value, both to me and to countless others; and what was more important many, from Christian friends to community nurses and hospital consultants, made this clear. She once said to me, 'I feel the Lord has thrown me on the scrap heap.' But this was not true. Her life was still counting, and all of us who cared for her were better people for our contact with her. Not least myself, who knew her best of all. I can watch that African mother struggling to grind a few grains of corn into flour to make a paste to feed her children and, heart-rending though it is, I am strangely a better person because of the example of her devotion and care. And she is a better person than she would be if she simply knifed the baby and herself to end it all.

Perspectives

Back in Frimley Park Hospital I empathised with those pied wagtails! The surgeon's skill had transformed our peaceful quadrangle into a seeming battleground. Had we known just how long the battle would take, or its outcome, I wonder if we could have handled it. Barbara made a recovery that startled both medical and nursing staff. There were bad days, of course, but her determination to recover and join me once again in our ministry gave her the necessary incentive. I shed much of my work in order to spend five or seven hours a day with her. The ward staff let me wander in and out as I wanted.

I was intrigued at the way my busy life, involved with national evangelical issues, had narrowed down. What mattered more than anything now was whether the physiotherapist would be able to keep our noon appointment, or whether today it would require only the physio, myself and one nurse to stand Barbara up and lay her back again in bed. We all knew that she could not come home until I could move her from bed to wheelchair on my own. Regularly and diligently Barbara exercised her limited leg movements to strengthen vital muscles. I counted, while she struggled to hold her leg a few inches off the bed in our daily 'work-out'. Suffering focussed our lives and made us appreciate so many of the 'incidentals' that often life was too busy to take in. It also put into perspective those 'big' issues that we think are so important. I hope I will never again assume that the only actions that matter in this world are those that affect the maximum number of people. I have learnt that, at a crucial moment, the warm smile and pleasant greeting of the lady with the meal trolley (and that's a rare thing in many NHS hospitals) can suddenly, even if only temporarily, make everything seem better.

I cannot pretend that we always found contentment in our experiences. I have often been challenged by Paul's claim to have learnt that whatever state he found himself in, he had learned 'to be content' (Philippians 4:11). What did he mean? He admits to his 'deep concern' for the churches (2 Corinthians 11:28), and to his troubles and burdens in Asia that caused him to 'despair even of life' (2 Corinthians 1:8). So, in what way was he content? I don't imagine that Paul hummed little tunes to himself all day when Demas walked out on the gospel in favour of the world, or that he set up a fixed smile to impress his visitors when Alexander the coppersmith caused him such hurt. What I do believe is that he had learnt to focus on both the here and the hereafter – at the same time. As he confessed to the Philippians, on the one hand he longed to depart and be with Christ, but knew that it was more necessary for him to remain here (Philippians 1:23-24). There was a life to live and work to do. This was a man with purpose, who knew that until God called him away from this life – in his case in the Roman execution yard—there was always purpose and meaning for him. Suffering helped us also to focus on the ultimate hope of heaven and to see it in perspective. Barbara and I often talked about heaven; she longed to be there and wondered why the Lord had spared her so often when she was near to death. But whenever we thought together about this, it was never long before the subject turned to now. We called it 'The meanwhile.' There was a life to live and work to do. Our task was to find that task and do it. We had to discover the value of meanwhile.

All of those whose story is told here have three vital ingredients to life in common. First, we are committed Christians. By this I mean that we have each come to a point in our lives when we accepted Jesus Christ as our Saviour to forgive our sin and rescue us from all its consequences, and at the same time we accepted him as Lord, to take charge of our life. Secondly, although it may not always be obvious, we all believe that our testimonies centre on the love of Christ and the daily courage, strength and purpose supplied by God himself. And thirdly, we have each determined to make the very most of the life God has given to us.

Re-reading each person's story, I doubt whether any of them could get much more out of life, or for that matter, put more in. In fact, that has been their unwritten secret. They do not talk so much about getting something out of life, but of putting something in. Their quality of life is measured not by what they get, but by what they give.

We each want our stories to encourage others. At times they may be deeply moving, simply humorous, or just ordinary, but our purpose is to convince the reader that there is always value in the individual, and meaning to life, however hard the path or bleak the outlook. All of us, whether carers or cared for, know the varied experiences of frustration and dashed hopes, aloneness and pain, as well as the joys, loves and hopes of Christian relationships. I suppose we have all, at times, passed through the tunnel of feeling sorry for ourselves, concluding that no one understands us, and wondering what on earth God is doing – or even where he is – when life hurts so much. Barbara once wrote, 'Suffering is a very lonely path, cut off from others but longing that someone would understand.' Claire, unknowingly wrote almost exactly the same thing, 'Sometimes I feel very isolated, even from my closest friends and then I get frustrated. I have days when I think just nobody understands, or ever can.'

For others who often feel the same, we want our stories to show that this is not the whole picture. They are not alone, because there are others who understand. However dark the room may seem, there is always a window of light. Barbara's comment went on to affirm, 'Suffering tests the reality of faith more than most trials. Instead of it becoming a source of bitterness, we must let it become a means of praise. God wants us to have peace, courage and faith in all the difficult circumstances of our lives.' There can be few things worse than suffering without hope – this leads only to black despair. But there is a rich value in disability when it is borne with horizons of hope – this leads to quality and purpose.

We want our stories to encourage others because, although we have not glossed over the hardships, frustrations and dark times, we have all found value in our experiences of life. A wise man in the Bible wrote, 'A man's spirit sustains him in sickness, but a crushed spirit who can bear?' (Proverbs 18:14). It is our prayer that our stories will not crush but sustain.

If I may employ the words of Paul in the New Testament and turn them just a little for our cases, 'We are hard pressed, but not hemmed in; we hardly know which way to turn, but we are not completely without a way through; we are constantly pursued by trouble, but we are never abandoned by God; we are knocked down, but never knocked out' (2 Corinthians 4:8-9).

The better side of worse

Brian and Barbara Edwards

From games captain to a wheelchair was not an easy journey, but Barbara never allowed her chronic disability to distract her from those things she counted important in life. Here, Brian opens a window into the roller coaster of their battle with disability throughout the thirty-five years of their marriage.

The ward Sister slipped into the side room and closed the door behind her. It was time to say 'goodbye.' For the past month she and her 'blue team' had carefully nursed Barbara from her admission as an urgent spinal care patient, through eight days on halo traction and through the trauma of postoperative care for a patient in a halo jacket. It was now time to leave hospital. We expressed our appreciation for the excellent nursing care Barbara had received, and our hope that she would not be returning for the foreseeable future. In response the Sister admitted, 'When we heard that we would be receiving a chronic rheumatoid arthritis patient on halo traction, we groaned. RA patients are the most difficult to care for; we cannot get them comfortable and can rarely please them.' Then she added with a reassuring smile, 'But you have been a joy to nurse.'

Those eight words accomplished far more than just feeding my pride for a wife who had been brave beyond measure and enduring beyond belief through forty years of pain and persistent erosion of mobility. They helped us to grasp something of the value of suffering and the purpose of battling through the dark days when you want to cry but can't, and when you want to die but don't.

All through our busy life leading a London suburban church for thirty years, Barbara had already confronted five major orthopaedic operations and the relentless deterioration of her physical health. The care of a loving church, the encouragement of a fulfilling ministry, and the support of state care for the disabled, all contributed to our ability not merely to cope, but to take on significant responsibilities and ministries. Above all, the courage and determination that God gave Barbara, coupled with her quiet acceptance of each successive loss of the things she loved and at which she was so competent, meant that we maintained our ministry long after we might have given up so easily.

Even when Barbara was wholly confined to a wheelchair we fulfilled two preaching tours in South Africa, took a party of young people overland to the Czech Republic, shared seminars together, and travelled throughout the United Kingdom for conferences and general ministry. It was not difficult to see that our shared ministry on two legs and four wheels was at least accomplishing something, however small, for the gospel of our Lord Jesus Christ. We knew precisely what our ministry was. We would love to have done more, but we did all that we could. Life certainly had obvious meaning. There was value in the meanwhile.

Frimley Park Hospital in Surrey challenged all that! Barbara had been transferred from Kingston as an emergency, and we met the surgeon within hours of arrival. He carefully explained everything to us and then offered to meet us again early the next morning when we could ask any more questions and give him our response; time was important. He would leave us to think it over. I thanked him and said we would talk a bit and pray a bit alternately. 'Why the prayer?' he enquired. I explained our Christian commitment in a couple of sentences and his reply was immediate, 'If you ask me to go ahead, you may like to know that your surgeon belongs to the same family.'

Providentially, Frimley Park Hospital was only five minutes from the home of our eldest son and his wife, Stephen and Fiona. That night, as I took advantage of their spare bedroom, I told God that I could not make this decision for Barbara but that I would support her in whatever decision she made. I called at the hospital early next morning and arrived before the consultant. Barbara looked up from her bed, smiled and said quietly but firmly, 'We must go ahead mustn't we?' The peace that we experienced at that moment was essential for what lay in the future. When Barbara cried in pain and weakness, 'Why did I ever go ahead?' I could remind her of that Saturday morning when we confidently said 'yes.' And when all I seemed to be able to do was to cancel preaching appointments, I had to remind myself also of that Saturday morning.

The surgeon never underestimated the seriousness of this latest episode in our lives. He carefully explained the dangers involved in degenerating vertebrae slowly crushing the spinal cord, and the risks involved in his proposed surgery; he frankly admitted that Barbara was 'an anaesthetist's nightmare.' A spinal decompression and an occipito-cervico-thoracic fusion meant fusing two pairs of vertebrae to relieve pressure and then bolting the head and neck together with a pair of titanium rods! It all sounded impressive reconstruction work, but it hardly appealed to our eagerness to return as soon as possible to our Christian ministry. Eight days on halo traction would be followed by the major surgery and then three months in a halo jacket. The jacket sat for a week in the corner of Barbara's room like an exhibit from the Inquisition, and when eventually fitted, it left her like a bird in a cage. For the 'normal' person a halo jacket would be unpleasant, but with a will to survive they could cope well enough; for Barbara, her minimal ability to do anything for herself was reduced to zero.

I am still amazed that we said 'yes' to the surgeon. 'If you ask me to go ahead', he warned, 'this will be more traumatic than anything you have been through yet and there will be times when you will hate your consultant.' Five months later we told him that he was right about the first and that Barbara had got close to the second. It was only then that he confided that the outcome of his surgery offered only death, paraplegia or success, 'There could be no in between.' And he added with a smile, 'Yours was success.'

The following notes are from the diary that I wrote each evening during Barbara's stay in Frimley Park Hospital. I have changed nothing, although I have omitted most of the medical notes and some other asides that would have taken too much space. I include them here because they are a time capsule of so much that we went through together in our marriage: operations, recoveries, and new ways of starting life again. The notes portray Barbara's strength just as they betray my fragility; but they are expressions of my real thoughts, since, at the time of recording them I had no intention that anyone else would read them. For the first ten days in this hospital Barbara was lying on her back and could see nothing but the ceiling.

Monday April 14 1997 (day 3)

Barbara is incredibly patient and bright. I really don't know how she keeps smiling, except that Hook Evangelical Church had a second prayer meeting for her on Sunday; around a hundred stayed for it.

Tuesday 15th (day 4)

More cards and flowers. The staff read Barbara's cards to her and some are moved by the messages. Barbara has some good opportunities for witness. One member of staff commented on the 'old Bible' lying on the locker, to which Barbara responded, 'No, it's not old, just well used.' One nurse seems to be searching for the truth and sometimes closes the door to talk further. Barbara's patience, courage and gentleness are incredible. The prayer of Christians all over the country humbles and encourages us. It has been a beautiful day and I'm sorry Barbara has to miss it, though she enjoys the dawn chorus; it must be those two dozen or more wagtails roosting in the quadrangle outside her room! A beautiful evening as I left. The sky was deep blue. It was not hard to leave everything in the hands of a loving and all-powerful God. I have said and written that the forthcoming operation is risky. But there are no risks for the Christian—only the unknown. There is no risk to Barbara; she is safe and secure whatever happens. The omniscience of God's omnipotence is where I place our lives, our future, and our ministry. I don't find it hard to trust God, but then, whom else can I trust? I hope I will always be ready to trust God, even if things do not go as I long and pray for.

Wednesday 16th (day 5)

Today Barbara was told that the operation will be on Monday. The weights on her head were increased to 15 pounds! Slowly they drag her up the bed and every two or three hours staff have to pull her down again. Everyone here is very approachable and encouraging. The nursing care continues to be excellent and caring, and the food is appetising. I know, because I eat half of Barbara's! However she is eating well. I think Adele spent today at school making cards for grandma; she brought three into hospital today. Susanna brought a teddy, which I have stood on the TV brackets on the ceiling so that Barbara can see it. Barbara was discouraged for a while today, mainly because I was late in. She continues to be so patient, a great witness surely. So many cards that, having filled the pin board, I started a scrapbook. When the post arrived a member of staff called out, 'If anyone has two hours to spare would they like to open Barbara's cards for her.' Pity no one had time to, because they missed the messages.

Thursday 17th (day 6)

More cards, more flowers, more care and prayer. We both continue at peace. Barbara patient as ever. I'm getting very little work done, but that is not my priority at present. It is encouraging to learn how highly the staff regard Barbara for her quiet patience. And even more encouraging to learn how highly they regard her surgeon!

Friday 18th (day 7)

This evening the Staff Nurse in charge slipped into Barbara's room with a cup of tea and flopped into a chair. We were glad that she felt our room was peaceful. The flowers and cards certainly brighten it up. Barbara is still bright and brave and trusting, even joking frequently with the staff.

Saturday 19th (day 8)

Barbara has now been just over one week on halo traction. She was low last thing this evening and I was very tired so was little help to her. What a poor support I am when I'm tired. However, Andrew visited, and Stephen and Adele and Cara. Also her brother Norman and Pam called; they came a long way and so it was good of them to come. More cards, more flowers. I wish Barbara could see them all. The room is very bright and cheerful.

Sunday 20th (day 9)

Quiet and calm day. Stephen and Andrew came in, as well as Barbara's brother Graham and Jean. I managed to spend most of the day in the hospital. We gave a copy of *No Longer Two* to a Staff Nurse who is to be married in August. Barbara's surgeon came in this evening to discuss the operation with us. I told him that hundreds of people were praying for him also all over the country. He replied 'Yes, so I understand from other sources.' I left Barbara confident and at peace.

Monday 21st (day 10. The day of the operation)

At 10 am. I met the anaesthetist. She was kind, patient and reassuring. She explained the procedure. Barbara is still quietly at peace, and we are both confident in the Lord. Barbara's faith has been tremendous; though she will not admit this. All we preach and believe has proved very true for us. Barbara said to me, 'If I come through this operation it is because the Lord has more work for us to do together. But if the Lord takes me to glory, I will be free from pain and suffering for ever.' I could only respond, 'So you win either way.' Selfishly, I want to work with Barbara beside me. We're so part of each other's life that I can't conceive of my ministry without her. There were no tears as we said goodbye, just strong confidence in our Father who always does best.

I came home and mowed the lawn! Andrew cooked pizza and chips for lunch and then I pottered in the garden. That is the only way I could occupy my time, by being busy and praying. Perhaps I should have spent the whole time in prayer; but I just keep saying the same things to God. I feel more at peace than before any of Barbara's previous operations.

8.15 pm. the surgeon phoned to say he had completed the operation as planned and that Barbara was now in intensive care. He was satisfied that all has gone well. The operation took four and a half hours.

10 pm. I called at Intensive Care Unit and spent ten minutes with Barbara. She is deeply asleep and on a ventilator. The Sister assured me that they are satisfied with the progress. Banks of monitors and tubes from everywhere ensure that the patient would have to work hard to die in a modern ICU. I would not have recognised Barbara. She was pallid and cold. They found a use for the halo by tying the airline to it with a white ribbon and a neat bow!

Tuesday 22nd (day 11)

Called at ICU at 11 am. Barbara is awake but still breathing with the aid of the ventilator. They hope to be able to remove it later today or tomorrow. She tried to speak but could not. She can nod and shake her head, and by this means communicated that I was not to come back today. That's one order I told her I would disobey!

7.50 pm. called to see Barbara. Stayed fifteen minutes. I feel guilty for being well when Barbara is suffering. I know this is foolish, but how can anyone watch someone they love suffering so much without feeling the frustration of helplessness. I want to cry and cry—but where can I? Someone will hear and offer sympathy, and I can't stand that. If the people I have tried to help in the past are like me, then much of my support and sympathy has been useless. I value knowing that Christians are praying, but all I want is to be alone and cry. But that would not help Barbara.

I read Don Cormack's *Killing Fields, Living Fields* today and realised that in comparison to the suffering of Cambodian Christians under the Khmer Rouge our suffering is nothing. That helps me to get things in perspective but it can hardly comfort Barbara fighting for survival in the ICU. Lord, I will try to sleep, but I ache for Barbara and somehow feel she was distant from me this evening—and that is scary.

Wednesday 23rd (day 12)

When I phoned ICU at 3 pm. Barbara was being moved back to her room. I went straight over. She now had only a saline drip, feeding tube to the stomach, a drain for the wound, and catheter. That's progress! Neither of us wanted to talk over the last three days. We agreed to swap stories when Barbara is stronger. She had no idea that it was Wednesday; the last three days have been a hazy blur. The surgeon called and claims to be well satisfied with progress: 'You are at the head of the field in recovery.' Tomorrow they will sit her up and fit the halo jacket; it was all said as if this was a reward for good progress. I groaned silently for Barbara—she was clearly not excited at the prospect either.

Barbara was closer to her real self now and managed to smile. She wanted me there and wished I could stay all night. This was a great relief to me. Her back and buttocks are horribly bruised. There is steady progress and I'm grateful to God for this.

Thursday 24th (day 13)

This morning Barbara was sat up and fitted with the halo jacket. It is much larger than I expected, and she seems like a bird in a cage. It will be her constant companion for the next two to three months at least. There are amusing aspects to it, particularly with the spanner and Allen key taped to it! But Barbara is, understandably, not yet ready to laugh at it.

Friday 25th (day 14)

Two weeks since Barbara came to Frimley Park Hospital, and they must be the most traumatic two weeks of her life. Yet the massive prayer response all over the country and the excellent nursing and medical care, have combined to give Barbara an incredible recovery. Everyone is amazed at her progress. Barbara is more cheerful today at the prospect of being home within a week.

Saturday 26th (day 15)

Barbara had a bad night last night but overall is still progressing well. Because the jacket is too large it is rubbing badly. She is still keeping bright and eager to get home. However, there are going to be a lot of adjustments and a lot to handle. Our Lord alone knows what the future holds for us and what we can effectively do for him.

Monday 28th (day 16)

After a good night, today was the day for standing up—and that is about all Barbara managed. When I arrived she was very positive about her achievement. I reminded her that one week ago she was fighting for life and now she is fighting to get home.

Thursday May 1st (Day 19)—election day!

But more significantly Barbara stood up twice—albeit with two physios and a nurse helping her. Incredible how ambition and objectives shrink in hospital; it becomes a small world of the tiny and painfully slow achievements. Every new thing is something to be celebrated. Tomorrow I will help the staff to stand Barbara; it's strange that I'm quite excited at the prospect. I can honestly say that I am more eager for this than the publication of a book. Barbara's small 'steps' of progress give me a buzz. How odd that the whole focus of life can change so rapidly.

Friday 2nd (day 20)

A bad day for Barbara. We worked the few leg exercises but today has been lost. Both very disappointed. I spent five hours with her but I feel I help very little. What can I say? Life is hard and prospects are not encouraging. I wish I could lift her when she is down. Came home and worked on sermons till 2 am.

Saturday 3rd (day 21)

Preaching at Tunbridge Wells and went straight on to the hospital. Beautiful weather, so much colour in the garden; it is sad that Barbara is missing it all. How can I possibly get her home by the end of next week? Today I cancelled an evening meeting on Thursday because I must give Barbara so much of my time. Her poor body is so battered and bruised.

My sermon today from Revelation 1:12-13 challenged me to believe in the hidden purposes of God. We have work to do together.

Sunday 4th (day 22)

Barbara was bright today. I preached this morning and then went to the hospital. Mahen and Chris Mutthiah called and that greatly encouraged Barbara. Later this evening the Sister and two Staff Nurses assisted me to stand her up. We did this twice and that was all Barbara could manage. I guess that is encouraging! Until she and I can do that on our own, and I can transfer her to the chair, she has to remain in hospital.

Monday 5th (day 23)

A long day for Barbara. Being a bank holiday, many patients have been discharged and the ward is very quiet. We carried on with bed exercises but no other progress. Barbara is bored and frustrated not being able to do anything. I spent almost seven hours with her today, but we can't even think of a game that we can play together. I read a chapter of a book to her, played music, ate, chatted and sat quietly. Barbara thinks she is not handling the situation well, but in fact she is responding to it brilliantly. To sit all day, unable even to scratch her ear or blow her nose, is not an easy burden to carry. We are praying for a miracle of progress this week so that she could be home on the weekend.

Tuesday 6th (day 24)

I spent seven hours at the hospital today. We agree that I will invest whatever time it takes to get Barbara home this week. It is likely that I will make the investment without the return! We knew it would not be easy, but neither of us expected it to be as hard as it is. Two sessions, exhausting work for Barbara, and all I achieved was to stand her on the turn-table, turn her around 90 degrees and return her to the bed—twice! And all with the help of a physiotherapist and a nurse. That's a long way from me being confident and competent to handle her on my own. The surgeon reiterated today that many of his halo patients stay in hospital for the entire two to four months; but that is not an option we are prepared to accept. Just about the only productive work I achieve at present is to make phone calls cancelling my appointments! The future is still so uncertain. Tomorrow we hope to sit Barbara in a wheelchair; the anticipation of an outing round the corridors of the hospital is really exciting.

Thursday 8th (day 26)

We both came to the end of the day exhausted! After lunch we explored the hospital a little further with the wheelchair. More hard work with the physiotherapist. Barbara needed to sleep, and I went to the van and crashed out for forty minutes, then prepared sermons, prayed and dozed a bit. I feel shattered. Returned to Barbara at 6 pm. to give her the evening meal. I was short-tempered once and that was enough to dissolve Barbara to tears! I tried to say I'm sorry, but the damage was done. Good news, an ambulance has been ordered for Monday afternoon. But I have a busy weekend ahead with a lecture and a sermon on Saturday, and Sunday morning preaching. I will certainly need the Lord's help.

Sunday 11th (day 29)

Barbara's final full day in Frimley Park Hospital. I can now transfer Barbara from the bed to a chair on my own. We will improve as time goes on.

Friday 16th (home)

Barbara came home on Monday and life has been crazy ever since! So much to do. I'm at least ten days behind in even opening my mail. Today was a joke. At one point, one of the members of the church was here cleaning for us, another arrived to help make necessary alterations so that Barbara can safely stay in her wheelchair in the van, the Community Nurse manager and supervisor called, and a mechanical digger unit arrived to begin work to renew our crossover. The day continued like that and I finally got to my desk at 9 pm. Barbara is working hard to do as much as she is able, but she is totally dependent. It is amusing to see how our world of priorities and achievements shrinks at a time like this. Just one small step of progress, like doing something a better way from yesterday, provides a great sense of achievement. Perhaps I'm learning just how insignificant the 'big issues' really are. Frankly I haven't yet found time to discover what I am supposed to be learning in all this, I just know that my ordered life has gone crazy.

Sunday 18th

Today I was able to get Barbara from the bed to the wheelchair, down in the lift and into her chair in the lounge and later back to bed—all unaided! That's fair progress in less than a week. Praying with Barbara tonight I heard myself asking God why we have been taken out of the race; then I corrected myself. We're not out of the race but transferred to a different track; one that he knows we must run. I wish we knew how we should plan for the future. It is hard to see what my ministry can be. But then, Christians often have to walk in the darkness of unexpected and unexplained events. We are the only people who can bask in the sunlight even as we walk in the dark. I know I'm learning lessons, but it is hard to feel so useless. Barbara continues to be brave, patient, and a challenge to me.

Sunday 25th

Life is very strange at present. We hardly seem to be 'connected' to the rest of the world. Most of our time is spent caring for ourselves in one way or another, and that is contrary to all our preference and experience. Never is this disconnection more evident than on Sunday. Barbara has not been to church for six weeks and it is so odd listening to tapes when we would love to be among God's people. More flowers and cards this week. Slowly we are overcoming difficulties and we can be almost independent now. Barbara is still brave, patient and sweet-natured. I snapped at her two or three times this week, which shows just how impatient and hard I can be. Often we talk of the future, but with no more light. We know only that there will have to be a radical change in pace. A friend reminded me this week that my public prayer frequently included the phrase, 'Lord, we have no cause to complain against you.' I believe that without hesitation.

Anywhere, except London!

Barbara and I first met in our teens. I had accepted the invitation of school friends to a boys' Bible class and was impressed at this new experience of a room full of boys of my own age listening to the Bible. I was even more impressed when I learned that there was a similar class of young girls a few doors down the road! Barbara came from a family of eight brothers and a sister, and was the only one to take the claims of Christ seriously. She committed her life to Christ at the age of ten and in spite of teasing and taunts she never wavered. She was now in that girls' Bible class.

By the time she was seventeen Barbara had been diagnosed as having rheumatoid arthritis. In the late 1950s, steroid was the wonder drug for this condition and so she began a course of treatment that was to stay with her for the rest of her life. I went up to college in London and although we were engaged in 1959 we knew that it would be at least another four years before we could marry. I had a four year course to complete and Barbara went to a training college for two years to equip herself for what we already knew would be her role as a pastor's wife. We were both country kids at heart and told the Lord that we would go anywhere to serve him—anywhere, except London. As two penniless students we married in 1963 and settled into our first appointment; I was assistant to Derek Prime at an evangelical church in West Norwood, in South East London! Barbara worked in the office of a local printer, I took on secondary school teaching part time, and we moved into a small flat where my study furniture was made from orange boxes. Three years later and with six month old Stephen, we moved to Hook Evangelical Church in Surbiton, a south west London suburb. We decided against telling God where we would not go!

We learned to adapt to changes throughout our lives. They came slowly but with a steady deterioration of Barbara's health and ability. At times she hobbled like an old lady, then the centre of attack shifted to her hands and wrists. Pain—hot, nagging pain—became part of daily life. By the time Andrew arrived, seven years after Stephen, Barbara could no longer play with the children easily. Caring for a baby became a painful exercise. On the other hand, her devotion as a Christian wife and mother, and her commitment as a member of an evangelical church, was a significant example. Barbara loved all that she did for the home, and entertaining was her speciality. We gave hospitality regularly, and the boys would complain if we dared to take a Sunday free of company. We opened our home for long-stay visitors as well, from 'drop-outs' to overseas missionary students. They were full and rewarding years.

Barbara taught in the Sunday school, commenced a girls' Bible class, started a young wives' fellowship and then a day-time playgroup. One of her greatest contributions to the life of the church was the Young Disciples class. This was designed for children who professed Christ, and with her first class of thirteen children she developed a syllabus that was

later adopted by many churches across the country. It expressed her practical, down-to-earth approach to everything. She taught them not only the great Christian doctrines, but also how to pray, read the Bible, witness to their friends, and even how to listen to sermons. She loved these children and treated them as young adults; they retained their love for her even when they passed into their teens.

But perhaps Barbara's greatest single contribution, and the one for which she will be most remembered, was the Pastors' Wives' Conference. It was borne out of a realisation that so many wives 'in the ministry' felt inadequate, even intimidated, because of the expectations of many churches. Others felt lonely or hurt by the attitude of the church to their husband. Although we worked with a united and caring church ourselves, Barbara understood the needs of these wives and wanted to do something to help.

Our church hosted the conference for twelve years, and those two days away from home and family was appreciated by many of the wives. At first they travelled from as far away as Scotland and Cornwall but Barbara, never an empire builder, felt it would be wiser to start regional conferences that would run their own programme. In the event, five were started. Scores of pastors' wives across the country expressed their appreciation for the help that they had received. Many got to know each

Above: By 1960, the year of their engagement, Barbara had already been on a course of steroids for five years

other for the first time, and they felt valued in themselves and not just as the wife of their minister husband; often at FIEC Caister and other conferences, pastors' wives would take great pleasure in introducing husbands to each other! The most moving picture in my mind is of the pastor who presented Barbara with a single red rose 'as an appreciation for all that you have done for my wife.' Barbara loved this work, and perhaps thought of it as her main ministry beyond her home and church; but it took its annual toll on her and left her utterly exhausted. I kept that weekend free just to be available to help her.

During all these busy years the rheumatoid arthritis was grabbing at Barbara. Over a period of twelve years she spent sixteen weeks in hospital undergoing five major operations for orthopaedic surgery. Life began to change more rapidly. Her daily pain was compounded by very little mobility. She needed help with many ordinary tasks. I had to take on some new duties: housework (but kind volunteers helped with this), washing (easy in today's world), cooking (which I dislike) and shopping (which I hate). With a growing and active church and family, and increased demands upon our time, there had to be constant readjustments. Only two things were constant: The reassurance from the

Above: Brian and Barbara married in 1963 and settled into their first appointment at an evangelical church in West Norwood, in South East London

Bible of God's love and wisdom, and our love for each other which matured and grew stronger with the passing years. Without these ingredients our marriage could never have survived; the pressures at times were immense. As a girl at school Barbara had been very active—and from games captain to a wheelchair is a hard route to take.

Gradually every joint in Barbara's body was attacked and deformed by this unstoppable disease. We maintained a busy programme and shed virtually nothing. Barbara learnt to live with pain as her daily companion, and most of the indignities of helplessness we laughed at.

Eventually, I resigned the leadership of the church we had served for almost thirty years and we took up a new role. For two years we travelled widely throughout the United Kingdom visiting churches, speaking at conferences and attending committees. We designed our own motor home suitable for Barbara's needs, and we travelled everywhere together. Andrew was still at home, but well independent. Stephen was married to Fiona and they had three delightful girls. Life was hard, but rewarding.

Behind the smile

Three months after leaving Frimley Park Hospital the infamous halo jacket was replaced by a more aesthetically pleasing, though even more uncomfortable brace. Four weeks after this, a soft collar became standard uniform and the consultant expressed himself well pleased with the result of his feat of engineering. Certainly some of the earlier symptoms of spinal compression had disappeared. By the late summer we were preparing for a few days away to make up for the cancellation of our planned holiday. We were hoping that, after all, some of our autumn schedule might be redeemed.

Barbara was known for her smile. It was not merely a facade; she was determined never to bore people with her disability and she only spoke of it in detail with a few friends, and then only when pressed. Otherwise she would quickly change the subject. It became a joke in the church that Barbara was the biggest liar in membership! Whenever anyone enquired how she was, the reply was always, 'I'm fine thank you.' But then, as we explained, given that she could not walk, use her hands, or do anything for herself, and was always a short distance away from the next crisis, she was often quite well.

But although her smile was not simply for show, it did mask many of the fears and frustrations that lurked in her mind constantly. 'At night' she once told me, 'I dream of all the things I would love to be doing; then, when morning comes, reality hits me and I can do nothing but lie and sit. Sometimes I think I should just enjoy everybody doing everything for me, but that isn't me. I can't be like that, I want to be helping others and running the home and actively involved in the Lord's work.' By this time she was finding it much harder to find value in the meanwhile.

By the summer of 1997, just when things looked as though they were improving after Frimley Park, Barbara's general health deteriorated. Slowly at first, but then more rapidly, it became clear that she was seriously ill. She lost her appetite and what she did eat was hard to retain; she was in constant pain and discomfort. Visits from the doctor and various changes in medication brought no relief. The spiral was downward and gathering speed.

Life soon became a constant round of visits from doctors, community nurses, occupational therapists, and physiotherapists. For hours on end it became impossible for Barbara to get comfortable. As the days dragged on she just wanted to die and be with the Lord. She bore her suffering with the patience that I had become used to in her, but I suffered with her when she cried, 'My body is all tense with pain. People tell me they remember my smile, but I can't smile anymore, the Lord has taken it away.' That was sadly true; I can recall a period of three weeks when I do not think I saw Barbara smile. Often I would come into a room and discover her quietly sobbing with pain and frustration, 'I'm tired of just sitting, sitting all day, I want to get up and walk. I want to do something on my own, for myself, unaided.' By now she could not even turn the page of a book or a magazine.

This inevitably led to her self-worth being attacked. For many years Barbara's health had been finely balanced. One over-stressed day, one night in an uncomfortable bed, one meal with wrong ingredients, one draughty seat, and the results could be traumatic. Now every new day was a new mountain to climb. She felt useless and was convinced that she was spoiling my life and ministry. 'I was sure when we began our ministry', she sobbed, 'that God would give me the health and strength to support you in all your work—but he didn't keep his promise, he has let me down.' In her mind she knew that this was not the right conclusion, but I was glad that she felt she could confide in me what she was feeling. Some people understood this. I recall the close of a conference I had ministered at when the leader prayed a brief but beautiful prayer for Barbara; Eddie Vass touched every trigger point, 'Lord, you know that we live in an age when people are judged by appearance, power and material assets. Help us to see the value of every individual. Barbara must be feeling a lack of worth and value. Lord help her to see her value and worth in you.'

We cried together and prayed together. I struggled on with a reduced ministry, but at times my heart was not in it. I hated leaving Barbara and wanted to hurry back to her. I was fine whilst I was preaching, but I am ashamed to say that at times I couldn't care whether I preached or not. I never preached what I did not believe, but I often preached what I could not feel. In thirty years of Christian ministry I could never recall seriously wanting to quit my work—until now. The effort of giving Barbara total nursing care, with no realistic hope of improvement, and at the same time maintaining a full ministry of preaching, writing and leadership seemed just too much. I would lay a letter of invitation on my desk, look at it and then leave it for another day. Maybe tomorrow things will look different and we will be able to go; but tomorrow they weren't different, and we couldn't go. For the first time that I could recall, it seemed more attractive to give up everything and simply care for Barbara; this way I would not get ratty when I was under pressure with loyalties divided between sermons, publishers, committees—and Barbara. I bounced from one plan to another. We talked endlessly about what we could do and how this and that might be possible. Then another downturn in her health scuppered our plans and sent us back to square one.

The worst part of all was when Barbara's faith was attacked. I overheard her sobbing through her pain, 'Lord, I'm walking through the wilderness alone; you're not with me anymore.' And the sad comment when she woke up one morning, 'I suppose I should sing "This is the day that the Lord has made"—but I wish he hadn't.' She alternated between hope and despair, that paradox of the Christian with a firm faith in the future and a painful experience of the present. More than once I heard Barbara pray, 'Lord, I'm tired of the struggle. I just want to die.' But a day later her request was simply, 'Lord, I long to feel better.'

Inevitably another stay in hospital could not be far away. It came one morning when I noticed a large swelling in her back. Nine and a half hours in casualty was our introduction to six weeks in a local hospital. Here, cared for by a senior consultant who was both a friend and a Christian, two large abscesses took a month to drain and her slow road to recovery was hindered by contracting the infamous hospital bug MRSA (Methicillin Resistant Staphylococcus Aureus). Weeks passed in a long struggle for survival. Fluctuating temperatures, a constant fight to keep down the little food she could eat, scans and examinations of every conceivable kind, massive doses of antibiotics, these all became our regular daily round. Eventually I spent all day every day with her in her side ward in order to keep up her determination to fight, and to care for her above the limitations of a busy ward staff.

It seemed just about every consultant in the hospital came to see this prize exhibit of something or other! But they were all very kind and reassuring. When Barbara was particularly anxious about the nature of yet one more unpleasant examination the consultant touched her arm and reassured her, 'Come on, you are a star patient, and a very brave lady.' 'I might seem like that outside' she responded, 'but inside I'm terrified.' On another occasion when a consultant kindly commented that he counted it a privilege to meet her because everyone was talking about her, Barbara responded, 'I don't want to be a hero, I just want to be well.' The senior radiologist remarked to two visiting medics that Barbara was the most severe case of rheumatoid arthritis he had ever seen. Far from upsetting us, this in fact reassured us. We were always afraid of making too much fuss about her disability, and a comment like that at least confirmed that we weren't.

Barbara had long since learned to cope with the indignities of hospital life, especially as a patient who could do nothing for herself. To be prodded and poked by doctors, stared at and lectured on in front of inquisitive students, and to be totally dependent for everything, including feeding, is hardly a recipe for feeling a valued and respected member of the community. 'When you come into hospital', Barbara advised, 'just leave your dignity at the entrance and collect it on the way out.' Yet, somehow her dignity never quite left her. A consultant understood this when she wrote of Barbara, 'Her courage was magnificent and very few of us would have coped with such daunting problems with the dignity which she managed to produce and with a smile and with exceptional cheerfulness.'

Light in the Tunnel

For my part, all I had ever preached with conviction and passion was being thrown back at me. All through Barbara's declining strength, I had never for a moment doubted the wisdom and care of God. But it was hard to make any sense of it all as I watched her in pain every day, sometimes all day, then crying out in her sleep, and with a catalogue of medical conditions from joints that burned with inflammation, to pressure sores, mouth ulcers, bladder infections, days that frequently ended in violent vomiting, and now two large abscesses slowly poisoning her. However, when we are so close to the event we often cannot make sense out of suffering.

I longed for Barbara to be home again, and I knew that around the country hundreds continued to pray for her. Sometimes I felt selfish in praying for her recovery! I wanted her home more than anything in the world, but I knew that life for Barbara would continue to be a knife edge of relative health and dangerous illness. Pain and weakness would be a permanent part of her life. So why didn't I pray for God to take her to that better home where there is no more pain or tears? Because I knew that the timing of our departure is for God to decide, not us. Where there is life there is meaning. We never doubted that God had plans, and his plans, however hard at the time, would always, ultimately, prove to be 'good, pleasing and perfect' (Romans 12:2).

There were times when Satan tempted me as Job's wife had tempted her husband, 'Are you still holding on to your integrity? Curse God and die' Job (2:9). I prayed for a little respite for Barbara—but things got worse. I felt exhausted and wanted to swear! Anything to relieve my feelings. What was the point of my theological integrity? In the roller coaster of our experiences, when one good day was no guide to what would follow, I sometimes felt that God was playing with Barbara as a cat with a mouse. I knew that he didn't really behave like this, but there seemed no reason why she should be so tormented with pain, discomfort and disappointments.

Unintentionally I expressed our deepest confusion in my diary when Barbara's wound from a Girdlestone operation to remove her hip had broken open and was long, deep and oozing.

Saturday December 6th 1997

I failed Barbara by being tearful before I left her. No one can ever know how much it hurts me to see her pain. What is almost worse is the strong way she takes it all. I fail beside her resolute will; and yet I know that inside she is more churned up than I am. Tonight we both agreed that we felt we were living in a strange surreal world. Our world seems divorced, or at least separated, from the real world around us. We feel guilty that so much of our time—all of Barbara's time—focuses upon ourselves. We can barely pray for ourselves, let alone for others. As we read the Scriptures, promises from God and descriptions of his character come before us almost mockingly. They hardly seem true for us. We look at each other and honestly confide, 'But he's not like that to us, is he?'

Is Barbara only here because I have asked for her? And is God piling more and more suffering on her until I *want* to let her go for her sake? If ever I have been glib about suffering in the past I never will be again. Our life is one long surreal confusion. Barbara lives with pain in her body, and I live with pain in my soul. If she has to suffer like this, I cannot again ask for her to stay here. I want Barbara to be taken to heaven, peacefully, for her sake. Yet for my sake, I desperately want her to stay with me. Who can make sense of all this? I will preach tomorrow on Revelation 1:5-6. I *know* my words are right, but will I *feel* the truth of what I say? I fear that I will preach from a well-informed head but with an uninspired heart.

In the event I noted that the Lord helped me to preach with heart and conviction. But this was how very low we both were. It was hardly the time to be making our own serious decisions about the future. What I did not know was that we still had some terrible days ahead, but also some of our most beautiful times together, times that I am so very glad we did not miss.

For months on end there seemed no light at the end of the tunnel, until gradually it dawned on me that perhaps I was expected to find light *in* the tunnel, rather than just at the end of it. Life after Adam's fall into sin has been chaos. Only God can ultimately make sense of it all, and meanwhile Christians are caught up in the horrendous holocaust of mankind's madness. We live in a world of misery and sadness, disease and death. In *The Moon and Sixpence*, Somerset Maugham puts these words into the mouth of poor Dick Stroeve, 'The world is hard and cruel. We are here, none knows why, and we go none knows whither.' That must certainly be true for those who live and die without Christ.

Back in Frimley Park days I wrote in my diary that, 'Christians are the only people who can bask in the sunlight even as we walk in the dark.' It was only later that I came across the force of Isaiah 50:10, 'Let him who walks in the dark, who has no light, trust in the name of the LORD and rely on his God.' Walking in the dark with God is in fact walking in the light. We may not be sure where we are going, or even where we are, but the absolute certainty of knowing that God is there is sufficient light. I don't think we ever doubted this. There were times when we felt desperately desolate, but we trusted in the confident certainty that not only was God true, but that he was also true to his word. Our strength lay not in how we felt, but in the friendship we had with God as our Father through Jesus Christ, and in the many assurances in the Bible that he whose ways were always wise, would never leave us.

I am a very impatient person. Barbara's calm concentration on the present always contrasted with my hurry to get things done and move on to the next project. Interference annoyed me. I watched her attempts at writing, and was unkind enough to laugh as the spidery letters slid slowly down the page in an illegible scrawl. She laughed with me. Years before, when her ability to play the piano and touch-type came to an end, she would painstakingly continue by pressing the keys of her laptop with the knuckle of one of her ten floppy fingers. In earlier years I never ceased to marvel at the hours she would spend decorating a sponge or cake that the guests would demolish in minutes. The finest and most intricate embroidery was a challenge to her. She bore her pain and limitations with dignity and determination. For my part, I got frustrated. I inwardly rebelled and often outwardly snapped as more and more of my programme was shed to make way for Barbara's needs. I challenged the Lord, 'How do you expect me to continue with my ministry *and* look after a disabled wife?' I don't know when or how, but it dawned on me that only two people got hurt by this attitude, Barbara and myself.

Many years ago I watched one of my senior elders, a relatively young man, slowly degenerate with Multiple Sclerosis. When he was finally confined to bed and his wife, Joy, had to care for his every need, I asked Philip how he, an active, visionary businessman and Christian, could possibly be coping so well with the indignity and disappointment of his steady decline. I have quoted his reply often, 'Brian', he said with a look that told me I would understand one day, 'there is no future in frustration.'

At last I was about to learn what he meant.

Up until this point Barbara and I had never allowed her disability to hinder our work for Christ and his church. We worked hard and long and we saw the church grow. I hope I cared for Barbara and the family, but at times I know they were neglected. During our two years of itinerant ministry we travelled together and thoroughly enjoyed being together and working together. We camped in our motorhome, and could be on the road for days without needing any supplies. We enjoyed each other's company immensely. Barbara bore patiently my impatience when, short of time for a meeting, I still had to dress her and get her off the van in a howling gale and pouring rain, tidy her up, settle her in a strange building and then appear calm and collected to a congregation. But it was all so worth while. Barbara was not only my best critic, but also my greatest friend and companion in the work. She often learnt far more about a church than I did. People talked with her freely. Her variety of experiences in the way people respond to someone in a wheelchair gave us a lot of fun and stories to tell! However, this could not go on, it was clear that our programme would have to change.

Barbara survived those stomach abscesses, but a few weeks later an MRSA abscess in her left hip led to a Girdlestone operation to remove the hip altogether. We still hoped to travel. However, pressure sores soon confined her to bed for much of the day and MRSA abscesses demanded more hospitalization. Travel now became out of the question. I came to the conclusion that Barbara was my first priority, and that if necessary *all else* must go. Once I had come to this conclusion, had cancelled all my planned conferences, limited my preaching ministry, and come off almost all my committees, I had great peace! I had found light in the tunnel.

My days revolved around Barbara, and I enjoyed it. After the community nurse left in the morning, I would try to get three or four hours work in the study whilst Barbara rested. From lunch on, the day was hers. We worked on revising our marriage preparation book *No Longer Two*, and if the weather allowed we would go out. We remodelled the garden, and perhaps for the first time in our lives had time to enjoy it. I was no longer frustrated. This was God's new plan for us both. Our love was deep and strong, and I marvelled constantly at Barbara's fortitude and faith. They were some of the hardest months of our lives, yet some of the most beautiful. We both knew that our time together was on loan, but we also knew that when our Saviour called in the loan, we had nothing to fear. Value was back in vogue. I am so grateful not to have missed those months.

Be careful with grandma

I know what Barbara found hard in her disability. High on her list was not being able to cuddle the grandchildren or play with them. It was hard for her to watch them rush up to granddad who could run away and hide or chase them or swing them around; and it was harder still to hear the wise warning from Fiona, 'Be careful with grandma when you kiss her goodbye.' But the upside was their thoughtfulness. When they excitedly shared their adventures at a theme park and seven-year old Susanna advised, 'And you would enjoy the boat ride grandma because it had a place for wheelchairs', that simple observation was heart-warming. The grandchildren never showed embarrassment at a grandmother who couldn't walk or play like other grandmothers, and they would love to walk beside the chair and hold on to its arm-rest in lieu of a grandmother's reassuring hand. When Barbara came home from hospital probably no one was more relieved than Adele's teacher; at last her pre-occupied five-year-old could stop making cards and return to the curriculum the government had planned for her.

It was hard not being able to cuddle or be cuddled by anyone she loved. A squeeze of the arm or a firm hug would be grinding bone against bone. In her greatest distress of pain and the despair of never feeling well again Barbara once cried, 'I just want someone to hug me'—my only response could be a gentle arm round her shoulder and a soft kiss.

Cake decorating, flower arranging and cooking were all major interests for Barbara. I know that I am highly biased, but she was good at them all. She decorated cakes until it became impossible for her to spread the icing or work the intricate lace-work, she was in demand for floral decorations at weddings until the effort became too exhausting, and she gave up hospitality long after many would have quit. I tried to act as a back up, but decorating cakes is definitely not my scene. At least we managed the occasional floral decoration, with me pushing blooms in where I was ordered. To give up these loves one by one was hard to accept. But always Barbara would find something to take their place.

She longed to go for walks, shop on her own, and just be like everyone else. So, to claim that Barbara became accustomed to her disability would not be true. She simply accepted it and saw herself, not as some great hero who knows no fear and feels no pain, but as a reluctant trooper, who just knows that this is the way it is, that there's a job to be done, and that we must get on with it. I felt the same way. Perhaps the only difference was that I gained some comfort in my pride of such a courageous and devoted wife and in the fact that those who knew her best admired her the most.

Interestingly, but perhaps typically, when I talked with her about what she found hardest, Barbara never mentioned the matter of living with daily pain. Her pain tolerance was incredibly high and more than once I have stood by as she negotiated a lower dose of pain relief with the palliative care team. In reply to a doctor's enquiry, 'Are you in pain Barbara?' she would often reply, 'Well, it all depends what you mean by pain; it's a bit uncomfortable.' Sometimes they would make the decision for her, 'Well, you ought to be in pain, so I'm writing up pain relief for you on your chart.' When I caught her sobbing with pain, I knew it hurt a lot.

Barbara left school at sixteen and trained as a bookbinder in a large printing firm. She never gained academic qualifications, and because of this was never above people. Perhaps because of this also, she had a judgement and assessment of people that I relied on heavily. She was an excellent listener and our two boys knew that she always had time for them to talk. They, like most other people, also knew when she disagreed with them; Barbara was never a very good hypocrite.

Barbara's mind was always full of ideas. Sometimes I thought they were far too ambitious and I was less than enthusiastic, but her dogged perseverance carried others with her. As a young Christian she had longed to serve God in India; my arrival on the scene changed that, but she never lost her passion for evangelism overseas. As a member of our church World Vision Committee, Barbara was determined to change the stereotype 'missionary weekend' into something valuable and exciting. The first year we had over two hundred people on the Saturday afternoon and evening, a third of whom were actually involved in the presentation. It set a pattern that is still followed at Hook. Most were worn out by the end of it, but she rarely took 'no' for an answer and encouraged people to achieve what they never thought possible.

The better side of worse

A friend once said to us 'You two never seem to grumble.' I had to be honest, 'Oh we do', I replied, 'but not to you, there's little point in that; we grumble to the Lord.' In more recent years there were many times when we just cried out for a little space. As soon as Barbara got through one crisis, another tumbled in. And each time she could never quite make up the ground she had lost from the time before. But then we felt guilty, and in asking God to forgive our ingratitude, we surveyed all the benefits of our life. We knew that there is always a better side of worse.

We enjoyed a lovely house and garden. When we brought Barbara's bed into the lounge it meant that she could lie and admire the changing colour of our garden with, as the estate agents would describe it, a south facing and secluded aspect. Our two sons and daughter-in-law were Christians and all busily involved in Christian work, and we had three delightful granddaughters. Friends all over the country, and beyond, regularly assured us of their prayers. Others were even willing for us to join them on holiday!

Throughout our ministry at Hook Evangelical Church we were surrounded by Christian friends who cared and who wanted to help. For years they complained that we were too private and independent about Barbara's disability. But we had no intention of becoming dependent before time. For twelve years they never saw her out of a wheelchair, but we did not slacken our pace. Perhaps it was typical of Barbara that she often wished her wheelchair would go faster; she hated to be overtaken on the way to church by Graham and Tessa in their faster electric buggies!

However, when eventually we needed help, it was ready to hand. Ladies from the church came to clean, prepare meals, shop, or just to stay with Barbara when I had to be away for a day. Whenever Barbara was in hospital, a team ensured that someone called in at midday every day to give her lunch. Without this she could not have survived, or I would have had to give up all ministry long before. A modern NHS hospital cannot cope with a patient who is totally disabled. The Christian family can either be a tragic failure at such times, or a great example of what Christianity stands for. Hook Evangelical Church was the latter. The value of a Christian family that behaves like one, is beyond price.

Barbara's skill in her wheelchair opened the house and garden to her. But it did more than this. She was incredibly adept at manoeuvring;

unerringly she could negotiate round a large store, or back into a 'parking lot' between pews. At conferences she could be independent of me and choose her own seminars to attend.

Every new decline has to be accepted with courage for the disabled. But they must prepare for it with a blend of their own time and the right time. The two are not always the same. Taking to a walking stick is not easy, a frame is yet a further challenge to our pride, but a wheelchair is perhaps the ultimate. For our part we always planned ahead and prepared for the worst scenario. We tried to gauge what the next stage would be and how we could be ready for it. This was far better than a rush to meet a crisis.

Barbara received her first hip replacement at the age of thirty-nine. Eight years later it broke down and she spent two months in hospital while the hip was replaced, the bone grafts healed, and then the other hip was also replaced. We were warned at that time that she might never walk again. I arranged for a vertical lift to be fitted at home so that her wheelchair could be taken straight to the bedroom. This time it was the men in the church who undertook all the preparatory work; they made what the lift engineer called, 'The neatest hole I have ever seen.' In the event Barbara was able to walk a little for a while, but I never regretted the lift, which soon became a necessity. Similarly, we entered the motor caravan market before Barbara could no longer get into a car. Eventually we designed our own van, which included a lift for the wheelchair, and this made our wider ministry possible. Forward planning is vital for someone with a degenerative disease. You can either look at it as morbid pessimism or as practical wisdom. I know which served us best.

We were blessed with a local medical practice that never questioned the expensive drugs Barbara was on. On one occasion I came home from the pharmacy with eighteen hundred pounds worth of medication in a carrier bag. A team of excellent Community Nurses came daily to care for Barbara's wounds and to administer her antibiotics by injection. They were totally supportive. We were relieved when the team expressed their willingness to care for Barbara's large open wound on her hip, complete with the MRSA bug, so that she could come home from hospital. They willingly took on the responsibility of injections through a central line, and even trained me to give the evening injection so that we could be a little more independent. When Care in the Community works, and ours did, there is nothing better. Our local hospice took us under its wing just in case Barbara needed respite care, and their constant contact was reassuring. Later, the provision of an Environmental Control Unit by central government meant that at the press of a touch-sensitive pad Barbara could answer and open the front door, close the curtains, make and receive telephone calls, or switch on the light, television or hi fi. This gave back a little of her lost independence. Government disability pensions kept us mobile and active. We never ceased to be grateful for how well provided for we are in this country.

It is not easy being on the receiving end of kindness, but we had to learn that actually everyone benefits. We had spent thirty years serving others, arranging rotas of care and visits, sending cards, and counselling and providing hospitality. It had been our privilege to give, and through those years we were involved in many tragic disruptions to people's lives. But now the tables were turned. People came into our house and just got on with their job; we felt we were losing our privacy and even our own home. But there was no alternative. Between them all they made us feel that we mattered. From those who came with medical help, to those who came to clean, cook or shop, or just to sit with Barbara, no one gave the impression that we were a nuisance—though we constantly felt we were. The quick-fix solution of the euthanasia lobby denies everyone the rich experience of caring and being cared for. The hospice movement encourages the Christian view that life is valuable and meaningful, however painful. It may be tempting to find a way out, but it is far more valuable to find a way through.

When the writer of Proverbs 5:18 encourages husbands to 'rejoice in the wife of your youth', he did not mean simply 'rejoice in your wife in your youth.' He meant that the love and joy that we had in our youth should continue. It is even better when the varied experiences of life enrich it. Our love grew deeper with the passing years and everything we taught—and finally wrote—in our marriage preparation series, we both believed and experienced. Humanly, the best side of worse for us was our trust and confidence in each other's love. That made the suffering, and the final separation, harder, but it meant that we shared every success as well as every failure. We never tired of each other's company and nothing was a greater delight than when Barbara could travel with me. That bond turned even those common duties of caring for someone who was totally disabled into a privilege—though I do not pretend that I always saw it this way!

Our hope of heaven also showed us the better side of worse. Typical was Barbara's response when I woke one morning to hear her quietly sobbing to herself. When I tried to comfort her she apologised, 'Darling, I'm sorry I keep crying. I just feel it all boils up inside me and every now and then the lid has to pop off. Oh won't it be wonderful in heaven.' We talked often of heaven, not in a vague and detached way, but with the certainty that when it was all over we would be there with our Saviour Jesus Christ for ever. Neither of us feared death, though we didn't relish the thought of what form dying might take.

Undoubtedly our greatest strength of all was drawn from our faith in God and the Bible. Isaiah 41:10 was always a special verse for us, 'Do not fear, for I am with you; do not be dismayed, for I am your God. I will strengthen you and help you; I will uphold you with my righteous right hand.' Of course there were moments of despair and questioning, but always we fell back onto the unchanging character of a faithful God. Even when God seemed a million miles away and Barbara admitted that she could not even cry to him for help, even then we knew that he would never abandon us. We believed firmly in the God of sovereign authority, and we had confidence in the fact that, 'The LORD does whatever pleases him in the heavens and on the earth' (Psalm 135:6). However, we learned that not all his ways are pleasing to us, though they are always right. And if they are right, then they always please him. So, we learned to thank God that he always does what he wants.

From death into life

When the Lord finally called Barbara away from her suffering into the pain-free joy of heaven I was overwhelmed with almost five hundred cards and letters. Light in my darkness came from the rich tributes that letter after letter gave to the value of Barbara's life. She may have felt that the Lord had thrown her on the scrap heap, but no one else seemed to think so. The following expressions are typical of scores:

'Barbara's influence will continue, not only through the wives' conferences... but through the indelible example she has left of persevering faith in the face of so much affliction.'

'Barbara was truly a shining example to us all of humility, wisdom, patience and courage—to say nothing of her special sense of humour!'

'You will know better than anyone will how special Barbara was, but others of us will retain precious memories of her courage, warmth and spiritual perception. These and other gracious qualities brought enrichment to us.'

'Barbara's indomitable spirit was an encouragement to us all.'

'We remember her fortitude and courage, her incredible patience and her smile which often belied her suffering. We are so thankful to have known her. She was always an inspiration to us.'

'It has been a great privilege to know and admire Barbara for her love and dedication to our Lord Jesus Christ, and we are grateful for our personal indebtedness to her.'

'Barbara never handled her life as if it was 'for worse.' There was no collapsing into a private world of self-pity; always, rather, a lively interest in other people and in Kingdom work outside of herself.'

'Barbara was unique—she touched the life of each person that met her, including me.'

'Her bravery and her example... will urge us on to make the best use of the health we have been given.'

I know exactly what Barbara's response would have been, had she seen such tributes: 'Rubbish. They don't really know me.' But they did, and I, who lived with her for thirty-five years, can confirm it. I saw Barbara at her lowest ebb and at her most determined. The first was rare, the second was the real Barbara. The reason why Barbara never wrote or spoke publicly about her suffering was that she never considered that she was anyone special. And in one sense she wasn't. She was simply a country girl who trusted Christ as her Lord and Saviour and promised to serve him. She kept her promise. She loved God's world and God's people and threw herself into God's work with all the strength that he gave her—and then asked for a little more. Anyone can do that. None of us knows the impact we make on the lives of others by just being what we are and doing what we can do. Only eternity will reveal this.

I was given a number of test runs for the end, and I became accustomed to answering the question, 'Mr Edwards, what do you want us to do in the event of cardiac arrest?' On one occasion when Barbara's temperature soared and her blood pressure plummeted she had slipped into a coma before we reached the hospital. Suddenly her room was filled with doctors, and when the senior medical registrar informed me that she was fighting a serious infection and pneumonia I knew there was no hope for her recovery. They suggested ICU and ventilation, but this meant a cross-country dash of twenty miles to find a bed. I could see no value in prolonging her misery and made the decision. I told him that we were deeply committed Christians and had no fear for Barbara's future; I strongly opposed euthanasia but could see no reason why Barbara should go through such trauma when the end was inevitable.

The Registrar and anaesthetist agreed, and they made preparations to keep her comfortable. I called Stephen and Andrew to join me, and we settled down to wait for what everyone knew was the end. The boys were brave and supportive and the nursing staff were caring and thoughtful. As the night wore on we prayed, sat in silence, chatted, drank tea, swatted the flies and wasps that ventured through the open window, and waited for the inevitable. By 5.30 am Barbara was breathing normally and two hours later was asking for a cup of tea! When the Registrar arrived for his morning round, his first words were, 'This is not the lady I was dealing with last night.' Then, turning to his clinical assistant he dictated the first words of the medical report,

'Miraculous recovery.' I watched the doctor write it down.

But it was a short-lived miracle! More emergencies, a stubborn MRSA abscess on the knee, discussions about the possibility of amputation as the only way forward and finally an early morning dash to the hospital with a soaring temperature and plummeting blood pressure. I watched Barbara and had some idea of how many things were wrong—though in reality there was much more. I wrote in my diary:

'Oh Lord, all that Barbara and I have dreaded you are allowing to happen. An operation? Barbara's poor body cut and mutilated even more. But what can it achieve? Lord, if the end must be slow please give us both 'sufficient courage that God may be glorified in our bodies.' Give me faith and strength not to fail you Lord. To see Barbara hurts me so much. I always asked to be able to care for her at home to the end. But can I? Oh Lord, these are terrible days. When Barbara looks up and says, "Brian, help me!" it's awful. I want to; I always do – but now I can't.'

For the first time ever, I stood beside her bed and prayed that God would take Barbara to himself. The end was not slow. I returned home and heard myself sobbing, sobbing. I was back at the hospital shortly, and at 2.10 pm on Monday November 16 1998 Barbara passed from death into life. I was with her as she slipped into glory. Andrew and Stephen arrived, and in her room we stood and held hands and prayed. A wonderful moment! There had been value in all our meanwhile. I closed my diary for that day with these words, 'Only I know just how wonderful a wife and mother Barbara was. Her patient endurance, deep love for the Lord and longing to serve him. Thank you Lord, for Barbara.'

More than skin deep

Andrew and Helen Bryant

With the arrival of Charlotte, Andrew and Helen looked forward to a fourth, healthy child to add to their lively young family. They had no idea that Charlotte would be born with a rare and serious skin disorder that would radically change their lives and challenge their faith in ways they had never imagined. With courageous honesty, they share with us their fears and failures, as well as their times of confident success, as they cope with Charlotte's disability.

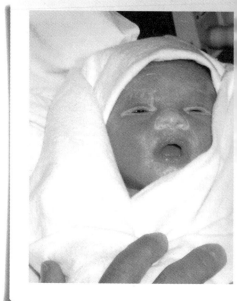

It was 2.30am at the Neonatal Intensive Care Unit in Harold Wood Hospital. Anxiously we peered through the sides of the incubator. Inside was our newborn daughter, barely one hour old. Charlotte Ellena, our fourth child, was born a month premature and she came in a hurry. We had been enjoying a day out with friends at Legoland in Windsor when Helen went into labour. The theme-park nurse was most helpful, but urged us to travel home immediately. Never had we driven so enthusiastically around the

M25. Thoughts of an emergency delivery on the hard shoulder held little appeal for either of us. Charlotte arrived in the early hours of Wednesday August 28 1996. She was duly named, held and photographed, but as the midwife attended to her medical needs, murmuring began. It was obvious something was wrong, and her swift removal to the special care baby unit caught us by surprise. After three healthy babies, we were somehow not expecting there to be any problem with the fourth.

It was Charlotte's skin that gave cause for concern. It appeared tight and brittle, particularly across her chest and tummy. It was something like that of an over-cooked chicken, and looked as though it would crack to the touch. Her eyes were fixed open, the nose and cheeks discoloured. Her tiny hands and feet were shiny, as though encased in plastic. The duty paediatrician acknowledged that there was a problem, but the words he used made little sense to us at first. On repetition, we understood that she had a condition called collodion membrane ichthyosis.

Charlotte was branded a collodion baby, which meant that she was cocooned in a thick, outer layer of skin that needed to be shed like an emerging butterfly if she was to survive. Infection and dehydration were the greatest dangers at first, so she was kept in a warm, humid incubator. Helen was allowed to hold our little daughter for just a few short moments.

This was so different from anything we had ever previously experienced. Having always opted to have baby's cot by the bedside throughout her post-natal stay in hospital, Helen found the next day or so strangely empty. As the medical staff tended to Charlotte's physical needs, the normal bonding between mother and child was more difficult to establish. It was possible to breast-feed Charlotte, but this had to be fitted in between the frequent creaming and washing of her skin, and the various tests that were being carried out. By midday on Thursday Helen was discharged and had the agonising experience of travelling home and leaving her newborn behind. The following few days became a constant round of juggling hospital visits, feeds, the needs of the older children and the search to understand more about our baby's condition.

Left: At birth, Charlotte was branded a collodion baby, which meant that she was cocooned in a thick, outer layer of skin that needed to be shed if she was to survive

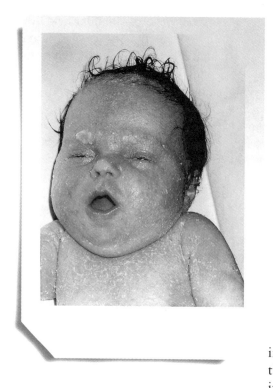

The first thing we discovered was that information about ichthyosis was scarce. The standard family health books said virtually nothing, and the hospital staff could be seen looking up entries in their own medical textbooks. We had recently connected to the Internet, and a search of the worldwide web yielded some material. In particular, we discovered an American support group, the Foundation for Ichthyosis and Related Skin Types (FIRST). This was to become an invaluable source of information and provided the impetus for our own involvement in the setting up of a similar group in the UK.

An early appointment with Charlotte's consultant, Dr Prasad, proved especially helpful. We learned that ichthyosis is a rare genetic skin disorder. In its more severe forms around one in six hundred thousand children are affected. There is at present no cure. The word 'ichthyosis' is derived from the Greek *ichthus*, meaning 'fish,' and is used to describe a number of conditions in which the skin can appear thick and scaly. Either too many skin cells are produced, or the millions of dry, dead cells stubbornly refuse to shift. As well as being unsightly, infection becomes more likely. Movement and co-ordination may be inhibited, and other medical

Above: After three weeks of an intensive round-the-clock regimen of bathing and skin lubrication, Charlotte began to emerge from the cocoon of outer skin. This relentless treatment is ongoing, and for life.

complications can occur. The cause is faulty copies of genes that are passed on from one generation to the next. We were told that, in a case such as Charlotte's, both parents would have contributed faulty genetic material. So in every respect we were very much in this together. The chance of us producing an affected child was one in four. As Charlotte is our fourth, at least the statistical probabilities proved correct.

Collodion is the name given to a gluey solution used in photographic processing. With ichthyosis, the 'collodion' label refers to the thick, plastic-like outer coating of skin that needs to be shed. Charlotte's incubation was intended to regulate this process. If it happened too quickly, she would suffer rapid dehydration. The risk of life-threatening infection was high. Once the outer layer of skin had shed, it was just possible that she would be left with nothing more serious than rather dry skin. There was a far greater probability, however, that her skin would remain excessively dry, requiring a life-long regime of creams and ointments, with the inevitable practical and social implications. Several changes of clothes a day, and a somewhat different appearance from other children, were predicted.

We were grateful for the frankness of Charlotte's consultant. It would have been so frustrating to be presented with only partial explanations. We wanted to know what we were dealing with. In addition to our own anxieties, our families and the church members were keen to be kept informed, and to be able to assist and to pray for us.

Roller-coaster emotions

Quite apart from Charlotte's arrival, this was already proving to be an eventful year. A few weeks previously we had moved south from Derbyshire because Andrew had been invited to become minister of Romford Evangelical Free Church. The last few months in the Midlands had involved some sad farewells, but we both had a firm conviction that the change of pastorate was the Lord's plan for us. Our new church must have wondered what they had taken on. The induction service took place just three days after Charlotte's birth. Helen managed to take time out from the hospital to be at the service, though she sensibly declined the invitation to sit on the platform and 'say a few words.' As soon as the meeting was over she hurried back to the hospital for the next feeding session. It was also an encouragement to be joined at the induction by some of the members of our previous church. They have faithfully maintained their interest and prayer support.

Meanwhile, the skin-care regime continued. Every two hours Charlotte was covered from head to toe in a thick, greasy substance, and other procedures were carried out to monitor her condition, with varying degrees of success. Helen remembers the quiet evening when she was sitting by the window reading. A doctor entered the room and made several attempts to insert a 'line' through Charlotte's tummy button to allow for rapid injection of fluids should she dehydrate. Helen simply sat and watched all this happening to 'our' baby. We were later told this was the third attempt. X-rays had shown the needle was going too far and ending up in her liver! It is at times like this that one feels the urge to complain, 'Don't you realise that is our child you might be damaging?' However, we were conscious that, as Charlotte's condition was so rare, even the medical profession were to some extent working by trial and error. We found ourselves simply asking God for more wisdom—both for ourselves, and for those into whose care we had entrusted our child.

Amazingly, another child had been born with ichthyosis in the same hospital just nine days earlier! Charlotte and Lily shared a room. Lily had progressed remarkably over her first two weeks and was able to go home. This really did raise our own hopes, and the medical staff decided to try Charlotte out of the incubator, with a view to letting her leave hospital also. Unfortunately, we did not see the same level of improvement. Further complications were to come.

Andrew will never forget the day we tried taking her home. With three children already, he saw himself as an 'experienced' dad and this was supposed to be a special occasion. As we strapped Charlotte into her child-seat, we were conscious of little other than the pungent odour of the dead cells her body was refusing to shed normally. The plan was for us to continue a two-hourly skin care regime. We set the alarm clock twice a night to remind us to cover her in yet another layer of grease. There was little time for anything else. The family and our new church friends were frequently in the house providing so much practical support. Overall, however, we can remember little—except that after another fortnight, Charlotte was deteriorating, and we were exhausted. It became obvious that she needed re-admission to hospital; this time not to the neonatal

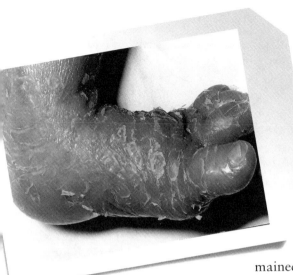

unit, but to the children's ward. Stripped and returned to the incubator, our little daughter immediately won the hearts of the nurses, but she was still very ill. The staff were trained literally to scrub at the thickened patches of skin and then grease her all over. During the three further weeks she remained in hospital, the general pattern of three baths a day with applications of grease every four hours became established. Four years on, we still follow the same routine. Helen well remembers the day when the crusty skin around the eyebrows had finally been scrubbed away. That was quite a milestone.

Looking back over these first few weeks, there seemed little time to pause and think. This was perhaps a good thing. People would ask us, 'How are you coping?' The truth is, we just got on with whatever needed to be done. Only later did we begin to realise how much others did for us on a practical level. Meals were prepared, cakes delivered, children collected and catered for, cleaning of the house arranged. We experienced the kindness of the Lord through the graciousness of his people. This was to be a recurrent and dominant theme as time went on.

In reality, our own prayer and Bible reading was at best sporadic. We were offering up brief and sometimes frantic requests, but were not managing to create time and space to meet with God on a consistent basis. This tended to fuel feelings of guilt and inadequacy, particularly as we

Above: Hospital staff had to be trained to scrub at the thickened patches of Charlotte's skin and then grease her all over

realised others were looking to us for spiritual leadership and direction. Already we were wondering what lay ahead. Obviously we had concerns for ourselves and for the implications of Charlotte's condition on the rest of the family. Laura, Alice and Thomas were understandably troubled by the amount of time mum and dad were at the hospital. The sense of disorientation must have been all the more intense since they were themselves getting used to a new home and a new town, and for Laura, a new school. On the whole they responded well to the needs of their baby sister. Thomas, who was two, jealously stood guard over her in church. Laura, aged eight, was keen to help as much as possible, but three-year-old Alice seemed perturbed, 'Mummy, Charlotte's funny skin keeps touching me.' This concern was short-lived, and soon they all simply accepted and welcomed her into the family. One or other of them will pray about their sister's skin at family prayers around the breakfast table. Sometimes they will ask God to 'make it better', or else, 'help Charlotte not to get too upset when she isn't allowed outside to play in the sun.' We certainly have not issued instructions on what is reasonable or legitimate for them to ask for in relation to her condition. So far she has not been old enough to tell us what she thinks of these petitions, but no doubt she will soon express her opinion!

We are especially thankful that Charlotte has a brother and sisters with whom to play and learn. We suspect that, had she been our only child we may have been prone to over-protect and therefore isolate her from other children. Instead, she has quickly learned to join in with the others, and is sometimes the most adventurous of the four. Beyond this, however, there was our apprehension over what Charlotte herself could look forward to. It was one thing to acknowledge that God was sovereign over every aspect of our lives, including her birth, but it was quite another to presume that she herself would grow to accept this. As a father, Andrew found himself developing an attitude of fierce protectiveness and a determination to fight for her interests. Maybe this gave us a faint glimpse of the Lord's zeal to protect the lives of his own loved ones. Helen found that her time and energy was fully taken up with the sheer practicalities of the daily routine. We both knew already that Charlotte would need all the tender love and biblical wisdom that we could possibly give her. We also saw that like all children she would need to grow to acknowledge Christ in her own life.

Ultimately our responsibility was simply to pray that, whatever the challenges ahead, her heart would be opened to receive him as her Lord.

Learning to accept help

At six weeks, Charlotte was referred to the Great Ormond Street Hospital for Sick Children, known as GOSH to the 'regulars'. She travelled by ambulance in a transportable incubator, and was seen by consultant dermatologist Dr David Atherton. He had been overseeing the advice given to our local hospital, and he was eager to examine her in order to confirm the correct diagnosis and to decide on further treatment. This was the first of many visits to GOSH, where she is now a regular visitor to the Outpatients' Department. There was, apparently, little doubt that hers was a severe case of ichthyosis. She was sent off to be thoroughly photographed, both for her own records and doubtless for the doctors' own collections. We were able to obtain copies for ourselves. We are so glad we did this, as they continue to provide a valuable reminder of how far she has progressed since then.

Soon afterwards Charlotte came home, but not before Social Services had arranged a package of help in order for us to be able to care for the needs both of our youngest child and the rest of the family. The ensuing case conference seemed to us to be a remarkable example of inter-departmental politics working in our favour. About eight medical professionals had been gathered together by our young daughter's local paediatric consultant. The purpose of the meeting was to assess the implications of Charlotte's condition on our family life, mainly for the benefit of her newly assigned social worker. Helen was told beforehand that a few tears shed at the appropriate moment would not go amiss! Thankfully there appeared no need to resort to such a tactic, which we felt was hardly appropriate for the wife of a minister anyway.

Shortly afterwards we were offered the support of carers in the home for several hours a week. This meant that Helen would be able to take some time out from the intensive and potentially all-consuming regime of skin-care. We would also receive the on-going support of a social worker specialising in the care of children with disabilities.

Andrew confesses to some initial embarrassment at our having been assigned a social worker. He found himself emphasising to others that this was *Charlotte's* social worker. The thought of our family needing such input was a greater threat to his pride than he had anticipated! This was one of several ways in which we have found our personal prejudices and presuppositions challenged over the last three years. Maybe this is just one aspect of the honing and purifying process that God promises to all his children.

For Andrew, the first few months in Romford meant getting to know a new congregation, preparing two sermons most weeks, and seeking to identify priorities for the church in the months ahead. For several years there had been three full-time pastors, but Andrew was now the only paid minister, though supported by an able and experienced team of elders and deacons. We confess there were times when we wondered how we could possibly fulfil the hopes and dreams of those who had called us to help lead the church at Romford. We were especially sensitive to any comments that could be taken as expressing anxiety over our ability to give of our best. Even in our bleaker moments, we were able to find encouragement from the very clear way in which the Lord had opened the opportunity to move south, and the overwhelming vote of confidence we had received from the church membership regarding Andrew's appointment.

Soon after Charlotte's return from hospital we decided, as a treat for the children, to return to Legoland, where it had all begun. We had a great time, and although we made regular trips to the nappy-changing facilities, we managed to take in plenty of the rides. On returning home, however, we became aware that Charlotte's breathing had become laboured and noisy. We telephoned the on-call doctor, and had our first experience of trying to explain her condition as best we could. This time the problem was the much commoner bronchiolitis, but it required immediate hospital admission for one so young. As it was half term, Helen was able to stay with her. Andrew had a week's holiday booked, but this was not quite how we had intended to spend it. Five days later she was home again, and the domestic routine recommenced.

A well-oiled family!

Helen's schedule revolved around grease, baths, washing clothes, and then more grease. The first bath of the day was at six o'clock. This involved washing down with a special soap substitute and attempting to remove surplus skin. A good soak in emollients to seal what moisture the skin could retain was followed by the application of a thick greasy substance made up from 50 per cent soft white paraffin and 50 per cent liquid paraffin. A complication in Charlotte's case is that she also suffers from eczema. Unfortunately some of the ointments which might alleviate the symptoms of her ichthyosis tend to exacerbate the eczema. As with a great deal of her care, we have tended to rely on a trial-and-error method to discover what works best. On occasions this has produced angry-looking rashes on her skin. Thankfully, however, these soon disappear when the offending medication is stopped. We managed to obtain a very expensive cream from America, which had been seen to achieve significant results on a number of patients. Unfortunately Charlotte's skin was unable to tolerate it.

Right from the start we were told that the greasy ointment was by far the safest and most effective treatment for ichthyosis, particularly on the skin of one so young. This was fine in theory, but the practicalities are that both Charlotte, and everything with which she comes into contact, become very greasy. Imagine coating a toddler liberally with petroleum jelly and then letting her loose on your best furniture and carpets, not to mention your dry-clean-only suits and your mother-in-law's new curtains. We didn't need to imagine it—it was our constant experience! The resulting stains and the additional dirt are enough to try the patience and test the friendship of many. We began to wonder why the other children's socks were becoming dirtier than before. Then we realised that the grease absorbed by the carpets was attracting every piece of dirt. We had already been warned that Charlotte would need frequent changes of clothes. We were also soon to discover that the grease would take its toll on our own wardrobes, and we would need to take thought for the clothes of our friends and fellow church-members. Our delight that others were eager to hold our new daughter and give her a cuddle was tempered by a realistic concern that they should not ruin their best clothes.

Everything Charlotte wore quickly became impregnated with the grease. How ever much we washed them, a residue always remained. As she grew, we were to discover that elasticated items suffered most. Trousers and pants would no longer stay up! We had been advised to dress her only in pure cotton clothing, therefore many of the items passed down from the other children had to be discarded, and we needed to purchase more new clothes than we had anticipated. We were greatly helped, however, by several families in the church who specifically sorted out their unwanted cotton baby and toddler clothes.

The grease factor is one of those issues which has challenged our cherished scale of priorities. Whilst we cannot presume on the indulgence of others, surely we should not be concerned if we go out with the odd mark or two on our clothes. We were deeply moved when one of the church members eagerly asked if he could hold Charlotte. He was wearing his best suit, and he knew the possible implications, but he didn't seem to mind at all. That meant a great deal to us, and challenged our own attitudes. We have no doubt at all that Jesus would have gathered her in his arms—even if the disciples had been scrabbling around looking for a stick of *Vanish* to rub on his clothing. More than anything, we want to avoid giving the slightest hint to Charlotte that we are less keen to hug and hold her. We really do love her—grease and all.

Then there was the long-running saga of the washing machine. We soon discovered that the ointment attacked the rubber door seal and pump. As a family of six, our use of the appliance was already heavier than average, but now it was in use for most of the day and late into the evening also. Within two months it was beginning to malfunction, and soon after came the first of many visits from the engineer. Water over the kitchen floor, and clothes literally stuck inside the machine, were regular occurrences. After a while we wondered if we should try to secure the engineer a designated parking space outside the house.

It surprised us how a seemingly mundane problem could create such worry and stress at home. Helen confesses to this having been a real source of discouragement at a time when the larger part of her day was already taken up with caring for the family's regular needs. Once again, we saw the goodness of the Lord when a friend suggested we might be eligible for practical assistance from the Government-sponsored Family Fund; this fund exists to help lower-income families with a severely disabled child. We initially balked at this description. We would not immediately have described Charlotte as 'disabled'. Yet, a major genetic defect affecting the whole of the skin, which after all, is the largest organ of the human body, has the potential to cause considerable limitation to movement, co-ordination and overall health. We were assessed and found to meet the relevant criteria. Not only did they provide us with a new washing machine, but also agreed to pay for servicing and repairs as required. The same fund has also provided help with bedding, and towards the cost of a family holiday.

When each of the children reached their first Christmas, Helen introduced them to the glorious experience of messing with paints. Taking her cue from a friend, she coated a tiny hand in paint and made a handprint on paper. Alongside, she would write a poem, frame the result, and wrap it up for dad as a Christmas present. The idea is popular with playgroups and toddlers' groups, so for Laura and Alice, Helen was able to use the well-known accompanying verses. For Charlotte, however, she felt she needed some 'customised' lines. Overcoming the slight worry of what the paint might do to her hand, and how to remove it from the cracks between the scales, she produced the following:

I guess it should be greasy,
This handprint sent from me.
But here it is in red paint,
For everyone to see.
It seems to be much smaller,
Than from the other three!
Telling of other struggles
That you have had with me.
But I'm glad to be a Bryant –
To have you as my Dad;
Because whatever happens
You'll make sure it's not so bad.

Whilst this may not win any prizes for poetic skill, it was sufficient to bring a tear or two to dad's eyes.

The birth of a support group

We soon discovered that although ichthyosis is a rare disorder, it is not so rare as to exclude the chance of meeting other sufferers and their carers. Therefore we eagerly accepted the invitation to a meeting to be held at Great Ormond Street Hospital for past and present ichthyosis patients and their carers. As we travelled into London with our new member of the club, our emotions were somewhat mixed. Whilst we were keen to learn all we could, we were nervous about what we might see and hear. How does an affected child cope at school? What about the struggles of a teenage sufferer, with all the normal pressures of adolescence combined with the added burden of noticeably different skin? Would adults be prepared to talk of the particular challenges they faced at work and in their social lives?

In the event, we were able to meet children of varying ages and with skin displaying different degrees of abnormality. Some had distinctly reddened faces, tightness around the eyes, or skin that had the appearance of desiccated coconut. A few hid behind hats or sunglasses, noticeably self-conscious about their appearance. Others appeared much more confident. We talked with a young man in his early twenties who had tried various treatments, and had for several years been taking a retinoid (Vitamin A substitute) drug; we were to learn far more about retinoids over the next couple of years. He spoke of having endured some teasing at school. 'Skinny' was one of his nicknames, and not because of his physical stature. Having recently qualified as a mathematics teacher, he had begun his first job. His mother spoke of her tears of joy the day she watched him walk down the road hand in hand with his first girlfriend. One of the fruits of this day was the setting up of the Ichthyosis Support Group, specifically to link families together and to provide friendship and encouragement to those who have an affected child.

We had originally been disappointed to discover there was no support group for families like us. This inevitably reinforced the impression that we were very much on our own. Therefore this meeting with other parents and sufferers seemed to offer an excellent opportunity for such a group to be established. One mother had already been looking at such a possibility, and others who might be interested in joining her were invited to come forward. This was too good a chance to miss. Contact a Family, a charity experienced in assisting parents to develop their own national or local support groups, offered their assistance. Within a few months, more contacts had been made, and a steering committee was taking shape. At this point the need for a chairperson was becoming evident. Almost before she knew it, Helen was given the job! We both agreed that this would be a very useful way of broadening our own knowledge of ichthyosis, and hopefully, a means of making a worthwhile contribution to the needs of other families. In some ways it would prevent us from narrowly focusing on our own problems alone. It would have been far too easy to become so immersed in our family situation that we would be hard-pressed to look beyond.

The group developed rapidly. Within two years, the initial handful of contacts had grown to over a hundred families. In order to ensure the quality and accuracy of information given by the group, a medical advisory board comprising specialists from around the country was established under the leadership of consultant dermatologist, Dr John Harper, of Great Ormond Street Hospital. At their initial meeting they were asked to write leaflets on the various forms of ichthyosis. These are now available, and provide a valuable resource for those encountering the disorder for the first time. When Helen saw the initial draft submitted about lamellar ichthyosis, she almost cried. It contained in one simple sheet just about everything it had taken us nearly two years to piece together. For the first time, families could receive that information immediately a diagnosis had been made.

Further activity followed. A request was made to BBC Children in Need for a grant towards the cost of the group's first national day. The application was successful, and the event took place at Great Ormond Street Hospital on 13th March 1999. Over fifty children were taken on a trip to London Zoo, whilst many more stayed in the crèche, with the occasional appearance of Pudsey Bear adding further excitement. Meanwhile parents and relatives were able to participate in a day of lectures and question-and-answer sessions; it was so valuable to be able to talk at leisure with other families experiencing the same challenges.

After two years, we decided it was time for Helen to step down from the role of chairperson. The increasing amount of time the job entailed, combined with the ongoing demands of family life, were beginning to take their toll. In the meantime she had also been invited to become part of the advisory committee for the Rare Disorders Alliance (UK). This is a new venture currently working within the auspices of Contact a Family, but specifically aimed at networking the rare disorders which, because of their very rarity, have little voice of their own.

Breakfast TV

It was in connection with Helen's work with the Rare Disorders Alliance that she and Charlotte were asked to appear on *GMTV* to publicise Rare Disorders Awareness Week 1998. This was actually their second appearance on television; the first was for a London-based cable channel, which closed down a few weeks afterwards! This time, we were driven to the studios on the South Bank at an unearthly hour of the morning. Following a quick résumé of the kind of questions to be asked, Helen and Charlotte were whisked into the make-up area. They wisely decided not to tamper with Charlotte's skin, but Helen received the necessary 'treatment'. This was one of many occasions when our family circumstances have brought some unlikely fun into our lives. Helen sat next to an actor from a well-known soap opera who had been 'killed off' the previous week, but Charlotte was much more interested in another guest: 'Woofy' the dog had recently been rescued from an untimely demise after biting a postman's leg. The interview went ahead without hitch, and the publicity led to several people contacting the support group. These included two women who had both been told that their condition was virtually unique.

The same week we were able to invite our local Member of Parliament to a tea-party at the House of Commons; this was sponsored by the All-Party Disabilities Group to coincide with the awareness week. She was happy to attend with her husband, and was prepared to spend some time discussing the issues arising from living with a rare disease. Once again we were struck with a sense of having moved into what was to us a whole new world of living with disability. Maybe, even in our own weakness and lack of knowledge, we could make some small contribution towards helping others in a similar or far more difficult situation.

The great home-schooling disaster

Family life invariably brings its share of the unexpected and unforeseen. Like most parents we have an overwhelming desire to do the best for our children, and as Christians we have a particular sense of accountability, not only to our fellow believers, but also before the Lord. We have prayed about the decisions we have made along the way. Sometimes we believe we have known a deep conviction about the right course of action, whilst on other occasions, we have simply tried to exercise our God-given responsibility to make sensible choices based on all the available information, including the wisdom and suggestions of others. At times, however, we have made decisions, which in retrospect have appeared ill considered. Our experiment with home schooling was one of these.

When we started, some said we were daft to try. Others, we suspect, thought the same but kept their counsel. The decision followed several months during which we believed the older children had been suffering as a result of the amount of time Helen in particular was having to spend attending to Charlotte's needs. We had recently been impressed by the example of some friends who taught their children at home, and had been challenged by the extent to which our children's minds and hearts were being shaped by influences that were largely outside our control. Add to this the very real concerns we had about whether or not Charlotte would cope with the school environment at four years old, together with Helen's training as a primary school teacher, and we were building what we regarded as a fairly compelling case for home education.

Early on we attended a conference extolling the virtues of teaching at home and highlighting some potential horrors of the state system, 'Would you entrust the training of your children to humanists, atheists, and hedonists?' We were all too aware of what is quickly picked up in the playground. So often home-schoolers are criticised for trying to insulate their families from the so-called 'real world'. However, we felt there was a strong case for taking time and trouble to prepare our children for the world at large.

Rather than using one of the pre-packaged schemes available from America, and favoured by many home-schooling families here, we settled for a mixture of 'Christian' and mainstream British materials. Initially Laura and Alice appreciated the novel approach. The Local Education Authority inspector who visited gave us a very positive report. Yet the sheer weight of responsibility, the hours required for preparation, and the increasing concern for Helen's own health meant that soon into the second term we knew that a return to school was inevitable. We felt very foolish. Our friends were exceptionally kind and understanding. Next came the challenging task of having one child re-admitted, and starting the second in the infants' school. Given the heavy demand on a popular school, we really do praise God for this provision.

Why did we try this experiment? Surely we should have listened to the wisdom of those who warned of the intolerable burden it would place upon Helen in particular? Were we not able to trust the Lord's sovereignty over every aspect of our lives, including the spiritual well being of our children within what is definitely an excellent local school? On reflection, we suspect that we had simply allowed ourselves to become so consumed with worries about what might or might not happen in the future that we temporarily lost touch with the common sense required to get through each day. With hindsight, it does seem ridiculous to have been worrying about Charlotte's possible difficulties at school when she was barely a year old. For all we know, she may integrate perfectly well into mainstream education. We are learning that children, whilst being capable of cruel and spiteful attitudes, can also be far more accepting than adults of those who may appear somewhat different. Most of all, the decision to home-school probably illustrated that we were beginning not to cope with the seemingly relentless juggling of skin-care regime, hospital appointments, family and church commitments. Our pride urged us to carry on as though everything was fine. It was not long, however, before we were compelled to admit that we were in need of some additional support.

When Charlotte was two, we spent a day with some friends on a canal boat. The highlight for the children was a mile-long tunnel just north of Watford. As we entered it, we were soon engulfed in darkness. After a while we could just see a faint light in the distance. But it was not the light at the end of the tunnel. Instead it was another boat coming towards us. Would we be able to pass this large vessel within such a narrow space? Our friends knew that we could—and we only slightly bumped once. Not long after, the end of the tunnel was in sight and we were outside in the bright sunlight of a July afternoon, ready for a barbecue tea. In a similar way, there have been times when we have felt as though we were confined and enclosed. We have had no alternative but to move forwards, but with seemingly few options and minimal light. In our case, matters came to a head in the early months of 1998.

Struggling to hold on

Charlotte has always brought a great deal of pleasure and delight into our family. As a baby she quickly won the hearts of friends and neighbours, and she would even engage the attention of shoppers at the supermarket. Just occasionally we would receive less welcome comments. Her ointments can give her the appearance of being hot and sweaty, although ironically the thick scales can severely inhibit the sweating process. From time to time we are asked bluntly, 'What's wrong with her, then?' Depending on our mood at the time, we either say briefly that she has a skin condition, or occasionally we risk giving a longer explanation, which can lead to embarrassment on the part of the questioner! Right now she is a bright, perceptive and determined pre-schooler, who simply loves life.

It was the relentless and unremitting nature of the skin-care that gradually wore us down, both physically and emotionally. Apart from the average of three and a half hours a day spent in the bathroom on the soaking and oiling routine, there are the regular appointments at the hospital and the doctor's surgery, the seemingly unending piles of greasy clothes to be washed, plus the regular demands of family and church. For the first year and more, Helen found herself able to cope with it all. Eventually, however, the strain began to tell. Helen's journal entry for 17 October 1997 hinted at problems to come:

'End of an absolutely terrible two/three weeks. I've just caved in and can't seem to get myself back together again. Have spent a lot of time crying—which is probably long overdue. Just feel totally drained and exhausted.'

This realisation in itself was painful to confront. Helen now speaks of the overwhelming emotions of guilt and failure that were threatening to cripple her at this time. She found herself taking out her frustration and pain upon those whom she cherished the most:

22 February 1998: 'A holiday week for Andrew and I can't cope! Pathetic! What does a holiday week mean any more? He gets a break from work; the routine goes out the window and I genuinely don't know what to do. My whole being craves for doing absolutely nothing, yet the basics continue to have to be done. I just feel as if I'm making a fuss—God has given me this load and I must get on with it, and he will give me the power to do it—will he? What happened this week? Why was I so utterly hateful to and about all that I love most dear? All that I have ever wanted, I was trying to destroy. Why? All I have ever wanted is a husband and four children—and here I have them and am throwing it all away. I'm just *so* tired. Tired of not being able to get "untired" and there is seemingly no end in sight. Everybody says it will get better, but what about enjoying something now—these are precious years the children are never going to have again … Is it the combination of factors or am I just making excuses, fighting it all … I want to run, but that fills me with even greater guilt.'

We were beginning to panic. Andrew found himself reacting to Helen's distress with a mixture of sympathy, fear and anger. Most of his emotional resources were being consumed at home, and he struggled both with his preparation of Sunday sermons and with the ongoing load of pastoral responsibilities. We were concerned that this would soon be perceived as a lack of vision and commitment to the church work. And after all, it was the church that was paying the salary and providing our home. The children were, understandably, showing signs of insecurity. Something had to give.

Looking back, we realise we were scared to seek help. It was one thing to request occasional favours with baby-sitting or shopping, but quite another to admit that we were not coping at all with our situation. Others, we reasoned, were probably dealing effectively with far heavier demands than we were. Andrew had certainly preached sermons about the need to admit our human weakness. The Lord's promise to Paul that, 'My grace is sufficient for you, for my power is made perfect in weakness' (2 Corinthians 12:9) was often in our minds. Yet if we admitted our struggles, would we be perceived as too weak to remain in the pastorate? Would we even come under scrutiny from the local authority as being inadequate parents?

At last, we had no option but to ask for help. We contacted Charlotte's social worker and she quickly arranged a visit to assess our needs. She organised carers to come into the home virtually full-time during the day and evening for two weeks. She also made provision for further help with cleaning and ironing. This was to let Helen have some time for rest and recuperation, whilst Andrew could continue at work. Meanwhile we shared our situation with the church elders, who proved very supportive and were concerned to allow us whatever time and space we needed.

Helen spent a few days with friends near Chichester, sleeping for much of the time. We then arranged for her to stay with a mature couple who are involved with a scheme operated by Care for the Family, which offers short breaks for those suffering particular stress. Following this we were able to spend several days together at Stanton House, a Christian retreat centre near Oxford. This gave us precious time to talk, in peaceful rural surroundings. We took our time getting up in the mornings, enjoyed leisurely meals with the staff and other guests, and rambled around the surrounding countryside. It may all sound rather indulgent, but we recognized the Lord's goodness in restoring our souls and our bodies. We began to talk about establishing more realistic routines at home.

Meanwhile the children were coping very well with what must have been a deeply unsettling and uncertain time. Several friends from church, together with Helen's sister, and carers provided through Social Services, ensured they were looked after and given plenty of treats. It was around this time that we made two decisions which at first felt like admissions of failure, but which both led to significant progress in the months following.

First, we contacted a Christian psychologist and asked whether he would be willing to see us to help us work through some of the conflicting thoughts and emotions of the past couple of years. We really were unsure what to expect, and our expectations of the 'therapist's couch' owed far more to popular caricature than to any proper understanding on our part. Our caution was fuelled by our subconscious acceptance of the popular Christian mythology, that it is somehow a shameful expression of inadequate faith to seek help of an emotional or psychological nature. For ourselves, we would still be hesitant about receiving such assistance from a non-Christian practitioner. Therefore the provision of one who shared our Evangelical faith gave us the courage we needed. The willingness of our local fund-holding doctors' surgery to cover his fees was even better!

The sessions exposed some of the conflicts, which we had not managed to resolve. There was the gulf between what we wanted to achieve for the Lord in our own lives and the church, and what was realistically possible given the intensive and unremitting nature of Charlotte's skin care. For Helen especially, there was the disappointment, until now largely unacknowledged, of not having been able to cuddle and 'show off' her new baby in those precious first few weeks. There was the sheer exhaustion of lost sleep, and all the emotional anxieties that accompany caring for a child with special physical needs. More than anything, we were helped to see that the overwhelming sense of guilt—some of it subjective and false, rather than objective and real—had been clouding our perspective and robbing us of joy.

We were helped to consider workable, achievable strategies for coping. In particular we were urged to create time for our family, time for ourselves as a married couple, and time alone with God. Although this may sound obvious and simplistic (and is the kind of advice Andrew often gives out in the course of his pastoral ministry!) we attempted to put this into practice more rigorously than before. Whilst it remains an ongoing challenge, we do believe we have made some progress.

Our second significant decision was even more difficult. Our GP had diagnosed that Helen was suffering from some form of clinical depression, almost certainly triggered by the exhaustion of the past two years. He advised that she might seriously consider taking a course of anti-depressant medication. Our first reaction to this was decidedly negative. We reasoned that this was yet another sign of faithlessness. If we ask the Lord to lift this depression, could he not do it without us resorting to drugs?

After a while, however, we realised that Helen did need some form of additional assistance to lift her out of what was fast becoming a severely depressed state. If we accepted that medicines to treat physical ailments were ultimately gifts of a gracious and compassionate God, then why not something that would help with a condition of a psychological nature? Even if it is one to which physical exhaustion had, we suspected, contributed a great deal? Our greatest fears concerned risks of long-term dependency. However, we were assured that with the tablets in question, there was little if any risk of this. Therefore we eventually agreed. We decided at the outset that whilst we would not make a point of telling others about it, neither would we keep it a secret. With children observing most things that go on at home, this would be pointless in any case. On a couple of occasions one of them has been known to ask innocently, and in company, 'Have you taken your tablet today, mummy?'—yet another lesson in humility!

The FIRST Conference—Insights from New Jersey

By early summer 1998 we were both feeling far more positive about our situation. Some months previously, we had discovered that the Foundation for Ichthyosis and Related Skin Types was to hold a family conference in New Jersey from 19th-21st June. There would be a large contingent of dermatology specialists and others with particular knowledge and expertise. We wondered whether it might be possible for us to attend. We were keen to learn all we could from others who had far greater experience than ourselves of living with and caring for a child with ichthyosis. There were so many questions we would want to ask. How have other children with ichthyosis coped when starting school? Have they experienced rejection or teasing from others? What are the best ways to keep your child cool during the summer months when overheating can be a real problem to a child who is unable to sweat normally? Is the condition likely to change in severity or in manifestation as the child grows? Are there other creams and treatments that have been found to be effective? In particular, is there something less intrusive and more user-friendly than the ever-present paraffin grease?

At the time, one of our greatest concerns was about the retinoid medication, Acitretin, which Charlotte had recently been prescribed. The potential side-effects are formidable, and we had already ascertained from our surfing of the Internet that American paediatricians seemed even more cautious about it than their British counterparts.

Arrangements for the trip came together in a most amazing way and at a time when in ourselves we had little energy to organise the details. Members of our church were swift to offer help in caring for the children whilst we were away. We decided that, given Charlotte's young age, she would do better to remain at home. We were given considerable financial assistance, and before we knew it, we were on board a British Airways 747 bound for Philadelphia.

We travelled from the airport to the conference hotel with Tracy, an ichthyosis sufferer in her twenties from Ohio. Immediately we had to watch our reactions. She was quite severely disfigured, walked with a pronounced limp, and her skin was a deep red with sores and lesions all over. Her eyes were somewhat sunken—a characteristic trait, due to the tightening of the skin around the eyes. Knowing of this, we have always tried to pay particular attention to greasing that area of Charlotte's face. Tracy talked in a very matter-of-fact way about her condition. It was obvious, however, that she had suffered through the years.

What really worried us was that her physical disability is attributed to the effects of the retinoid drugs she took for twelve years. Tracy was involved in the original clinical trials of an earlier form of the medication that Charlotte takes. Apparently her dosage was far higher, and the drug has been developed and refined since then. Nevertheless we were disconcerted by the evidence before us. Tracy had suffered damage to her bone structure, especially around her hips. This was not exactly the greatest encouragement to those of us who administer retinoids to our children. This in itself ensured that we would attend to the lecture on the use of that drug with total concentration.

The FIRST conference surpassed our expectations. We laughed and cried, counted our blessings and worried about the future. We exchanged e-mail addresses with dermatologists and shared experiences with parents of children older than Charlotte. The children present provided a striking testimony to the love and dedication of their parents. Some were much more obviously affected than others were. Severely receding hairlines on little girls, eyelids gaping outwards on young lads, and deep red or fungus-like skin on others gave an indication of the level of disfigurement that often accompanies the various forms of the condition. On the other hand some adult sufferers looked remarkably normal.

We were shown a most powerful short video. Lasting only four minutes, it was called *Butterflies* and was narrated by youngsters through their own letters and descriptions. The 'butterfly' is the real person, desperate to break out of the 'cocoon' of their special skin. This is especially poignant for those who, like Charlotte, have had to shed their extra layer of collodion skin. The message was breathtakingly simple: 'Ichthyosis children really love their mums and dads because they teach us that "different" is okay.' A father spoke movingly of his son, 'He is our pride, our joy.' They had suffered much with him during the first few months of his life. The video was dedicated to him because, two weeks after filming, the little boy died. As the closing titles faded, we discreetly wiped tears from our eyes and recovered our composure for the remainder of the session.

The apparent self-confidence and love for life of many of the children and teens struck us. Some were, by any standard, noticeably 'different' in appearance. The receding and tangled hair was a recurrent feature. One or two wore hats, but most did not. Of course they were among friends. Other guests at the hotel seemed noticeably to flinch, then smile an uneasy smile, or look away, embarrassed. The Cherry Hill Hilton is, after all, an environment in which there is much elegance and beauty that is little more than skin-deep.

The session on retinoids did, as expected, give us some cause for concern. The panel of dermatology specialists indicated that Acitretin was rarely prescribed for toddlers in the United States. They emphasised the necessity of regular testing of liver function, white blood-cell count and skeletal formation. We resolved to arrange an early appointment with Charlotte's consultant upon our return.

Parents of a child with any kind of special need will inevitably be called upon to make decisions that may have long-term consequences. Looking further ahead still, severe deformities in babies are known to occur where the mother has been taking retinoids during pregnancy. Having maintained a good level of skin integrity for many years, a mother would be faced with the possibility of a much-worsened condition in order to have a child. At times we have found ourselves overwhelmed with our responsibilities, and have sought the Lord for wisdom and direction. In the absence of some dramatic and unmistakable guidance, we have gathered and assessed as much relevant medical information as we are able. Charlotte currently appears to benefit from the use of that particular medication. It may even give her skin a limited capacity to sweat. Eventually such drugs may be developed still further, with less possible side effects. It is this kind of research that both FIRST in America and the Ichthyosis Support Group in Britain are seeking to promote.

Charlotte—a person in her own right

Charlotte brings so much joy into our family life. Her beaming smile, her eager quest for mischievous adventure, her sheer love of life. All of this deeply enriches our lives. Adults frequently stop to talk to her, and other children display what can seem like a combination of instinctive protectiveness and straightforward enjoyment of her company. Yet we have to admit that there have been times when we have found it a struggle to identify with those who say of their disabled child, 'But we wouldn't be without them.' Inevitably this has contributed to feelings of guilt and failure. The relentless routine of days divided into four-hourly segments is sometimes suffocating and always hard work. Married to a pastor, Helen often sees jobs that need doing within the church. She recognises the hurts and needs of others and at times feels powerless to offer any help other than to make a mental note to pray.

From time to time we do pause to wonder what God is teaching us through our present family circumstances. Nevertheless, we try to be aware of the dangers of undue introspection that can lead to a distinct brand of selfishness. We are convinced that God is sovereign over all the challenges of family life, but when we look at Charlotte, we find it very difficult to think of her as being a 'thorn in the flesh', or a trial sent from heaven to test our faith! She is our precious, precocious and deeply loved

Above: Charlotte aged three. Children who meet her display what can seem like a combination of instinctive protectiveness and straightforward enjoyment of her company

daughter. She is also a person in her own right, a unique individual created in the image of God.

Prominent in our thinking is how Charlotte will grow to think and feel about herself in years to come. We long that she should both accept her physical limitations and live life to the full despite them. In the summer of 1999, Andrew took Laura on what proved a memorable and challenging weekend at an outdoor pursuits centre in North Wales. The weekend was organised by Care for the Family and was designed for fathers and their daughters. Canoeing, abseiling and orienteering were among the activities we were able to sample. Instinctively we found ourselves assuming that Charlotte would not be able to attempt such pursuits. Yet the more we think of it, the more we ask, 'Why not?' Certainly we do not want her potential to be limited by our own preconceptions. More than anything, we long for Charlotte to learn to trust Jesus Christ as her Lord and Saviour. This will surely include being given the grace to accept the weaknesses of her physical frame, and gaining a rich, biblical perspective on the contrast between the provisional nature of our present condition and the glory that is yet to come.

Hopes and challenges for the future

Should we pray for the healing of Charlotte's skin condition? This question has seldom been far from our minds. Andrew vividly recalls being present at a meeting of the Council of FIEC (Fellowship of Independent Evangelical Churches) soon after Charlotte's birth, when fervent prayers were offered for her healing. So far, these and other similar requests have remained unfulfilled.

We must confess to a certain tension in our thinking. If it was our own physical health that was the object of prayer, we would perhaps be more readily content to say, 'your will be done,' and to conclude that the lessons God wishes to teach us concern the nurture of such character traits as patience, endurance, and hope. However, because the focus of our prayers is another individual, and our own daughter at that, we are far more reluctant to leave it there. When she is struggling with the heat of summer, or when she wakes in the night tearing at her reddened skin, what parent would not seek the healing touch of the Lord? We reason that a genuine organic reversal of a genetic condition appears at variance with

God's regular manner of working today. And yet the very nature of a miracle, as an unusual and possibly unprecedented divine act, compels us to cry out with such a longing from time to time. If this is not to be, we pray that Charlotte herself will be given the mature faith that is able to accept her situation.

We find ourselves extremely hesitant to draw lessons from our experience so far. We are still relatively new to the reality of disability within the family, and have already become aware of how quickly circumstances may change. We have certainly had to learn to receive acts of kindness from others. Within the context of pastoral ministry, we have long understood our role to be primarily that of encouraging and supporting others in their struggles and trials. We have found ourselves reluctant to show weakness or to betray a lack of composure. There have certainly been lessons of humility, which have been painful but valuable. When the church elders asked Andrew to speak publicly about our situation, he did not feel at all comfortable. Somehow the perceived security afforded by the pulpit was insufficient to prevent an

Above: The family in 1999: Andrew and Helen, Laura, Alice, Thomas and Charlotte

open display of emotion from both speaker and congregation. Afterwards, however, we saw a level of sharing and honesty within the fellowship that both humbled and amazed us.

A challenge, both for Charlotte and us, will be the beginning of her school education. On a practical level, she will probably need help with her skin-care during the school day. Almost certainly we will have to adapt her routine. She will be unable to have a bath in the middle of the day! The first day at school for each of the children has been a somewhat emotional experience. It is quite a milestone, with the recognition that there will never again be the same level of dependency upon the parents. When it comes to Charlotte's turn, we suspect we shall be more than usually anxious. We will wonder how she will be received in the classroom. Will other children ask about her skin? Will they want to touch and feel it? Will she make friends who hold her hand in the playground? How will her school uniform cope with the grease? Will she be self-conscious, or simply go for everything she can?

Surely this is where mum and dad need to build upon what we have already learned. There really is a limit to the number of questions we can usefully ask about the future. We cannot possibly anticipate all that is going to happen. Neither can we protect Charlotte from every possible instance of rejection or misunderstanding or cruelty. What we do know is that there is a loving, heavenly Father who is more than able and abundantly willing to protect and guide her. Although our prayers range far and wide, they always return to that all-consuming longing of every Christian parent: that our daughter should come to trust and worship the Lord her God with all her heart and soul and strength and mind. We pray that Charlotte, together with her brother and sisters, will be assured that the value and meaning of their lives are so much more than skin deep.

'Life is an adventure—dare it'

Claire Salter

Claire is 25 and has recently completed a post-graduate Masters Degree in Social Work at the University of Reading. As a child she was diagnosed as having cystic fibrosis, a progressive and life-threatening lung disease. Claire is no stranger to emergencies and hospitals, but she remains active and determined to put into life all that she can. Here, she allows us into her private world of fear, frustration, faith and hope.

Descending the steps to Eliot dining hall at the University of Kent, I was confronted by the chatting of students, the clatter of crockery and the smell of food. It wasn't exactly cordon bleu cookery, but it was my university and I loved it. Eliot halls are strategically situated so that the huge dining room windows provide a panorama over the city. This particular autumn evening offered a magnificent view down the hill to where Canterbury Cathedral could be seen, lit up in all its splendour in the distance. Ali and I had never met before, but we happened to sit next to each other at dinner that evening and when she coughed, it sounded so familiar that it was rather eerie. We introduced, and she told me she was Alison Browne. We chatted about irrelevancies initially but I just couldn't get her cough out of my mind. I remember feeling quite rude when eventually I asked her if she had cystic fibrosis (CF). I just had a feeling that she did, but it would have been a terrible assumption if I was wrong. That was when our friendship began and I always admired Ali. I was touched with how brave and also comfortable she was about her disease; cystic fibrosis was part of her and she was not ashamed of it.

Whenever we saw each other on campus we would check to see how we both were—there is companionship in sharing the same illness. We often bumped into each other in sick bay or in the medical centre, and Ali and I were also treated by the same hospital. It was at the Royal Brompton Hospital that I saw her before she died—just before the end of her course. We hugged and said goodbye, little knowing that was the last time we would see each other. I found Ali's funeral extremely difficult personally, and cried very much. The church was absolutely packed and it has left a lasting impression on me. So let me tell you a little about the illness Ali and I shared.

All I remember about my diagnosis was that the boy being tested before me was crying so much he was almost hysterical. My dad came with me and told me that the tests were quite harmless. Although I was put off by the little boy screaming I also remember having lots of attention. Of course at the age of five I didn't know the seriousness of the issue, but to me it was brilliant because my family were so attentive to all my needs, especially my love of chocolate!

I had been ill on and off in my infant years and had pneumonia a couple of times as a baby (not that I remember any of this). Prior to the diagnosis being made, my mum was certain that there was something wrong with me, but the doctors thought she was being over protective. Our General Practitioner didn't believe that I was seriously ill so Mum took me to the local hospital (mum is a nurse). From Epsom Hospital I was transferred to the Royal Brompton Hospital in London, where they specialize in heart and lung conditions. The hospital is also a regional centre for cystic fibrosis. At Epsom the paediatrician was a great support and someone who was to oversee my care locally throughout my childhood. I got to know the consultant very well and she always spent time explaining to me what was happening and why she was prescribing various treatments. She had a fantastic bedside manner, something I think is very important in any doctor, and I constantly badger friends who are training to be doctors just how crucial this is for patients.

There is an abnormality of salt transfer within the cells of people with CF, which results in the production of sticky mucous in the affected organs. The lungs are the main organs that are affected as the thick mucous is difficult to clear and is an ideal breeding ground for bacteria, leading to lung damage. Cystic fibrosis shows itself by lots of chest infections, so antibiotic treatment plays a major part in trying to combat infection. Physiotherapy goes hand in hand with this. Physio consists of breathing exercises and 'clapping' with one hand over the chest area to help dislodge the mucous in the lungs. It also involves lying at different angles to 'drain' the lung areas. Altogether the physiotherapy takes about fifteen minutes, three times a day—well, it's supposed to if done properly. I'm afraid physio is not one of my priority activities!

My younger years

My parents were told they could either wrap me up in cotton wool or let me lead a normal life—they chose the latter; had they not, I would probably have chosen that route anyway. My parents were good in allowing me to do such things as sleeping under canvas, even though they knew that damp conditions were not the best environment for me to be in; however, they let me go and I am very grateful to them for that. They did set certain boundaries when I was a teenager that I was not so keen on, such as ensuring I was in at a certain time so I wouldn't get overtired. They gave the reason that there were physio and health needs to attend to when I got home in the evening; but leaving church or social events dead on time often made me resentful as I felt I had lost face with my friends.

When I was younger, I had a lot more energy than I have now! One of my first memories was that in primary school I could take time off if I felt unwell. Because the teachers knew I had cystic fibrosis, if I said I was ill they were very concerned about what would happen if they made me stay at school and I became seriously ill. I'm afraid that I used to play on that a bit, especially when I was keen to go home and watch television—which was much more preferable to lessons!

I have vivid memories of being in hospital when I was younger: memories of falling out of bed and giving myself a nose bleed, riding on the rocking horse in the children's playroom, which I did constantly, and having my first intravenous antibiotics when I was about eight years old. This was quite traumatic for me especially as the doctor kept swearing because he couldn't find a vein to put the needle in. I remember thinking that because I had been in hospital for so long and was now on a 'drip' I must be very ill, because when I used to see other children with drips I thought they were seriously ill. However, I also remember thinking it was quite funny because I didn't really feel too bad. I can't say that I ever wanted to be in hospital, but there were times when I enjoyed it because I made a lot of friends. When I meet up with some of the other CF patients I got to know in hospital, it's interesting to compare ourselves with one another. We chat about the hospital staff who looked after us so well, and generally catch up on news!

But there were other things to be getting on with. Part of living a normal life for me was camping under canvas with the youth group at Hook Evangelical Church in Surbiton. It was at one of these camps that I became a Christian. Church activities had been a part of my life since I was a baby, and as I became older I learned that God, in his love, had sent his son Jesus to die for my sin. It didn't matter whether my sins were great or small, none of us live up to God's standard, and I needed to say sorry to God. By doing this and asking him to come and help me and share my life, I became a Christian.

Youth camp was an annual event and I have definitely benefited by such positive experiences of being able to do all the things my friends did. I even enjoyed camp food, except the dessert we called 'slop' that was served from a bucket! My auntie, who was one of the youth leaders, made sure I was OK. However, she did have an annoying habit of doing some of my physio in the breakfast queue. This involved 'clapping' my back in front of all my friends, and I found that very embarrassing! I didn't want to be any different from the other children, but this was like advertising it to the world. My CF wasn't that much of an issue when I was a child, at least not to me. I just had all my treatment and went into hospital when unwell, had two weeks off school watching T.V. and I didn't think too much of it. I knew I had cystic fibrosis and that meant I had a bad cough most of the time, but I didn't grasp the impact and consequences of it until my teenage years.

When I was nine years old, I was given a great opportunity. I went to Florida by courtesy of a charity that sponsored 'holidays of a lifetime' for children with life-threatening diseases. It was a really fantastic experience. In Florida the main aim of the trip was to go to Disney World and Sea World; this was brilliant for a nine-year-old who had never dared to dream of such experiences. We went to other theme parks in Orlando and it really did prove to be a holiday of a lifetime. However, that was the first time I came into contact with a lot of other CF people and it was quite a shock to me, because at that stage I was very well compared with some of the others. This was the first time I remember feeling guilty about my better health compared with theirs. I shared a room with a little girl called Rachel and she seemed very ill to me. Lots of the children were thin, and when we had our physiotherapy they coughed up a lot of mucus, yet when I had physio I hardly coughed at all. Some were wheelchair bound because of their breathlessness. It was very sad to see them and I found it hard to understand how ill some of them were. It dawned on me that there were other people who had CF far worse than me. I wondered why I was so well and why they seemed so ill.

Despite all this, it was a wonderful holiday; I never thought I'd ever have the privilege of visiting America. Sadly Rachel died a couple of years after we returned from Florida and that was my first experience of death. I was upset, but at ten I didn't really grasp the full implications of someone dying from CF. I wondered why Rachel had died and not myself. I was upset that I had not had the opportunity to say goodbye and I felt sad for her family too. I was also aware that this had implications for my own life and death; however at that age I couldn't fully understand. I remember fooling myself into thinking that maybe she had died from a car crash and not CF and that made me feel better about it.

My adolescent years

As I grew older I had more of an inkling that I was a bit different from the others. Of course I knew that I had CF but I don't think it really affected me at the time. Every year I would go into hospital and have intravenous treatment and try my best not to miss too much school, but then, when you are ill, you're ill. However, I hated being away and missing out, and I was absent for only about two or three weeks a year. I enjoyed my time at secondary school, despite all the hard work and the pressure to do well. I met a lot of very caring friends with whom I still keep in touch. They continue to maintain an interest in me and I appreciate as well as value their love and support.

I tried to be as active as possible, though sometimes I felt I was losing the battle. I was never very good at sport, as my lung function didn't allow me to be. Even if it had, I don't think I'm a particularly 'sporty' person. But I used to try and run the 500 metres because I was the only person who volunteered! What a mug I was, as I was always lapped, but at least my classmates cheered me on and thanked me! All the teachers knew that I had CF and looked out for me. It was that sort of school and I did appreciate it. I may not have done brilliantly academically but the ethos of the school was great.

I was involved in school plays and I enjoyed English, particularly poetry. I wrote an article for a Christian magazine about living with CF. My mum had written the previous article and I wrote the second one. I really enjoyed this and for a while after that I wanted to be a journalist! I felt I was giving back to society in a way by letting people know about CF. The article also helped me to be able to talk about my illness, which I had not done so publicly until then. Along with another pupil in the school, who also had CF, we spoke about it in a school assembly to promote 'CF week'. I hated standing up in front of the whole school but at least I was known after that.

Cystic fibrosis is the most common genetically inherited disease in Britain, and I had friends at both school and university suffering from it. Approximately one person in twenty-five carries the defective gene for CF. Carriers are completely healthy and can be tested to see if they carry the gene. If both parents are carriers, there is a one in four chance that a child will be born with the disease, a one in two chance that a child will be a carrier and just a one in four chance of being completely clear.

During my secondary school years I started helping with the seven to elevens in the church youth group. I loved this work and tried as much as

Above: Claire on Graduation day with her proud parents, John and Mave

possible to take an interest in looking out for others and I do try to empathize with people. For the past few years I have worked with older teenagers and find this a great privilege as well as challenging at times. I was also a prefect in my sixth form and enjoyed the social side of things at school. During the sixth form in my spare time I worked for an elderly neighbour. He needed his cleaning done so I was earning some money and that made me feel quite independent. My parents used to get infuriated with me at what they called 'burning the candle at both ends'. I guess I'm a firm believer in living life to the full, even though I do get so tired. I knew I had cystic fibrosis, but that was that; everyone knew so I didn't have to tell anyone. It was accepted and no explanation was needed. I felt very safe and secure.

University—a new life experience

I completed my A level exams and in 1993 started at the University of Kent at Canterbury to read Social Psychology. I found the statistics part of the course incredibly difficult. Not being a mathematical person at all, I hated maths with a passion—and still do. However, I surprised myself by passing the stats exam and confess to being quite proud of the achievement! I enjoyed university tremendously. I loved student life and being away from home. But my health started to deteriorate during the first year at university and my CF became more apparent. No one can particularly see there is anything wrong with me. I'm not very tall, which may or may not be linked to CF, but apart from that I can pass as an average person in the street. Once I started to tell people, the news spread, so I didn't have to tell all my friends; it was like being diagnosed all over again—explaining things to people. The Christian Union was very supportive, as was my church in praying for me, particularly when I was unwell. Their love and concern has always meant a lot to me.

I had some great friends in my college Hall of Residence who always looked out for me and encouraged me to eat when I didn't particularly feel like it. My next door neighbours were a great support, and one evening one of them knocked on my door to ask me if I wanted help with my intravenous antibiotics. But instead of saying, 'Do you want help with your IVs?' she asked me if I wanted help with my IQ! However, she was a bit tipsy and in no way fit to help; we still laugh about that incident. At the end of my first year at university I became quite ill. I had lost weight and contracted a bad chest infection; the day after I was bridesmaid for a good friend from church—I think I just made it up the aisle in one piece—I was taken into hospital.

In cystic fibrosis, as more areas of the lung become 'fibrosed' due to the repeated chest infections, so breathing becomes more of a problem, which impacts on how much exercise you can do. Even walking up one flight of stairs becomes difficult for some people with CF. A few years ago scientists isolated the defective gene in the DNA and this has added to their knowledge in treating the disease. It is anticipated that in a few years time gene therapy, a technique to correct the faulty gene, will halt some of the damage to the lungs that frequent infections cause. Although gene therapy can prevent ongoing damage, it cannot correct the fibrosis that has already occurred; but it is the nearest thing to a cure, and when it becomes available, patients should benefit.

Antibiotics are taken in a combination of oral, nebulised (via an aerosol) and, when infections really get a hold, intravenous injections. It is not uncommon for people with CF to have two or three different bacteria at one time; so, long-term antibiotic therapy is normal. Other drugs to help breathlessness are taken via a nebuliser as an aid to easier breathing. As chest infections take a hold, maintaining adequate food intake is a problem; when anyone has 'flu', for instance, they are sometimes off their food. Feeling one (or a few) degrees under occurs frequently with people who have CF and it can be difficult to maintain body weight; therefore high-calorie drinks are needed as well as high protein food.

For many people, the digestive system is also affected, leading to difficulty digesting food. This is another reason why people with CF are low in weight. Pancreatic enzymes, that help digestion, are required before each meal. Sometimes people with CF need to be fed by a tube inserted into their stomachs. People with CF can become diabetics because of the effect on the pancreas. Thankfully my digestive system is not affected yet and hopefully this won't develop in the future. However, CF is not just confined to the lungs and digestive tract, it is a multi-system disease that affects the liver and other organs. One new finding is that osteoporosis (the bone thinning that is common especially among the older population) is found at a much younger age in people with CF, so this is another area that needs regular follow-up. Cystic fibrosis is a chronic condition that can deteriorate each time a new chest infection is present.

Needles, needles and more needles

Ending up in hospital on a bright Sunday morning was inconvenient; I had an exam to sit the next day! But CF is often inconvenient—it interferes with my plans, which annoys me. The doctors wanted to give me intra-venous antibiotics to treat an infection I'd had, but unfortunately my veins had completely collapsed. After four hours of trying (including attempts at the veins in my feet and neck), they decided to give up. By this time my arms and feet had been soaking in hot water for ages. This supposedly 'warms' the veins and makes them more prominent. The doctors were really frustrated; there was blood everywhere from their aborted attempts. They finally decided I would need to have a portacath, (an implant that makes it easier to administer intravenous medication). They recommended this approach because it would save a lot of trauma in the future. I had had the 'portacath talk' prior to this because it is a much easier way of giving intravenous medication.

The talk emphasizes all the positive sides of immediate access to the veins, and I was introduced to other patients who have one and I listened to them promote it. However, I had only had minor surgery before, and although it is a small operation, I didn't want scars on my body, especially at eighteen! A portacath is a metal-coated device that is inserted in the chest wall. The size and shape of a ten pence coin, it is inserted surgically under the skin of the chest wall, giving access to a central vein. The fine tube—or 'line'—attached to the device, is tunnelled under the skin, the end of which lies in the right side of the heart. It works wonders because it is permanent, avoiding the need for the sometimes painful and messy search for a vein (Portacaths are often used for cancer patients when they have chemotherapy). Now when I have intravenous antibiotics, a special hooked needle (it's not as gruesome as it sounds) is inserted into the portacath under my skin, and there is immediate access to the veins. When I was younger I had horrible experiences when the doctors put little venflons (needles) or even 'long' lines up the veins in my arms; they took hours to put in because my veins are so small and fragile from years of intravenous antibiotics.

Before the portacath operation I had to return to university to complete my exams. When I arrived that evening, my friends were there to make tea, run errands and one even promised to walk me to the exam the following day. They were so good to me, especially as I was feeling quite fragile and very grumpy at the time. After the exam I had to return to hospital for the portacath operation.

Like most people, I hate needles, but they are a major part of my treatment. I have a lot of bad memories about needles and blood tests as I've had so many, but I realize I have nothing to complain about when so many people live lives of continual pain. When the portacath was first mentioned, I must admit I wasn't keen to have surgery. I don't like anaesthetics, and the operation had to be done as soon as possible, giving little time to prepare myself for it. Four years later I now think it's wonderful compared to all the hurt before; I consider myself extremely fortunate to have it. One drawback is that the portacath protrudes from under the skin. I didn't want it just below my neck because I thought that if I wear V-necked T-shirts for instance, people would notice, so I had it inserted lower down, next to my ribs, so nobody can see and my clothes cover it. I have got a scar just below my collarbone, but it's quite small and I can cover it up most of the time.

After the portacath was inserted I went back to university with intra-venous antibiotics, which I had to administer myself. When I was about sixteen the hospital staff had taught me how to manage my own intra-venous drugs (IVs) because it gave me more independence and I wouldn't have to spend the usual two weeks in hospital whilst undergoing treatment. Instead, I live a busy life and continue with my treatment at home. However, to do my own IVs away from hospital and home is a big responsibility. I always prefer to have someone around when I'm injecting myself just in case anything goes wrong. I am very choosy about who helps me with my injections. I feel vulnerable to germs when I'm on IVs and am always washing my hands when preparing the injections. I think this is because my portacath did become infected once, necessitating further surgery.

Most people with CF have two different antibiotics as part of the course. These cannot be given straight after one another but have to be 'flushed' through with a saline solution to ensure they don't mix once they are in the system. One evening at 11.00pm, while drawing up my drugs and talking to a friend on the phone, I forgot to 'flush'. Fortunately nothing happened but I got my mum to ring the hospital immediately. I really panicked as I thought I was going to die, with only minutes to live. I asked my auntie, who was with me at the time, to hold my hand as I was sure any minute my heart would stop beating. We sat rigid for a few minutes until I realized I was OK. I felt so stupid afterwards, but I frightened myself enough to take better care in the future. I admit that I do get a little bit lazy with my intravenous antibiotics and sometimes I don't take enough time over them as I should. They interfere with my social life, and my family is always nagging me about my carelessness—but I suppose they're right.

Cough, cough, cough

I shared a room with Carol during my last hospital visit, and she just could not stop coughing. The CF cough could be classed as a trademark of the disease—and it certainly gave me an inkling that Ali had CF. As a child my mum was apparently told more than once by complete strangers that she shouldn't bring me out with such a terrible cough. As I grew older my cough was frequently mistaken for that of a smoker! Coughing can be as annoying to the person doing the coughing as it is to others. It's really difficult to try and control a CF cough, and most embarrassing when everyone looks at you. One of the amusing things about coughing in public is that it can often be misconstrued. For example, when I am waiting in queues such as a supermarket checkout and I cough, the cashier has interpreted it as my impatience. All people with CF have a cough and it can be quite distinctive. I remember being away with a group I had never met before; I had not mentioned to anyone that I had CF but one of the team members said, 'You've got CF haven't you?' It was my cough that betrayed me.

One of my few 'downs' at senior school was being seated near a window with the sun streaming through all day whilst taking exams. A teacher who did not know of my condition said that I disturbed everyone by coughing and that in future I must sit my exams in a room alone. Since then, even through university, I have sometimes sat in isolation for my exams, but I prefer that, as I hate having to disturb other people.

Ele, one of my good friends on the course at university, met up with another girl on the course whom I did not know. Ele happened to say she was meeting me later that day and the response was, 'Oh, is that the girl who coughs all the time?' It's funny how other people notice things that are so familiar to me that I forget I'm doing it. People who know me well can always tell if I'm in church, or in lectures, because my cough is very distinctive.

Friends and family

I'm a very active person by nature. I want to be going places, doing things, seeing people. One thing I find hard is demanding and expecting too much of myself.

There are times when I don't feel well, and yet I think that I should make the effort to do this or that when I've arranged to do things with my friends. Then I blame others and myself when life becomes busy and full and I haven't got enough energy to cope.

Perhaps selfishly on my part, I get frustrated that not many people understand about CF and its implications on daily life. I guess that is the same no matter what illness someone may have. This is one of the reasons why support groups exist. Part of their work is to educate people about certain issues. I remember having flu at a time when everyone else was suffering from it; mine went to a chest infection and made me feel quite ill. It didn't help to be told by one of my friends, 'We all feel ill when we have flu, Claire.' However, I know I'm my own worst enemy. I need to pace myself better because there are some days when I just wish I hadn't arranged to do things in the evenings. After work or a day in lectures, I get so tired and I must learn to say 'No'. But that's very hard for me, because my philosophy is that life is to be lived—to the max!

After one of my operations, my friends from the church and university just came and sat with me, and I really appreciated that. One friend particularly understood my need. I didn't feel like talking, but every time I opened my eyes she was there, just smiling and being with me; it must have been boring for her just to sit for so long. She was one of the few people who appeared to understand how I was feeling. I am indebted to my friends because they are so good to me. I am never in want for cards, chocolates, or visitors when I'm in hospital, or even when I'm unwell at home. I don't have brothers or sisters unfortunately, but God has really showered me with some wonderful friends and without their continued love, care and support I really don't know where I'd be. They certainly don't allow me to feel sorry for myself, which sometimes is a daily battle. I don't think I began to feel too sorry for myself until the last few years, when the reality of having CF became a lot more apparent. However, as time progresses I'm ashamed to say I do feel life can be hard. I try not to let it show because that is not constructive, but nevertheless it's a battle when I'm ill.

I know CF has had an effect on my family. They worry about me because I don't worry about myself enough, or at least I don't let them know I worry. They've had to wait to see if I can come home from hospital in time for holidays or Christmas. Christmas with IVs isn't unusual. When I'm ill it's my mum who knows about me best. She understands the real Claire Salter, because she has seen me at my lowest and my worst both physically and emotionally. I'm sure that if my friends saw me at these times, they wouldn't want to be my friends. She understands best, partly because she's my mum and partly because she's a nurse. I think my parents are very strong, especially as they have had to cope with so many difficult moments when even the doctors have been concerned. Unless I become a parent myself, I don't think I'll ever fully understand what they've been through.

I know that when I have intravenous antibiotics it puts quite a lot of pressure on my family. I'm grateful that my mum helps me draw them up into the syringes and sometimes she wakes me up in the mornings and gives me my IVs before I have to go to work or lectures, which saves me a lot of time. Mornings are not my favourite time of day! One thing I do find difficult when I'm on intravenous antibiotics at home is keeping going at work when I feel so drained and when I know that other people can have time off when they're ill; but because I'd already had time off, I feel I have to keep going and when I am exhausted and unable to concentrate I must go in to work. When I take time off I feel that the CF is winning and I don't like to be defeated.

Sometimes one of the signs of an infection is coughing up blood. I know I have to phone the hospital if I cough up a certain amount, and it's quite frightening not knowing whether it's going to stop. However, it always does stop. One dilemma I have is that if I tell my family, it worries them, but I feel that I want to tell someone because it worries me. Usually I just tell mum. She often calms me down and tells me not to worry about things. Being reassured that it doesn't necessarily mean I'm going to be seriously ill makes things feel better. So my family are the ones who do take the brunt of my illness. And they cope with me when I'm in a moaning mood.

When I was first diagnosed with CF, I really enjoyed all the attention, but after a while it contributed to me feeling different from other people. So I would downplay my illness because I didn't want to be anyone special; perhaps, adults saw through my facade. However, as I got older I realized how much I appreciated and needed the prayer and support of the church, even though I get a lot of attention through this. When I was particularly ill, on one occasion a hundred people met to pray for me. I know many other patients who don't have such a positive back up. However, when I'm feeling ill or down, it's easy to lose sight of these blessings. Hook Evangelical Church has been a tower of strength and encouragement to me. I try not to burden too many people with my problems. When people ask me how I am it's easy to become too introspective, so I generally try to respond to enquiries positively even when I sometimes feel rough, but I am learning more and more to let people know just how it is.

The touch of fear

Sharing a room with Carol on my last hospital visit was a big eye-opener for me. It was quite shocking to see her so ill. Her husband brought their five-year-old daughter to visit and all the little girl wanted was for her mummy to play with her, but Carol just couldn't muster the strength to do it. She kept saying to me, 'A couple of years ago I was like you, Claire, I could push my child up two hills without getting too breathless.' It was frightening to hear that I could be like Carol in a few years time. The doctors had just suggested that she consider having a heart/lung transplant. Carol amazed me how she coped with this news; she didn't cry, at least in my company. She was a great source of strength for me; I thought she was so brave. I don't think I could ever be that brave.

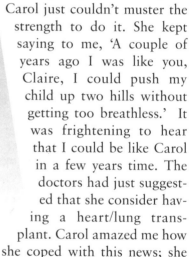

Each three-monthly outpatients visit for me means seeing the dietician, the clinical nurse specialist for CF, having blood and lung function tests, X-

Above: Claire caught the 'travel bug' when she was in her late teens and went 'interrailing' around Europe, visiting eight countries in just a few weeks

rays, visiting the physiotherapy department, and then waiting to see the doctor. An electro-cardiogram (ECG) once a year is also part of the process, not only because CF can affect the heart, but a lot of people with CF go on to have a heart-lung operation. Because the lungs may possibly need replacing due to the damage over the years, it is apparently easier to replace the heart at the same time.

The trouble with a heart-lung transplant is that only about one third of patients survive. This is partly due to the fact that they are very ill before the transplant and it is a big operation. But as more are being done, the survival rates are improving. However, because of the shortage of donors, some patients do not get a suitable donor in time. This is something that really worries me, the thought that I may be put forward for a heart-lung transplant and may not get it, or if I do manage to get a suitable donor, I may be too unwell by that time to go through the operation successfully. Taking it one step further, if I did have the operation, the new organs may not last long before they would be rejected. In terms of transplantation as well, it is difficult to comprehend what it would be like to have someone else's living lung inside my body. It is possible for 'matched' relatives (those whose body-type tissues are a good match with mine) to give part of their lung instead, and whilst I know members of my wider family would be willing to be tested, I'm not sure how I would feel about it all.

My experience of, on the one hand having an incurable illness, but on the other of being able to live life relatively well has meant that when I compare myself with others who have CF or different disabilities, I feel guilty because they may be worse than myself. This is especially so when I am with other CF people and they often look more frail and are, perhaps, coughing more; I wonder if I am an offence to them because I am comparatively well. At times I hate the fact that life is so unfair to me, and to so many others who suffer each day; so the guilt not only incorporates my feelings towards others, but of God too. But I thank God for the relative health he has given me and when I view this life in the light of eternity, I remember that he has a reason for everything. Although I don't understand it fully now, one day I know I will.

Often when I look at other people I wonder, 'My goodness, how do they cope?' I have difficult days, but when I see people so much worse than myself, I think that I've got away lightly. However no one can know how you're feeling and I try to avoid using the phrase 'I understand how you feel'. I can't fully understand what they are going through, just as no one can fully understand me in my position. There is some common ground, though, when we each experience illness. I believe that sometimes people who have gone through difficult times in their lives are often the best people to talk to because they do understand some of your feelings and experiences. Sometimes I feel very isolated, even from my closest friends and then I get frustrated. I have days when I think just nobody understands, or ever can.

I do struggle and I do find life harsh sometimes. I'm not pretending that I don't get frustrated with people who can't understand what it's like to be in my shoes. I have to admit that often I don't cope with my illness very well. So it makes me smile when I'm told that I cope so well. Sometimes people don't want to know when I'm having a bad day and who can blame them? Often we don't want to hear about each other's troubles because we've got enough troubles of our own. That's when I get a bit frustrated with my situation and with God, because day to day problems come as thick and fast whether one is healthy or ill. I think, 'Well, the next person hasn't got CF to cope with', even though the next person has probably many other problems. But that's part of the day-to-day struggles of living with a chronic, life-threatening illness… getting so tired, needing to take all my medication, do my physio and sort myself out before I leave the house in the morning.

Burghardt, a physician, wrote, 'In my opinion death is an insult; the stupidest, ugliest thing that can ever happen to a human being' (Burghart 1980, *Tell the Next Generation*. New York Paulist Press, p.315). Manning, a Christian writer, suggests that the 'separation from loved ones is too painful to consider. Perhaps for most of us, the frenetic pace of life and the immediate claims of the present moment leave no time, except for fleeting reflection at funerals, to contemplate seriously where we came from and where we are going. Saint Benedict offers the sober advice to "keep your own death before your eyes each day". And yet we are not cowed into timidity by death and life. Were we forced to rely on our own shabby resources we would be pitiful people indeed. But the awareness of Christ's presence, risen from the dead, persuades us that we are buoyed up and carried on by a life greater than our own. Hope means that in Christ, by entrusting ourselves to him, we can courageously face evil… we can then face death' (Manning 1994 *Abba's Child*. Navpress, Colorado, p148-150).

Euthanasia is a topic that frightens me and I worry that people won't want me around because I'll be a drain on society in terms of money. Some of my drugs already cost £8,000 per year and I'm worried that if euthanasia becomes legalized, the pressure from society not to 'waste' money in this way may be to my detriment. Euthanasia is, of course, such an emotive issue but I know that if it does become legal, there could be problems for those who have long-term incurable illnesses. I don't think society will know where to draw the line even though they may have good intentions, and I believe we will worry about who we can trust and what we say, whilst wanting the best medical advice. It is so important for a patient to have confidence and trust in the medical staff.

I do worry about the future—having CF is like having a big dark cloud hovering over me. I don't notice it all the time but it is always there. I don't know what the future holds; I don't know how long I'm going to live; I don't know which avenue my health will take. I might be reasonably all right for ten or twenty years, or only for two or three years—life feels so insecure. That's the hardest thing, it's like a time bomb inside you, the clock is ticking but you don't know when time will run out. I get so annoyed when people say they could get run over by a bus tomorrow, because that kind of reasoning doesn't allow me, as a person with a chronic illness, to feel my pain of the uncertainty of my life. It's the fear of the unknown, and perhaps people who don't live with an issue like this do not fully understand.

Because of my worries about my own mortality, I have recently had some very helpful chats with one of the community cystic fibrosis nurses. It has been vital for me to discuss how I feel about certain aspects of CF and how I can come to terms with it. I have found that I can really be open and honest with Liz, partly because she knows what I am talking about and she understands, and also because she is a professional rather than a member of my family or a close friend. All the issues around death and dying made me very tearful. I couldn't talk about this without crying, and Liz reassured me that she would have been worried if I hadn't talked about such important issues and that it was OK and natural to feel this way. I'm a strong believer in counselling and although this is not Christian counselling, I can honestly say that it has helped me speak freely of what I am afraid of. Even as a Christian, it is natural to have these kinds of feelings. What's important is how you work through all this with God. I feel I began talking a lot more about cystic fibrosis amongst my friends, which I had never really done before, or at least, not to such a great extent. They were very gracious in listening and showing understanding.

I don't mind admitting that often I'm very scared. I'm scared of what life may hold and I'm scared of being in pain. As one writer puts it, 'At the bottom of every one of your fears is simply the fear that you can't handle whatever life may bring you' (Jeffes. *Feel the fear and do it anyway*. Penguin, New York 1991.) I had begun to feel a sense of tremendous anxiety about being away from home and thinking a lot about dying and becoming seriously ill. I was in America at the time, taking a holiday after a friend's wedding there. I was very anxious about going, and just before the return trip I was really worried about not making it home. It was not that I was particularly ill, but I was worried about dying in a country I didn't know, and without my family or friends around me. This was quite frightening, because I suppose I am like everyone else in that I don't want to die alone. My friend Ali had died a year beforehand, surrounded by a loving family and caring friends and her death had affected me a great deal.

Ali's death brought my own mortality a lot closer, and issues that I had blocked out in the past, or did not fully understand, seemed much more apparent. I'm afraid of not being able to cope with my illness, and of being dependent upon other people, even being wheelchair bound. I'm very concerned with the logistics of how I die. Yet the irony of all this is that I might even outlive most of my friends and family and then I will feel very guilty about all the time I have spent worrying about my situation! But what if I die and leave a husband and young children, or even elderly parents and other relatives? There just seems to me to be so much to think about and there are no answers or guarantees for the future. Sometimes it's so hard to get on with life with so many imponderables. I sometimes find it hard to trust God with this big question of death. Before I feel ready to go he may say, 'OK Claire, it's time'. And I won't want to die. One of my prayers, and it's something I feel strongly that we all should pray, is that God will help me accept my situation and be ready to confront death.

There are times when I get tremendously excited about the thought of heaven and I just can't wait to go. I think it will be amazing to be free from all pain and tears. I cannot fully grasp it, but I guess that if we had a foretaste of heaven we'd all want to go right now. However, I know God wants to use me while I am here and I hope that, despite myself I can somehow reach in to other people's hearts and touch their pain. God has been so faithful and loving throughout my life that I know I can and must trust him for what lies ahead. But it's so easy to write that and a lot harder to do. Part of my anger is knowing that God is all powerful and could change my situation if he wanted; yet I know also that in his infinite wisdom he has chosen not to. However, I have very ambiguous feelings. It is frustrating that I can do nothing about my illness, and at the same time, I realize how fortunate I am. I try not to let these feelings alter my trust in God, because I know he has everything planned for my ultimate good.

I often think about marrying and having children, even though the opportunity hasn't arisen yet! If I do get married, I wonder if it would be fair to have children? When my health deteriorates, how would my husband cope and respond to major decisions that he would have to make about the future? So, is it fair even to get married? There are so many questions to consider and I'm not sure how, or if, they will be answered. I guess the hardest thing is just giving it over to God and letting him control everything.

In writing about my experiences, I feel very exposed. This is all the real Claire Salter! Not the one who so often hides behind a facade that everything is all right.

A silver lining

Are there any benefits in having CF? In recent years I have been able to experience different parts of the world, which has been a real privilege. I caught the 'travel bug' when I was in my late teens and I felt that I should get travelling in while I was sufficiently able to. My aim is to enjoy life as much as I can whilst I am able, and to see as many new places as I possibly can with the money and time that I've got.

The year after I had my portacath implanted, I felt reasonably well and a few of us from University went 'inter-railing' around Europe. We visited eight countries in a period of three and a half weeks and, although exhausted, we all enjoyed the experience. My family was quite

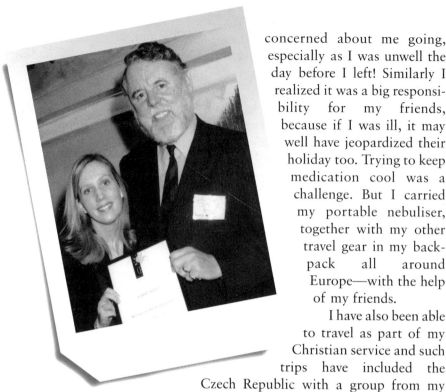

concerned about me going, especially as I was unwell the day before I left! Similarly I realized it was a big responsibility for my friends, because if I was ill, it may well have jeopardized their holiday too. Trying to keep medication cool was a challenge. But I carried my portable nebuliser, together with my other travel gear in my backpack all around Europe—with the help of my friends.

I have also been able to travel as part of my Christian service and such trips have included the Czech Republic with a group from my local church. We journeyed by road but this time medication went in a fridge in our pastor's motor caravan. The problem, however, was that the nebuliser wouldn't work. But there were a couple of nurses on the trip who really looked out for me. A further privilege was taking food parcels and visiting refugees in the former Yugoslavia with a Christian organization; this was an incredibly humbling experience. I have been fortunate enough to visit South Africa, Egypt and Israel.

Closer to home, I have undertaken a short spell of Christian service with the London City Mission and I have regularly helped with the youth work on the annual Caister week of the Fellowship of Independent Evangelical Churches. I continue to be engaged in co-leading a weekly

Above: Claire receiving her Cystic Fibrosis Achiever's Award by Terry Waite at The Park Lane Hilton in 1998

youth group at my church. I love working with teenagers, partly because I think I am still such a teenager at heart. After my first degree I took a year out and worked with the Christian School's Work Trust in Kingston-upon-Thames. It was a great experience. I enjoyed the work and benefited so much from working with the team. I would love to work full time in Christian service one day. It was exciting for me to take the Christian gospel into schools and to show the teenagers that it is a relevant answer for their lives.

In many respects I'm very blessed having CF! I think that if I didn't have it, I would not have experienced half of the things that I have, and I have learnt so much through it. I don't think I would have chosen to have CF, but I know God has used me and blessed me more by having it. In recent years I have appreciated so much what it means to live with an illness like this. I didn't fully realize before, but people do care about me. I think that if I didn't have CF I would not have experienced half of the things that I have done. Other people who are ill and yet who keep on fighting and don't give up are an encouragement to me. Some people keep me going just because they know what I'm going through. Meanwhile life continues on the fast track and I will shortly complete a two-year Master's course in Social Work. It has been my childhood ambition to be a social worker—though I am beginning to wonder why, as it seems to be one of the many stressful occupations!

Endings

When the envelope flopped onto the doormat, the Cystic Fibrosis Trust symbol was clearly recognisable. To anyone unfamiliar with the logo it would probably just be seen as another advertising ploy, but this envelope was to introduce one of the best days of my life. I had been selected for a CF Achiever's Award in the 'Services to the Community' category, and the envelope contained an invitation to the Hilton Hotel in Park Lane. I wasn't the overall winner, but I did come top in my category and benefited from a healthy cheque!

So on December 10, 1998 I arrived at the Hilton, went up in the lift and met with Terry Waite, who I later found out was to present my award. I met many other celebrities, including the television presenter Carol Smillie and the cricketer, David Gower. But my conversation with Terry

Waite proved to be the best. Lots of CF winners of different categories were there and it was so great to meet them and hear their stories. We were all treated like royalty and enjoyed a fantastic lunch while we chatted and took endless photos. Terry Waite is one of my heroes because of his loving and caring attitude despite the years he was held hostage, most of which was spent in solitary confinement. It was during his captivity in the damp, dirty, underground cell that he developed chest problems and found it hard to breathe; that's why he can empathize with CF people so well. The whole experience of that memorable day will remain with me for a long time and this is one of the many examples of my privileges.

It is fitting that, having started with Ali, I should close with one of the poems that she wrote. It was read at her funeral and it means a lot to me and to many others. Ali died in her early twenties and yet she was an inspiration to so many—a real fighter. Ali's earthly race has come to an end but this poem speaks so strongly about her faith in God for the future:

When I am strong
I will fight,
And when I am weary of the fight
I will rest in you,
Knowing that you can carry me for a time.
In my fight
I will draw strength from your love
For your love cannot be beaten.

When I am alone,
When I feel the icy touch of fear,
I will take it in my hand
And hold it out to you
And in the heat of your love
It will melt away.

When my heart feels isolated,
When no one can comfort me
And the crowd serves
Only to remind me of how alone I am,

I will look within myself where you wait
And I will remember to allow you to love me.

Then, when the joy is so strong
That I cannot take life in quickly enough,
I will remember to take a moment to sit with you
And appreciate the beauty you created.

And when the night comes,
I ask only
That I be alive with peace and faith,
So that I may not fear
The new day that lies beyond.'

Alison Browne, 1997

From chaos to control

Paul and Helle de Vere

Taking life seriously does not stop Paul from laughing at himself and his situation. Paul is something of an entrepreneur, with an independent and determined spirit. In his own humorous way he shares with us his journey in a wheelchair from 'flower power' to Jesus Christ; a journey that led him to his wife Helle and their busy life of helping others with disabilities.

Mine was a difficult birth that very nearly killed my mother. The doctor who delivered me at home was as shocked as everyone else present. Softly he informed my mother, 'The baby is not normal. It might be better if we don't smack him and just put him quietly in the other room. If the good Lord wants him to breathe he will breathe—otherwise he won't.' My mother's response was immediate, 'Give me my baby now' she protested. Two years previously she had a stillborn baby girl, so I was very much longed for. I was the second of four boys and one girl, and my mother told me later that out of them all I was the one with the strongest appetite for life and who drank the most! She was convinced that this was a sign from God that I was here to stay.

The only difference between the rest of my siblings and me was that I was born with a rare condition that the doctor impressively called Arthrogryposis Multiplex Congenita. Hardly anyone knew what this meant, but the fact was that my fingers and ankles were in-flexed and my wrists and knee joints were locked. Despite this, although I couldn't stand I was able to shuffle around on the floor in funny little 'bunny hops', as my mother affectionately still refers to them. This would often prove to be something of an obstacle, because people would trip over me. I remember once my mother dropped a whole tray of tea and cakes just because she didn't see me. Luckily the hot tea missed me, but I was able to assist her in pointing out where some of the cakes had gone, even if one or two were missing by then! My brothers and sister used to think that my method of moving around was great fun and would often join me.

I can remember my first spell in hospital after the doctors tried to convince my parents that if they straightened everything out (my fingers, arms, legs and feet), I would soon be running around like a two-year-old—which I found odd since I was a lot older than that already. My father, who was a doctor himself, agreed on condition that none of my ligaments or tendons would be cut. He would only accept manipulation, not operation. I was in hospital for what seemed like forever, but in fact it probably was no more than six weeks. I had splints and straps on my fingers forcing them

Above: Taking full rein. Paul and Helle enjoy taking a break from the pressures of life by pony and carriage driving. Over the years Paul has won a number of rosettes

straight. My legs and ankles were also splinted to force them out straight against their natural inclination. Then my arms, which don't normally lift above shoulder height, were strapped way above my head to the top of a board on which my body was strapped to keep me straight. It was agony, and by far the most torturous time of my whole life. The painkillers that I was given morning and night seemed to have less and less effect. Each morning when I woke up I longed for the night. At least when I was asleep there was some respite from the pain. However, the worst was not over. When all the splints were taken off, my joints, bones, ligaments and tendons slowly went back to their 'normal' shape. That was more agony. Despite all the efforts of the medical profession I was to remain the shape in which I was born.

Recently, I met someone who had undergone the very operation that the doctors had wanted to carry out on me. It meant replacing the knee joint and cutting the tendons of the legs to straighten them. But since this would have had the effect that I would not be able to feel my limbs, they might just as well have been amputated. I watched the poor man struggle to walk with the aid of elbow crutches; the sweat pouring from his brow as he dragged agonisingly one leg in front of the other. He had no feeling in his legs. He informed me that life was not easy for him, and I could see that. I was so glad for my father's wise decision.

'Paul told us to do it'

My parents believed in an 'open door' policy to the neighbourhood. People of all shapes, sizes, colours and creeds were made to feel welcome, and they all took advantage of this welcome. They were always coming and going. This was partly due to the fact that some of my father's patients boarded on the top floor of our large family house. The family lived on the middle floor, level with the street, and we had cooks, maids, cleaners and a nanny living on the 'lower deck.' These were the ones who really kept the whole show going. They were lovely and devoted people. There was always a job available for them, even if it was just taking me out to the park. Even in those days people would stop and exclaim, 'Oh, what lovely blonde curly hair he has.' Not surprisingly the family nicknamed me 'Bubbles.'

My childhood memories of home life with my brothers and sister are happy and amusing ones. I can remember my first wheelchair. It was an old-fashioned type of attendant pushchair with four small wheels, a canvas seat, and no suspension. In it I always felt trapped; so I spent as little time in it as possible. My resourceful brothers, seeing how much I hated the wheelchair, took it apart and made it into a soapbox trolley with two planks of wood. With the aid of a rope I could now steer the trolley myself and scoot around the house. This was a marvellous invention as I became instantly mobile and could join in with all the other children in their games. I was now sitting in a cart the same as the rest of them and the only difference was that I needed to be pushed up hill. My parents didn't know whether to frown on the invention or not. It would be difficult to explain when the health visitor called to find out how I was progressing with my wheelchair!

I was always an inquisitive child. I had a wonderful set of brothers who would do almost anything I asked, which often got them into trouble. Because I spent most of my childhood scuffling around at ground level, it was near enough impossible for me to open doors. I worked out that if the lower panel of the heavy oak door in the bedroom was not there, I would be able to see everything that went on outside. My brothers figured out that this was not a problem. They gathered the necessary tools, and before long a wonderful hole had appeared in the door through which I could see out. As I peered through the hole, I looked into four eyes peering in. In utter horror I realised that it was my parents. They were not impressed with my new invention. My brothers' despairing plea, 'Paul told us to do it' was not good enough. We were all sent to bed early that night and we could all feel the sting on our backsides. Our parents believed in equality in our family!

My elder brother and I used to collect Hornby oo train sets. We had a marvellous set-up with a station with people and lights, and more lights all along the track. We would turn out the room lights to enhance the atmosphere as the trains raced round. Annoyingly, the street light outside the window spoilt the effect. One day I decided that we needed to put that lamp out and I told my brother that if he sat me on the window ledge I would unfold to him my idea. I explained that if he fired some plasticine from his catapult at the streetlight, the light should go out. Juan promptly opened the window and started to take shots at it. To my complete surprise, after only a few attempts he hit our target. At that instant the whole street was plunged into darkness. Again our parents appeared at the door. My brother tried the same tactic, 'Paul told me to do it.' But it was no more successful than the last time, and again that night it was a painful couple of children who made their way to bed.

I can well remember the summer's evening when my father told us to play quietly, because he had an important guest, whom he had to see in the front room downstairs. Once again, my inquisitiveness got the better of me. My brothers and sister, and some friends who we were playing with, fastened a long rope round my waist and under my arms. Gradually they lowered me out of the window so that I could sneak a peek at whoever the mysterious guest might be. My poor father watched in horror as a small figure slowly lowered outside the window, swinging in the breeze. In a matter of moments I was hoisted very quickly back to where I came from—and came face to face with dear Papa. Once again we went to bed early and painfully that night.

In preparation for bonfire night one year, my brothers had made an underground camp in the garden by shifting lots of soil. They made a cosy dugout, which we called our 'secret place.' There we lit a little fire and sat and talked. One day we were all down there, cosy and warm by the fire, when my mother called urgently about some matter. My brothers shot out of our secret hiding-hole to find her. After some time it occurred to me that I had been forgotten. By this time the fire was low and smoking profusely. I heard my mother call, 'Where is Paul?' As she looked to the bottom of the garden she could see smoke rising from the ground. I heard the pounding of feet as the family suddenly remembered that I was still down in the 'secret place.' They managed to drag me out, coughing and spluttering, and I must have smelt like an old chimney. There were quite a few strong words from my mother and I was put straight into the bath and sent to bed. The house was very quiet that night!

My first teacher was marvellous. Mr Ellis used to take me out for geography lessons in his old Ford Prefect. I can still remember the smell of the leather and the way the indicators seemed to pop out at whim. He taught me the names of the different trees and birds. He was a fascinating character and looked a bit like Woodstock from the Peanuts cartoon, with his shock of white hair, which stood straight up on top of his head. One day I didn't feel like lessons at all, so I asked my brother Juan to put me up into the old tree house we had at the bottom of the garden. There I could hide from Mr Ellis. I sat quietly watching to see if he would come and then go again. My plan didn't quite work out. On his arrival he set about finding me. I can see him now, climbing the rope ladder with his books in his hand. He began by testing me on my knowledge of trees and birds. That impressed me, and we became great friends.

Plaster casts and mouth sticks

After the formation of the National Health Service in 1948, my father's private clinic and consultancy began to wane. Eventually we moved to Guildford, where my father started a business selling second-hand theological books. A prominent orthopaedic specialist at Rowley Bristow Hospital in Pyrford near Woking wanted to carry out some tests on me in order to establish whether it would be possible for me to walk on artificial legs. They made a plaster cast from my thigh to my knee in which I could rest my knees. At each side of the cast they put two metal callipers, with rocker-type feet on the ends of them. They also made me some crutches, into which I could fit my hands, the top part of which went under my armpits. For the first time in my life I actually stood and 'waddled', a bit like a duck. But I didn't feel human with all these tin bits clanking away, and my father was not impressed. 'What would be the first thing you do if you fall over?' he asked the physiotherapists. Their reply was, 'Cushion the fall with an arm.' 'Exactly', responded my father, 'And that is something Paul cannot do. He would just fall on his face.' So, they assessed me for a self-propelled wheelchair instead. It was a bit like a dumper truck, with large wheels in front and wooden hand rims at the back. But it was a great success. For the first time I was able to manoeuvre myself independently of anyone else; it was freedom!

I stayed at the Rowley Bristow Hospital School and one day, at about the age of nine, my father came to collect me and told me that he and my mother had decided to live separately. I stayed in the hospital but regularly visited my mother and father in turn. At the end of my assessment at the Hospital School my father wanted me to continue my education. I passed an entry exam to go to Lord Mayor Treloar College, which was a boarding school for boys with physical disabilities. I managed to achieve GCSE's in commercial art subjects and was often top of the class in painting or drawing pencil sketches of people or landscapes. I also studied Pitman's basic bookkeeping, but I didn't exactly excel in other subjects.

My wheelchair was fitted with ball bearing arm supports, which had a cradle at the end of each support, in which I could rest my arms. These allowed me sideways movements of my arms and if the desk was at the right height, my fingers were in just the right position over my workspace. By placing a pen or paintbrush between my first two fingers I could do my work. At the weekends, whilst at home, I used this method to help in the book business by pricing the books and writing letters to our customers. Later, an occupational therapist friend of mine told me about mouth sticks. With these I found I had much greater control in typing, and I improved my painting techniques.

Our family book business eventually dissolved, and as I had finished my studies at the Lord Mayor Treloar College, I wanted to be employed with my own income and a place of my own. I was quite used to living away from home so I tried a residential establishment at Newhaven. This seemed to be especially for those who had lost an arm or a leg. The employment was either heavy or awkward: surgical boot making, engineering or tele-phonist/switch-board operator. The latter was the only job I was able to attempt, but I had to stretch quite far to connect incoming calls by raising the necessary plugs into their sockets. Apparently the company couldn't consider moving the board to a lower position because all switchboard operators worked at that level. Besides that, the help that I needed simply getting up and going to bed couldn't be provided, so I was deemed to be unemployable. I came back home again.

By the age of twenty I found just being unemployed at home was quite depressing. I complained to my mother one day that I was bored. In frus-tration she responded, 'Can't you write a book or something?' So I did! I produced a number of short stories for children, about a parrot with a magic purple tail. Then a friend of my mother knew of a small firm that did sub-contract work for a pharmaceutical company. Basically the work involved folding boxes into shape and placing a sachet of four tablets into each box. I think I earned a penny for each box. Accessible transport could be provided to pick me up from home and return me at the end of the day, so I decided to have a go at it. This job lasted for over two years and I was reasonably happy because this was the first non-residential set-up I had been part of, and I could come home with some pocket money to spend like everybody else. The set-up was mainly for people that had some form of physical impairment. I made new friends, and a few of them knew of a publisher. I mentioned that in a bored moment I had written some stories for children. The publishers were interested in my ideas and characters, and detailed an artist to make pictures of my characters. They offered me £250 for my stories and characters. With this I was able to purchase my first brand new electric typewriter. Shortly afterwards, owing to some problems with funding, the wheelchair accessible bus that took me to work from Farnham to Guildford a couple of days each week was withdrawn. Those of us who relied on it were asked if we could get to work on our own, but as none of us had a car, the work came to an end.

Beards, bells and beads

It wasn't long before I became bored again, and so began an interest in the arts. My mother assisted at the nearby Farnham Art School, which ran regular lectures on various arts related topics. This meant that I could attend the lectures and learn without having to write copious reports and sit impossible exams. I attended a lecture on textile design. I was particularly interested in the use of coloured ceramic Japanese tiles in forming designs, and was given an address in Japan, where I could order such tiles. Once again my mother said, 'Don't just sit there, do something.' I decided that it was time I started my own business. I had had enough of working for everybody else. I began covering all sorts of fancy shaped bottles with tiles that I grouted to produce a smooth effect between the tiles. I then had a hole drilled at one end and inserted a light fitting and flex. These, I was able to sell at a fancy 'nick-knack shop.' They looked grand in the window, and although it only supplied me with pocket money, at least I gained a sense of achievement. Unfortunately, I quite often cut my fingers instead of the tiles and the work made my hands very sore.

My mother had many 'arty' friends and was always involved with some art project or other. I was often included in their painting soirees at our home and began to learn quite a lot more techniques. I particularly enjoyed working with watercolours. My younger brother Harry and his wife Deno, also knew many art students and business people in the town of Farnham and were always bringing someone different home.

Some of them were pretty 'way out' people. Most of them were knowledgeable in the arts and literature and totally eccentric, which fascinated me no end. There were poets, musicians, painters, some of whom were connoisseurs, or like myself mere novices, just interested to learn. One of these characters, Mike, was a self confessed follower of Zen and a prolific reader and writer. He kept himself alive by window cleaning. A cleaning rag filled one pocket and a notebook, in which he constantly wrote his profound thoughts, filled the other.

My mother moved to Scotland to help a friend start a small business there and I elected to stay in the family home. Mike offered to be my helper. I managed to persuade some art students from Farnham Art School into taking some cut-price rooms in return for painting my house. This fascinated me as I saw the rooms changing to multicolour with all sorts of odd designs. I took more interest in art and started painting on paper and canvas rather than the hard grind of cutting ceramics for designs. Soon I was getting assistance from many different sources, all of them a little unorthodox; but I needed help as Mike's window cleaning business was picking up and he was seldom seen.

To be in your early twenties at the time of the psychedelic sixties was a wildly impressive time for anyone who had a social conscience. In the

Above: 'Don't just sit there, do something.' So Paul decided to start his own business

main, we were people who wanted to break away from the traditional values held by our parents and explore 'new ideas.' The emphasis was on 'expressing yourself, man!' and to find 'peace, love and harmony, man!' The popular philosophy at the time was being fed to us by the expounders of Jung, Freud and Jean-Paul Sartre. There was a pot pourri of advocates telling us all to 'search one's inner self', and obtain true peace and happiness; or to meditate along with the Beatles' guru and the like. By staring at a mantra on the wall and reciting some incantation or chant, perhaps we could reach some astral plane! A friend of mine actually went as far as drinking salt water until he vomited, in order to purify the inner soul!

In contrast to all this mystical dabbling and introspection, the debate was often about whether anything existed except the 'here and now.' Some of us doubted whether anything existed at all! Others questioned that if anything did exist, what would it matter anyhow? This last group would often sit crossed legged on the floor round a smouldering joss stick, puffing at large hand-rolled cigarettes, nodding their heads in agreement with each other and exclaiming profoundly from time to time, 'Far out, man'! A few of them became addicted to hard drugs and sadly are no longer with us. A Beatles' song well reflected the mood of that era, 'There's a fog upon LA and my friends have lost their way.' Looking back I can thank God I was saved from the 'pusher man's' dose of death. However, most of my friends were 'together people' and were good painters, musicians, poets and philosophers. They were lovely people whom I found inspiring. They protested against war, hate and violence, and there was always someone to debate with who had a perspective about life, the universe and everything. 'Gentle people with flowers in their hair', sang the Flower Pot Men.

Most debates about God, ranged from whether he was an astronaut to the pluralistic idea that he loved everybody and everything; therefore we could choose whatever route to him we wanted, whether it be through Buddha, Confucius, Jesus or whoever. Life in itself was a spiritual celebration to God; even communing with the trees and flowers was an extension of one's spirituality! Although I had a knowledge of some of the famous Bible stories, and had even won some prizes in my Sunday school days for remembering different texts, it didn't seem to carry any relevance for me. On the other hand, searching my inner soul to find spiritual fulfilment left me cold and with a feeling that I had opened a can of worms that was far from spiritual. I never felt quite holy enough to really speak to God, nor felt that he would be particularly concerned with anyone who had some form of disability; surely he only wanted people who were whole?

From time to time my uncle would push me to Bethel Baptist Chapel in Farnham, but one particular visit was to change my whole outlook on life. A guest speaker had been invited in order to celebrate some special event; they were always celebrating 'special events', and the 'Chapel Teas' caused the local neighbourhood to flock in because enough food was provided for a week. Although I couldn't follow every point the preacher was trying to make, certain things fixed in my mind. To say the least his was a very direct approach and he thundered out his message from the *Authorised Version* of the Bible, 'The word saith, "The soul that sinneth, it shall die".' I nearly fell out of my chair—this was going to be some celebration! He continued, 'Jesus said, "I am the way, the truth and the life; no man cometh unto the Father, but by me".' He thundered on, 'No other is good enough to pay the price for our sin. It's no good coming though any other prophet, priest or king. Only the blood of the Lamb cleanseth us from all sin; though our sins be red as crimson they shall be as white as snow. "Whoever, cometh to me", saith the Lord, "I will in no wise cast out".' And so it continued. One quotation from Psalm 139:13-16 particularly stayed with me, 'For thou hast possessed my reins: thou hast covered me in my mother's womb. I will praise thee; for I am fearfully and wonderfully made: marvellous are thy works; and that my soul knoweth right well. My substance was not hid from thee, when I was made in secret, and curiously wrought in the lowest parts of the earth. Thine eyes did see my substance, yet being unperfect; and in thy book all my members were written, which in continuance were fashioned, when as yet there was none of them.'

Wow! When I unravelled it, it told me three things: The route to God was clearly defined, God himself provided the means of holiness, and God knew everything about us—even me! Despite all the difficulties and uncertainties of life, this was a solid foundation that I could trust. And trust it I did—from that moment on. I wanted to tell everyone about my new faith, and as I had never been baptized, I decided to honour God by doing so. The elders were pleased, and they explained that although they held to the mode of baptism by immersion into water, this would not present any difficulty; one of them could lower me from my chair to two others standing in the water where I could be quickly dunked! To be fair, the minister did suggest that if it was easier for me, I could be sprinkled with water instead.

It was quite an occasion. People packed inquisitively around the pool in the little chapel. Many of them had never set foot in a chapel before, let alone seen a baptism by immersion in water. I was assisted down to the edge of the pool where I sat for a while and looked around at everyone. It was odd to see some of my hippie friends with their frizzy hair, long beards and bedecked with beads and caftans, standing alongside others who looked as though they had just stepped out of the eighteenth century. The preacher explained what was going to happen, and the reason why I was doing this. My assistants lowered me into the water, and being so light, all I did was to bob around on the top! They had to push quite hard for me to be immersed. I'm sure some of my friends thought that I had volunteered to be drowned because they chorused, 'Heavy man—Far out!'

About this time the local parish church claimed to have 'The out-pouring of the Almighty.' It was recorded in the press that people were talking in strange tongues and some were being healed. My friends, who were always on the lookout for a new experience in life, offered to push me along to one of the healing services. So, caftans flapping in the wind, I agreed to go along with them. The look on the vicar's face as we entered through the doors was a picture. I don't think he had seen so many hippies in all his life. At the call to come forward for the laying on of hands, all my friends told me that they would be rooting for me if I agreed to go up. In my mind I argued that nothing would be impossible if God really was almighty, so I decided to give it a go.

After the service was over, we returned home, disillusioned by the whole affair. I was invited to come back the following week, because it was suggested that I didn't have sufficient faith for any miracle to take place. After one more try I became even more disillusioned, and even angry at God for not doing anything. I decided that this church and I were not really compatible. Some of my friends wanted to persuade me that faith worked and, in a desperate attempt to convince me that miracles do happen, someone laid hands on an old car which was about to be 'pushed through' its MOT. To everyone's astonishment it passed! This only made me feel worse, because I was convinced that there must be something wrong with me if even a battered old banger could get healed. I was to learn later that God was more concerned about the healing of my spirit and emotions than the healing of my body.

The Little Mermaid

Many of the students lodging with me came from different parts of the country and their studies were becoming more and more intense as their degree courses came to a close. I was getting less and less assistance at the times when I needed it. I was also getting depressed and even began to wish that my mother might return. To me this would mean defeat. A friend suggested that I might try an institution. My pride was outraged, 'I am not going to be put away like some unwanted dog in a kennel.' However, after much persuasion and a visit to a couple of possible places I eventually settled for Le Court near Alton in Hampshire. It was a Cheshire home and seemed a bit like a glorified hotel. I had my own room and a call button that would summon help if needed. This help often appeared either in the form of a longhaired and bearded care attendant, or far better, some nice looking young foreign girls. This, I decided, would make a suitable home. I will never forget my second morning when I received a visit from my social worker. She drove over from Farnham to Alton just to inform me that 'all my problems would be over.' How on earth, I wondered, could she know that? She had never been in my situation.

For the next six years I was happy and contented at Le Court. I made many friends, who enriched my life. All the residents had varying forms of disability, and each one had a story to tell. I could empathise with most of them. The place was less of an institution and more of a home in the sense that this was our home, and the assistants were there to help us in our lives. We had our own car, our own shop, and a resident's lounge bar where we could entertain guests. In addition, the house was set in lovely grounds, and we had each other for companionship, which was just as well because we were right on top of a hill in the middle of nowhere.

One of the care assistants was a young girl from Denmark called Helle. The extent of my knowledge about that country was bacon, Hans Christian Andersen and The Little Mermaid. I met Helle almost as soon as

I arrived at Le Court. I don't actually remember it, but she tells me that she was 'sold' right from the start. There was something about my brown eyes, she said, which made her want to get to know me more. It took her a couple of months, to make me aware of her. Everywhere I turned, Helle was there. When I had breakfast in the dining room, she came flying over to take my order. If I was reading the paper or watching the television in the common room, she would suddenly turn up and enquire whether she could bring me tea or coffee. It appears that 'the way into a man's heart is through his stomach', is international.

We first got to know each other better when I had a real problem one day. I had bought a new stylus for my record player, but it was so small and fiddly, that I could not keep hold of it and put it in the right place. In my frustration, I stuck my head out of the door to grab the first passer-by. By a neat coincidence that passer-by was Helle! 'Can you put my stylus in for me?', I asked. The only response was a blank stare and a refined English, 'Pardon?' I had learnt to be patient when talking with all these foreigners so I tried more slowly. 'This is a record player—yes? This is a stylus—yes? It goes into the arm there—yes?' 'Oh', she responded, 'You mean the "pick up".' Well, how was I to know that in Denmark they use the English phrase 'pick-up' for a stylus? Helle then caught sight of my not inconsiderable record collection. I am very fond of music. She told me that she liked the same type of music as me, so it was quite natural that I should invite her, in her off duty time, to come to my room and play any music that she liked. That very afternoon, after teatime, there was a knock at my door.

Helle was born in Vejle, on the east coast of Jutland. Her spiritual awakening was one of slow development. Although her father frequently scorned all things to do with Christianity, perhaps because he had a very strict Christian upbringing himself, which had completely alienated him, he also had a devout Christian sister, Anna, who often visited and had a great influence on Helle. Helle's mother never made any verbal stand for or against Christianity because of the friction it would cause in the family. It was through the RE lessons at school, taken by the local vicar, that Helle's eyes were opened to understand the finished work of our Lord Jesus Christ for her salvation. She realised that Christ had died for her personally.

Helle's father, Hur, was the director of a large company selling shop fittings and installations for bakery shops. Her mother was a softly spoken, hard working housewife who, because father was away on business so much of the time, ran the large family home almost single-handed. Helle's father was used to directing everything and he insisted on making all decisions and giving orders as if he was an army sergeant. However, there were at least two things which did not go the way he wanted them. Firstly, he very much wanted a son and heir to the business; instead he got two girls, neither of whom was the least bit interested in bakery design. Secondly, he wanted Helle and her sister Kirsten to study languages so that they could be useful to him in his work; but they both decided on other professions. Kirsten became a solicitor's secretary, and Helle took six months out from studying between college and university to go to England. Her plan was to spend a few months improving her English, and then to spend time in France improving her French. Only then would she begin her studies at university in Denmark to become a bilingual secretary. Helle never got further than England!

A friend of Helle had heard of a residential institution in Hampshire where a lot of foreign students worked. Most of them were taking time off in between studies, and most of them had before them a career in the health services, either as nurses, doctors, physiotherapists or occupational therapists. However, although Helle had no thought of the medical profession (she faints at the sight of blood), she looked on the experience as providing a bank of English speakers with a wonderful opportunity to learn about all those things that you cannot learn from a book, like different dialects.

Over a period of time we built a very close friendship. We went almost everywhere together. Helle worked on a different wing of the building from where I lived, but she only worked four days a week so she had plenty of leisure time, and there were lots of occasions when she was able to escort me on outings. Our first real date was a little out of the ordinary. I invited her to London to see a wrestling match between Giant Haystacks and Big Daddy at the Royal Albert Hall! I was offered the tickets free by one of the residents. He would let us travel up to London in his car if I could find him a driver. This was a challenge I couldn't refuse, especially as money was a bit short at that time. I assumed that our first date would either cement our friendship or Helle would never want to see me again.

Roger was our driver. He had been in the police force and stood about 6ft high and 4ft something wide. Although he was the sort you would never pick a fight with, in reality he was a gentle and softly spoken character with a marvellous Somerset dialect. When we arrived at the Royal Albert Hall I suddenly remembered that my wheelchair was still standing in the car park at the home. As I was only 5ft tall and weighed around 7 stone it was easy for Roger to offer to lift me. However, it doesn't do much for a young man's ego on his first date to be sat, like a glove puppet, on the arm of a burly friend!

Living at Le Court had been the means of my meeting so many people that had enriched my life, both residents and staff. Many of the staff came from different countries, and even after they had left they often kept in contact. I asked Helle to escort me on my holiday to Holland where I was going to see one of the ex-Le Court care staff Arie-Jan. We would travel with another resident from Le Court, my old friend Steve, and his escort. The four of us had a wonderful holiday, and it was during this holiday that I first got the idea, that I might be able to convince Helle to spend the rest of her days with me. I poured out my heart to Steve. His response was threateningly direct, 'If you allow that girl to disappear out of your life I am going to punch you on the nose, and I don't care who you are!' Steve, an ex-bricklayer, was a formidable opponent in spite of his MS, and I had no desire to pick a fight with him, so the idea continued to buzz round in my head. I also had a chat with some other good friends, Pete and Kay, who had already taken this great step. Kay had been working at Le Court where she had met Pete who was a resident. They were married a couple of years previously, and now lived in the community in a council house. They were very happy, and that was just the news I needed to hear.

Independent living

It was not long before I plucked enough courage to offer Helle an engagement ring, but my proposal was typically unorthodox. I borrowed the ring from a friend and took it with me to a disco to which I had invited Helle. I sat holding the ring tightly in my hand, waiting for the right moment to present it. I was so excited that my hand jolted and the ring was catapulted to the other side of the crowded dance floor. In as matter-of-fact voice as I could manage, I turned to Helle, 'Oh, I dropped something,'

I said, 'If you can find it you can have it.' She rummaged around on the floor and to my surprise found the ring quickly. Lamely I muttered, 'It's an engagement ring', and unceremoniously Helle responded, 'What's that for?' I took a deep breath and spelt it out, 'Will you marry me?' To my astonishment she accepted.

My family was delighted. But the news received a frosty reception from across the Channel. Helle's father was especially unhappy. Not only could I not speak his language, but he took a long time to be convinced that, in spite of the fact that I could not play football, I was neither seriously ill nor about to die. I could not live with the fact that Helle's father felt somewhat estranged to me, so after a concerted effort, I taught myself Danish through books and a Linguaphone course. I must say, he was considerably impressed, because not many visitors to Denmark ever bother to learn the language. We ended up good friends, especially when I took an interest in his first love—golf—and followed him round the golf course in my electric chair pointing out where all the lost balls were. His attitude towards me over the years has changed dramatically and he has now included ramps and wide doorways throughout the ground floor of his home. This, plus building extra space in the bathroom, makes it easier for us to visit.

I really knew that my new sister-in-law had accepted me as an equal when one afternoon I was staring lovingly at a plate of biscuits, which she had just made. She could tell that I was positively drooling over these Danish Delights. 'Please help yourself', she said. 'I am afraid that they are out of reach for me', I replied. Kirsten looked at me with a cheeky grin and replied, 'No hands—no cookies.' We both laughed and she popped one into my mouth.

The day following my impromptu engagement, we were bombarded with questions; When was the big day? Where were we going to live? What would we live on? Neither of us had realised how many battles we would have to win before we found somewhere to live. The managers at Le Court were immensely supportive—although they did keep my room vacant for six months just in case it didn't work out!

We acted quickly and put ourselves on the council housing list both of Hampshire and Surrey. We were warned that it might take a long time. After eighteen months, Waverley Borough Council offered us a bungalow in Godalming. At the time it was still on the drawing board, so we enthusiastically watched it being built and planned our wedding day around its completion. Pat, a close friend of ours from Le Court, offered to drive us over to view the building site. I will never forget the conversation as we looked around. We struggled across the mud and went in through the doorway. Pat looked quite pleased and exclaimed in her refined voice, 'Oh, what a nicely sized room.' The workman looked up in total disbelief and responded in his well rounded Farncombe accent, 'Madam, this is the 'ole 'ouse.' Well we liked it, even though the whole bungalow was no bigger than Pat's front room in Linchmere. It was in the right place and it felt right, shops were close at hand and there were good connections with public transport.

A college friend of mine sometimes lent Helle his old beat up Austin A30 so that we could drive back and forth to keep an eye on how our little bungalow was progressing. That little old car, affectionately called Peanut, played a very important part in making sure everything was ready for our moving in. The passenger door didn't have a doorstop, so it was able to open until it hit against the front wheel arch. This gave a lot more space to draw my wheelchair up along side and with a push and a shove I could slide from the chair into the car seat. It had a hot and cold heater— hot in the summer and cold in the winter. It also had automatically opening side-windows—they slowly opened whenever we went over a hard bump in the road. Peanut went like a rocket in fourth gear, which seemed to be the only gear it could stay in without jumping out again. It had a marvellous engine, which was the only part that always kept going. The only time we ever stopped was when we ran out of petrol. The petrol gauge didn't work and was fixed on empty.

About this time a group of my friends at the Cheshire Home were seeking to return to the community. As they began to see that it was possible to return to live in the community, we affectionately became known as instigators of the 'escape committee.' They managed to convince their sponsoring authorities that for less than the cost of staying in an institution, they could return to the community with enough money to pay their own assistants and be able to choose a quality of life that they wanted. They started a venture, which was aptly named Project 81, to coincide with the International Year of Disabled People.

Project 81 was the means of changing the course of life for many

Above: Paul and Helle at their wedding at Godalming United Church in 1981

disabled people throughout the country. It was the embryo of what became known as 'The Independent Living Movement.' Responsibility was handed over from the sponsoring authority to the individual, who would be able to hire his or her own personal assistants. In those days it was known as the 'Self Operated Care Scheme.' This tailor-made system effectively turned the disabled person into an employer. Often it worked out cheaper than staying at a residential institution, and certainly the quality of life improved immensely. The scheme was particularly useful for unmarried people. Many of our friends are still living within this system and are leading full and active lives in the community. We were privileged to be involved in this project even when we chose to get married.

Helle and I were determined to get married before moving into our home, but in the event we were given only four days notice before receiving the keys to the bungalow. We had been waiting for eighteen months and had asked the Council at regular intervals when the prospective moving-in date might be. In view of the shortage of time we had to obtain a special licence from Petersfield Registry Office, and grab a couple of friends from the home to be our witnesses. This was at the end of October 1980. From the day we moved, Helle's income changed from a standard auxiliary nursing pay scale to earning nothing at all. By marrying me she became 'just' a housewife, and she was expected to do the work of a care assistant for the sake of love. It was immaterial to the authorities that she was no longer able to hold down a job, or that she was providing the same level of care as was previously provided for me at the home. Many of our friends thought we were stupid for wanting to declare our love by getting married, but as Christians we had decided to do things properly, in spite of the penalties.

The first night in our own home was strange. The silence was almost deafening! For six and a half years I had lived amongst one hundred and fifty people, with the constant noise of a clattering lift, cups and saucers, people talking and so on. Now suddenly there was just the two of us living at the bottom of a cul-de-sac, where only the occasional passing of a car could be heard. It took some getting used to.

A new family

We had a 'proper' wedding ceremony at Godalming United Church on the 3 January 1981. It was a Methodist church, and we had met the minister of the church at the local post office, and during conversation with him established that his church was reasonably wheelchair accessible. We attended this church for more than two years, but when he left, the ministry changed dramatically. We had made many good friends at the church, and it had played a very important part in our first years together. Reluctantly however, we started looking around for somewhere new to worship.

In 1983 we undertook a survey of public buildings in our town to see how accessible they were for wheelchair users. Churches were included, and so we arrived one Sunday at Binscombe Evangelical Church. At that time, the building was not equipped for wheelchair users, but the positive attitude of the leaders encouraged us, 'If you come back next week, we will have a ramp for you.' They were as good as their word and when we returned after a couple of weeks, there was the ramp. Granted it was a little makeshift, but it was there. And they didn't leave it at that; soon a new concrete ramp was built. We were so impressed, not only by the practical ministry but also by the sermon, that we continued to attend, and eventually became members. I quickly realised that my disability was no barrier to being accepted by these people. We instantly felt at home and discovered that the teaching was directly in accordance with the Bible, with nothing added and nothing taken away.

It was not long before the leadership of the church started looking for ways to draw me into some more purposeful jobs at the church. When the treasurer moved away, the Pastor, George Goldsmith, asked me, 'Are you any good with figures?' I had to be honest, 'Well, not really, I have never done anything like that before.' 'Splendid', was the confident reply, 'That's what we like, a humble man. We will give you full training.' Before I could object, I was installed as the new treasurer, a position that I still hold more than a decade later—so I must be doing something right!

The church was growing and was considering running a club for children in the locality. The only problem was that there was nobody to run it. The pastor's wife was looking for volunteers and asked us if we wanted to be involved with the club. Helle responded that she never really knew how to relate to small children. Sheila enquired, 'At what age do you begin to feel comfortable with them?' Helle, not realising the trap, mentioned that she felt she could cope when they were able to understand what it means to listen quietly and be able to take correction without screaming or playing up—perhaps around eleven years of age or so. Sheila's face beamed, 'What a coincidence, we just need some leaders of the 11-14 group. You will love it.' In spite of the fact that I used a wheelchair, none of the children ever ridiculed me or made silly remarks. They just naturally took on board that this was my means of transport. We helped with the club for a number of years until we ran out of steam and felt we had to give it up. Even now, I often exclaim to Helle, 'Look there goes one of our children.' They are now all in their mid 20s and some have children of their own.

I get on well with children and they gravitate to me. Perhaps this is because I am literally on their level. In the earlier years of our marriage, when the neighbours' children were small, they would often knock at our door and ask Helle if I could come out to play! The fact that I couldn't hit the ball very hard never seemed to cause a problem. It was more fun for them to aim the ball at my bat and then someone would run for a six. After I had acquired my power chair, they particularly enjoyed it when I was able to tow them around on their skateboards.

Power to my elbow

One of the biggest 'steps' towards my independence was the purchase of an electric wheelchair, which I had seen and tried out at an exhibition. The cost of such a thing was far beyond my financial means. At the time there was little difference between the cost of an electric chair and an Austin Mini car! I used to dream about driving myself round the shops or down to the lake, instead of being pushed everywhere. Having spent six and a half years propelling myself round an institution where everything was accessible on one level, it was unnerving when Helle was negotiating busy roads and rough pavements. I was no longer in control.

One day we were handed an envelope by a friend, who said that he had been asked to pass this to us, so that we could buy an electric wheelchair. We were both totally taken back. It contained just the right amount to buy my dream chair. I phoned the company straight away. Now, at last, I could explore the area with power at my elbow; though for a while Helle would not let me out of her sight in case I ran into something. It also meant that she now had both hands free to carry a picnic!

It was a good, rugged chair made in Canada by a road construction company! The prototype was built for one of the company's workers who had become disabled, but who wanted to remain in employment. That chair got me to places that some wheelchair users couldn't reach; some people thought I was a little too adventurous. However, the one thing that it could not do, was negotiate steps over four inches high. Although I enjoyed this new-found freedom, I found it very frustrating when I tried to enter homes that do not have level access to the doorway. It's not surprising that elderly and disabled people often feel excluded from the mainstream of society.

Old Thor

I will never forget how we got our first wheelchair accessible car! I was out in the garden when I caught sight of someone walking around old

'Granny', as we called our little Austin A30. 'Ain't she lovely', he said in a strong West Sussex accent. 'Yes', I answered, taking it for granted that he was talking about 'Granny' and not Helle. During our conversation I informed him that I was after a vehicle large enough to be able to load my power chair into. It was my plan to sell 'Granny' that we had previously bought for £230 and use the money to put towards something a little larger. He looked a jolly sort of chap with his oily jeans, old jumper and woolly hat. He appeared to have only two teeth, and these definitely became apparent when he grinned at me from ear to ear. He peered underneath the car whilst slowly shaking his head. He gave a sharp intake of breath almost whistling through his two teeth. 'Won't get a lot for 'er, she's goin' 'ome a bit.' He adjusted his woolly hat, which by now was almost over his eyes, and stood straight up. 'Do 'ya know I've been 'ere for about 'arf an hour and you 'aven't offered me a cup tea, yet.'

Over tea we got his whole life story about his German wife and four children, who were now all adults, his life on the farm, and finally his interest in restoring old cars. He explained that he wasn't very good at remembering people's names, and he seemed to have problems pronouncing 'Helle', so he asked if he could call her Clara. Apart from his wife, whose name was Grete, he called every female Clara—even his daughters and grand children! We both became very fond of old Bob and enjoyed many a 'cuppa tea' together. One day he invited us to his house for a 'cuppa tea' and told us that he had something up the top of his garden that he wanted to show us. It was a beautiful garden, with colourful flowerbeds and rockeries. His 'pottering about' area, just inside the back gate, contained a shed full of spare parts for cars, and beside it what can only be described as a graveyard for old cars. 'Wha d'ya fink of this' he said, pulling the tarpaulin covering off a Florentine blue Austin A35 van, with side windows. It was restored almost to mint condition. She was beautiful. 'Wow!' was my only exclamation. 'Get 'yer chair in there awright. Back seat folds forward', he said beaming from ear to ear. He called it 'Thor', after the old Norse god of thunder. After the 'cuppa' Bob offered a deal that I couldn't resist: 'I'll gi' 'yer this 'ere van, 'Thor' for yer 'Granny', plus £200.' 'Done'—I quickly replied.

That little van gave us many years of service, including trips to Denmark where it became the talking point of most conversations. Thor was a classic vehicle and was the means of us making friends and acquaintances we otherwise wouldn't have made. These included classic car restorers both in England and in Denmark. One of the members of our church was a tutor at the Guildford Technical College and he arranged for his students to make some metal telescopic ramps for the back of 'Thor' so that my electric chair could be driven up into the van. This was their community assignment. One day I asked old Bob why he had named the van 'Thor.' Bob replied with a chuckle, 'Because there were so many times I nearly put 'ammer to 'er.'

Helle's parents came on holiday to England, to visit us in their own car. When they arrived, my mother-in-law looked as white as a sheet. We asked them how they had found the trip. Hur answered, 'I cannot understand why they all insist on driving on the wrong side of the road. It is very confusing.' Before the end of the holiday we visited an exhibition of wheelchair accessible vehicles, and I tried out a car, where the floor dropped down, so that I could drive straight into it. In addition it had four other passenger seats. Hur's mind went into overdrive, 'If I promise to get you this car, will you come and pick us up from the airport and drive us around when we next visit you? I just cannot cope with this crazy system.' That was another offer impossible to refuse. We have enjoyed the benefit of that vehicle for more than ten years now. My father-in-law particularly loves us driving him through the narrow leafy lanes of Surrey, especially the ones which are really single track with a few passing places.

DisCASS

Our involvement with the Independent Living Movement has given us a mind-set to help people to take control of their own lives, rather than being passive receivers of Social Services and Health Authorities funding. To achieve this can often give them a quality of life that far exceeds their previous experiences or their expectations. It was out of this concern that the philosophy of DisCASS developed. We found that generally people have little understanding of the basic services to which they are entitled. They lack knowledge of the necessary equipment that would enable them to live more independent life styles, and they have a lack of understanding about the basic disability pensions to which they are entitled. In addition to this, society is often unaware of the fact that some of the biggest obstacles of all are not the individuals' particular disabilities and what they cannot do, but the social barriers that exist. These are too often seen in people's negative attitudes and an inaccessible environment. When society makes the necessary adjustments, by providing information, equipment, care, support and home adaptations, people at last feel included in mainstream society. They are then no longer 'disabled' but 'enabled.' Our purpose is to pass on to our own community what we have learned from our personal experiences.

With this in mind we wrote an article in our local press in 1984, saying that we would be willing to co-ordinate a disability information service if that was felt necessary. We asked the public to respond by providing finance. The letterbox never seemed to stop flapping as cheques piled up on the doormat. Our information service became the forerunner of what was to be a countywide information service for disabled people. Our information is available in local libraries and on the internet.

The work grew rapidly. I had soon become the secretary of the fledgling set-up, and I worked in this position until I became the Chairman of the organisation. We called ourselves DisCASS, which is an acronym of 'Disabled Citizens' Advice and Support Services.' We have a small office in Godalming, and Helle and I work virtually full time for the organization. Our particular responsibility is for disabled people in the South West Surrey area. We are a little like a Citizens' Advice Bureau, but especially for disabled people, their families, carers and friends. In addition to providing information, we also provide advocacy and train disabled people to become advocates for others. We also provide Disability Training programmes for local authorities, education establishments and the business sector. We are fortunate to have the services of a retired RIBA architect, who draws up plans for making adaptations to people's homes and also vets the disability access of planning applications from the local council. We also have the services of a retired occupational therapist to provide assessments in individual homes, and this shortens the lengthy Social Services waiting list. Our services also include benefits advice and help with form-filling, and with tribunals, training, employment opportunities, equipment provision, holidays, transport and caring services. We are able to access our information from our comprehensive national and local database.

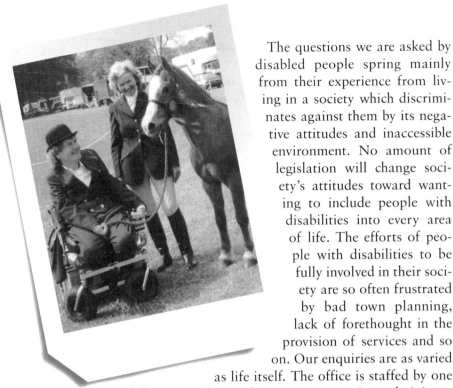

The questions we are asked by disabled people spring mainly from their experience from living in a society which discriminates against them by its negative attitudes and inaccessible environment. No amount of legislation will change society's attitudes toward wanting to include people with disabilities into every area of life. The efforts of people with disabilities to be fully involved in their society are so often frustrated by bad town planning, lack of forethought in the provision of services and so on. Our enquiries are as varied as life itself. The office is staffed by one full time paid co-ordinator, one part time administrative assistant and about ten volunteers. Most of us are either disabled people or carers or ex-carers, so that we all can be said to have encountered for ourselves how the system works—or doesn't work!

The demands for our services are increasing all the time. This is mainly due to the fact that Social Service budgets keep shrinking and they find it impossible to continue to provide the same level of service. The voluntary sector is expected to pick up the slack and replace what used to be freely available through statutory bodies. In order to readjust this imbalance, DisCASS has started its own wheelchair hire service, and an advocacy service to speak out for those who cannot speak out for themselves.

A horse and carriage

One of my best escapes from the pressures of life is driving a pony and carriage. My equestrian days began some years ago, when Patsy, a life-long friend of mine, took her horse to the local fete for children to ride on. Her daughter Gill and her boyfriend had offered to push me round the fete. 'How about a go on old Rondo, mum's horse', Gill suggested, 'I don't see why the children should have all the fun. After all, you already sit in the perfect jockey position.' Being a wild adventurous youth, I agreed. After much pushing and shoving I got on-board. They stood one on either side to support me, while Patsy led Rondo round. It was great to see all the events at the fete above the heads of everybody else. Everything was all right until the horse started to move. It felt as though my hips were being dislocated, and the ride came to a grinding halt after fifty yards. I yelled, 'Get me down, get me back to my own four wheels. The only way a horse is going to propel me along is if it pulls me along in my chair.' 'Oh', responded Patsy, always out to encourage everyone into the equestrian world, 'That's no problem. There is a small driving group in the Sheepleas in West Horsley. They do just that. You should try it some time.'

In spite of that encouragement, some time lapsed before I ventured back into her equestrian world. I had already discovered that Helle was mad on horses because she kept disappearing with Patsy to Shalford to exercise the horses in the field. When Helle also started to put pressure on me to try again, I thought, 'Well, if you can't beat them—join them.' We drove out to the pony driving group in West Horsley which had been set up especially for people who were not able to get on to a horse. It was the most amazing thing I had ever seen. The back of the carriage was on a hinge and folded down twice, turning into a ramp. This provided the means of getting on board. Beside you sat a non-disabled trainer. The pony was kitted out with two sets of reins, one set for the disabled person, and another set held by the trainer, which was only to be used in case of emergency.

We were tutored in all the different dressage techniques and the group was quite well known for its competitive spirit. Many of the drivers had won trophies and rosettes, proving their driving skills and abilities. The emphasis was strongly on enhancing our driving abilities rather than emphasising our disabilities. Our trainers were patient and saw no obstacles that could not be tackled. From the carriage I could see over the hedgerows and enjoy the view across the North Downs. We drove on what we call 'The Cabbage Patch', which is a one acre field. This was our practice area for our different competitions.

One reason I love this sport is that I feel in control. I am actually in charge of the animal. Because both trainer and driver are sitting down on the same level I am totally integrated into the carriage, and while I am driving my pony and carriage there appears no distinction between me as a person with a physical impairment and my non-disabled trainer, or 'whip' as they are known. In open competitions I feel that there is no difference between me and the Duke of Edinburgh, except that he drives four horses and I only have one pony. Probably, he doesn't have to clean his own tack either!

Over the years, the trainers have given me full rein and I have won a number of coloured rosettes to decorate the walls of our home. Because my hands are slightly closed-in, my fingers are not sufficiently straight or strong to be able to grip the reins in the more conventional way. However, the trainers have developed a pair of reins with discreet loops, which I can hook my hands into when driving. Sporting a bowler hat, suit, white shirt, suede tie and buttonhole at a competition at Royal Windsor or Royal Ascot with the rest of the team, gives me a sense of great significance. It is an honour to promote such a sport and I have made some wonderful friends.

I have one special pony. He's called 'Little John.' He is 11.2 hands, turns on a sixpence and is like driving an MG with fingertip steering! He only needs to see a set of cones and he is off like a rocket. He has also learnt to listen to my vocal commands, which makes it a lot easier on my arms. Her Royal Highness Princess Anne once commented to me, 'You must have been driving for years, because you seem so experienced.' I simply replied, 'Well, Ma'am, with this pony, I first show him the diagram of the course before we begin, and then he knows what to do!' I have won a number of first places and even a National Championship with Little John. On the other hand Little John has his downside. He is very fond of his stomach, and we once stopped in the middle of a course, when he suddenly realised that the obstacle we should negotiate was made up of hay bales. He decided to munch his way through it instead.

Helle became so impressed with the driving, that she wanted to be able to assist with the whole process. She joined a course to become a trainer and was trained by one of the nation's top carriage drivers. The course was very vigorous and comprehensive but being a tough Viking, she passed. Now we are able to drive together. On those occasions our roles are

Above: Paul and Helle refute the accepted society norm that defines Paul as the 'user' and Helle as the 'carer'. In fact they both equally have to give and receive, pointing out that their relationship together is something that they both cherish and continually nurture

reversed, and she gets her own back for all the times I am a back seat driver in the car!

We do not have children of our own, and although it has never been a big issue to us, it was certainly one of the biggest compliments we were ever paid, when Helle and I were considered worthy to become legal guardians of the three children of our very good friends, should anything happen to the parents. This, we consider a great privilege and not one to be taken lightly. We thoroughly enjoy being able to play the part of parents occasionally when their parents have to go away.

Without the assistance and encouragement from all those mentioned in this story, my quality of life would probably only have been half of what it is now. In addition, the various adjustments we have been able to make to our house has given me a greater level of independence. However, there is one small gadget, without which I would not be able to operate my computer, press lift buttons, answer the phone, scratch the top of my head and do so many little day-to-day things. It is a dowel rod with a rubber tip on one end and a plastic mouthpiece on the other. I call it my 'wonder stick'. With God on my side and the 'wonder stick' in my mouth I can take on the world.

Society often defines me as the 'user' and Helle as the 'carer.' This definition we both detest! It completely rules out the fact that I can contribute anything. In life, we both equally have to give and receive. Our relationship together is something we both cherish and continually nurture. The real elements of caring we consider to be love and trust.

Chapter 6

The silent preacher

Claud Trigger

A preacher for more than half a century, Claud Trigger literally lost his voice. Determined not to allow this shattering experience to destroy his service for God, Claud's story shines with his faith and courage. The love of Dorothy his wife, the support of his many Christian friends, and above all the strength supplied by his God, turned an event of frustration and despair into one of value and hope.

The dreamy semiconscious sense of unreality began to give way to the hard facts of the hospital ward. I had survived my operation and was still alive. A nurse noticed me and came with reassuring words, and I responded in the way I had been doing since I first began to say 'Daddy' and 'Mummy' over seventy five years before. The action of trying to speak brought the moment of truth—there was nothing there! My larynx had been completely removed, together with the cancer that had grown in spite of my life-long rejection of the smoking habit. I was literally speechless! My world of communicating as a preacher and pastor was reduced to a writing pad and a pen. The experience was shattering! When the surgeon came on his ward rounds with his attendant students, he greeted me with the thoughtless introduction, 'How is our preacher this morning?' I would gladly have answered him, but he could never have waited while I, still hazy from the anaesthetic, got out my paper and pen and wrote a reply. An uplifted thumb was all I could do. His greeting may have appeared insensitive, but it at least served to let all the patients and staff within earshot know that I was a preacher of the gospel. That public announcement paid off later when some nurses, whilst making beds, were involved in a religious discussion; they brought me into it by asking direct questions, even waiting for me to answer on paper!

When the eagerly awaited visiting time arrived and my wife Dorothy came to my bedside, we both realised that life would never be the same again. The normal responsive conversation with the immediate reply to remarks and questions, and the repartee that enlivens verbal relationships, was all now impossible. The incredible range of tone, inflection and pitch possible with the magnificent God-designed instrument—the human voice—was now a memory for me. The whole process of shared thought was slowed down as I filled sheets of paper with my indifferent hand-writing, hoping that it was legible to Dorothy. This was to be the pattern of our lives until I had explored the various options for more effective communication. Dorothy was very comforting and understanding, but there was a special poignancy in the timing. It was 1992—the year when we were to celebrate our Golden Wedding Anniversary!

My next shock was the first sight of my stoma, the technical word for the aperture in my neck. It was larger than I had expected. The operation involved the modification of the tissues of the mouth and throat and the complete separation of the lungs from the digestive system. The laryn-

Left: Claud and Dorothy at the final preaching engagement before the major operation which took away Claud's voice

gectomee, a patient who breathes through the neck, can only inhale air to the lungs through the stoma. Normally, breathing can be through both the nose and mouth but now, every inhalation for the neck breather is through a disposable medicated pad. My nose is for decoration rather than respiration! It is recommended that all such patients carry a card explaining this, so that in the event of an emergency, helpers will not apply inappropriate treatment. Mouth-to-mouth resuscitation is useless.

The medical programme continued with a course of treatment from a Speech Therapist. I attended the weekly session at the hospital clinic, where I was introduced to a method of communication called oesophageal speech. My air for breathing was now taken directly into the trachea or windpipe through the opening in my neck, which no longer had any connection with my mouth or lips. The aim of this method is to use the oesophagus or gullet as a small air reservoir that vibrates under pressure as the air is swallowed. As speech begins, the escaping air stream sets the narrow walls of the oesophagus vibrating, rather like the vocal cords do in normal speech. I worked hard at this, determined to be able to speak again. Week by week Dorothy would join me, with the other voiceless patients, as we struggled to form our words. Some did well, but while I managed small words, Dorothy observed that I made some very unnatural sounds and faces in the process. The surgeon suggested a valve should be plugged into the back of my gullet, a method which had been successfully used by some, but out of which I could not get a single sound.

Just when I was becoming frustrated by my lack of progress, the hospital loaned me an artificial larynx called a Servox. This was a steel tube about five inches long with rechargeable batteries. It was operated by me pressing a small circular vibrating pad to my neck under the chin. In a way that I have never been able to understand, when I used my palate, tongue and lips to 'speak', the vibrations are transferred to the Servox producing the electronic sound. It took time and patience to master the technique. I had to learn how to find the best spot when the tube was pressed to my neck, and I also had to remember to activate the on/off button only when actually speaking. If this is not mastered, the resulting sound is like a car alarm. However, I can still recall the thrill of being able to speak again. The sound was all on the same pitch and reminiscent of a Dalek, but it was like music to my ears and the beginning of a new experience in my life. I could communicate! My days of scribbling and waiting for people to read it before replying were over. This expensive equipment was not available on the NHS, but a kind friend bought one for me. Although the sound was artificial, I could use facial expressions, and in due course, even a trace of my West Country accent came through! My new found method of communication filled me with a deep sense of gratitude to God. Dorothy and I had a clear realisation of an overruling providence and that the Lord we had served together for 50 years was still in control.

Learning from disappointment

Those early days marked the beginning of many events that led me through the school of the Holy Spirit, and I began to learn some salutary truths. One early trial I had to face was that of disappointment. Following the first diagnosis, I endured thirty-three treatments of radiotherapy, which left me with vivid memories of the protective mask on my face and being strapped down on a hard slab for each brief attack on my cancer. Shortly after the completion of the course, the head of the Radiotherapy Department told me, with much satisfaction, that I was cured and had two perfectly healthy vocal cords. Thanksgiving, relief and a return to preaching shortly afterwards were my response. There was much rejoicing both in the family and in the church that the preacher had his voice back. Months of widespread ministry followed, but then came the dreaded huskiness, the weakness of voice so evident in some of the recordings of that period. The inevitable tests followed.

One afternoon will ever live in our memories. Shortly after these investigations, the telephone rang. It was my Consultant at the Royal Sussex County Hospital and he told me that a large cancer had been discovered in my larynx and that I was to report to the surgeon immediately to discuss surgery for the removal of my voice box. A cold, drained feeling swept over me. I could only barely imagine what would be involved. As I replaced the receiver, I glanced through the window and noticed a car draw up. Two visitors came to the door—Leith Samuel and his wife Elisabeth. Having been with friends in Worthing, they thought that they would call on us on the way back to Frinton. They had no idea about the grim news I had just that moment received, but they came as messengers of grace to us. Their loving words, the Scriptures read, and Leith's prayer was like balm to our troubled souls. We have experienced the Lord's wonderful timing in the past but never so immediately applied as on that afternoon. The sense of the Lord's presence during the brief visit of his servants is a living reality to us.

After they had left, Dorothy and I sat together and talked. I discovered that from the first diagnosis when the dreaded word cancer was pronounced, Dorothy had faced the possibility that I might not survive and that our long and deep marriage experience might come to an end. We realised that there was a big question mark on all our future, but the Lord was there and beyond it all. Dorothy was with me later when the surgeon, with tenderness in his voice, explained that my cancer was radio resistant, and that an immediate and urgent operation was necessary for the total removal of my larynx.

Such disappointments are part of the pattern of life for many of us. The wonderful reduction of the original cancerous growth on the first course of radiotherapy gave cause for much encouragement, but bitter lows and discouragement followed high expectation. Promising prognoses are not always fulfilled. It was a danger time when the seeds of despair and bitterness could be sown. It was here for me that the value of my Christian faith became a reality in the sharing oneness of a loving wife and the prayerful support of family and friends. I found that I needed to be reminded that my body was the Lord's and that while we are responsible for caring for it within our capability, we need deliverance from deep concern when there is nothing more that we can do. The reality of his presence can turn potential despair into peaceful confidence. I realised that I could only cope if I maintained a close and personal relationship with the risen Christ.

I early learned the lesson that we are dispensable. With a heavy heart, I cancelled three months preaching engagements as my voice rapidly deteriorated. But other preachers filled those pulpit appointments very quickly. Preachers are disposable, and the old saying is true that, 'Our cemeteries are filled with indispensable people.' Many church leaders have sustained nervous breakdowns, or at least a lack of real efficiency, by not realising this. The genius of leadership is delegation. We have to trust someone else to do things differently and perhaps, in our view, not so well as we would have done, but this is a pattern of sharing in the vital work of training new leaders. Paul urged his trainee Timothy to commit what he had learned,

'To faithful men who will be able to teach others also' (2 Timothy 2:2).

Another lesson that came home to me was that our strengths could also be our weaknesses. The Lord deals with our pride in this way. I am eternally grateful that I came to faith in Jesus Christ at the age of sixteen. A visiting preacher called Jack Rowlands, who worked among Indians in South Africa, took Acts 4:12 as his text in Horfield Baptist Church, Bristol. The uniqueness of Christ as the only name under heaven given for salvation, led to my deep experience of Jesus Christ as Lord. Immediately, I used my strong and clearly heard voice in public with Christian Endeavour, a church-based youth movement. It provided excellent practical training. We were encouraged to take part in every meeting. I began to grow in confidence as a speaker and enrolled on an evening course in public speaking and mental training.

Then came the invitation to be the speaker at the monthly visit to the lodging houses in the city; in these 'doss-houses', homeless and drifting people could have a night's lodging for fourpence. Determined to begin as I intended to go on, I wrote my outline notes on a postcard; as I stood up to speak, sudden panic fell on me and I found myself just reading through my notes and heading for the shortest sermon in living memory! God's dealings with me in the subsequent humiliation and distress showed that he had his own ways of cutting would-be preachers down to size early on in their career. However, the voice he had given me has stood the test of more than half a century of Bible preaching. I loved preaching God's word. I have vivid memories of occasions when the Holy Spirit took hold of me and his word went out in power. I was first and foremost a preacher. In these days of mumbling and whispering into microphones, I may have been a little too proud of my track record. Suddenly it was all over. I had to be content to communicate with an electronic instrument that made me sound totally unlike other voices around me! My strongest point had become my weakest. To say 'Why me, Lord?' would be presumption. I can only cry, especially in my moments of longing for the former days, 'Lord, make sure I really learn what you intend to teach me through this experience.'

Fighting frustration

Like many people with an obvious disability, I had to face the reaction of people. This first became evident in the family. One very early treatment was the removal of polyps on the vocal cords. This necessitated total silence for five days after surgery. Our grandchildren, welcoming me home from hospital, suddenly felt that because their grandfather could not speak, they could not talk to him either! They thought I was deaf as well as dumb! On my first visit to the Post Office with my new voice, the postmaster began to make hand signals, implying that the voice and hearing had both gone! He apologised afterwards, realising his mistake. People even asked Dorothy, in my presence, how I was progressing! The phrase 'does he take sugar?' took on a reality for me.

When I first began to use my new voice, I was embarrassed and inhibited. The normal human voice is familiar and part of everyday life, but mine, even with careful use of the volume control, is still penetrating. People guardedly look round to see where the strange sound is coming from. On one of my visits to the outpatients clinic with my daughter Gwen, I was chatting away to the Consultant while the patients in the adjacent waiting room, unknown to me, could hear the unusual sound, though not the words. On my return, I learned that Gwen had had to explain my situation to the inquisitive audience!

I dealt with my reactions to the behaviour of others by facing them squarely. It would have been all too easy to take the negative line, that I had enjoyed a long time with a good voice, I had had my day, and this is the end. I could have turned into myself and let the rest of the world go by. As a Christian, however, that was not an option. I was the Lord's child, my body was his, he would not forsake me in my deep need, and he had an ongoing plan for my remaining years. Besides, I could still communicate in a distinctive way. Perhaps even the difference could be useful. This was now my voice and I decided that it must be used as well and as often as possible. As a result of this decision I began to lose my inhibitions. Someone drew my attention to a letter in the *Methodist Recorder*. The correspondent had a laryngectomy and he could not face his inability to take part when the congregation was singing praise to God. He would choose a seat in a corner of the church building and read to occupy his mind until the hymn was over. I wrote to him to encourage a more positive approach. I explained how I stand with everyone else and mime the words, entering into their meaning, enjoying them with a facial expression as if I was vocal. I hope that it encourages the one who is leading the worship, but at least I have the advantage that I can sing the very newest song with confidence; I never have to worry about the tune! Any stranger would think I was singing my heart out! I never had a reply to my letter but I hope that the correspondent took my advice.

At the time of my enforced silence, there was the temptation to give way to despair. So many years of constant activity in Christian service had suddenly ended. Sadness, disappointment and longing took turns in overwhelming me. It seemed that the door to service for my Lord was finally and firmly closed. However, something happened early on in my treatment that was a great help in overcoming times of depression and frustration. Great store is set these days on being prepared for the Lord's service. There is a wealth of resource material; courses are available on presentation, counselling and a whole range of specialised training. Christians have no excuse for being ill prepared to be effective witnesses for the Lord we love. Yet in the darkness I discovered that he could take over in the most unpromising circumstances and speak through one who was in a most unlikely situation to serve him. I had been over an hour waiting for the surgical removal of some polyps on the vocal cords. A casual word from a junior doctor developed into a longer conversation, punctuated by his duties as the other patients arrived. He admitted that he had once been interested in Christianity and had even attended Christian Union meetings at college, but studies had overtaken him. The Lord had given me a deep peace, and when this doctor asked me how I felt, I was able to witness to him. Being a pastor gave an opening to a profitable testimony.

No course on personal evangelism would have chosen that situation for outreach. I had nothing on but the usual surgical gown open at the back, my teeth had been removed, my voice was like sandpaper on wood and I was lying flat on a trolley. Yet the Lord allowed me to have a short but serious conversation with a member of the hospital staff! The fact that he kept coming back to continue to talk, gave me encouragement. The doors to Christian service often keep open at unexpected moments.

The discipline of silence

Another lesson I learned was the discipline of silence. Of course, this was evident at mealtimes, which were now quieter than they had been. Any activity needing two hands renders me speechless. I discovered the lasting value of quietness especially in those first months of my vocal disability. My arm ached writing messages and answering questions. The rush of thoughts constantly overtook the committal to paper. The luxury of normal conversation was no longer mine. Too late I realised that perhaps people generally talk too much! A verse from an old hymn came alive to me:

'Speak, Lord, in the stillness, while I wait on thee,
Hush, my heart, to listen in expectancy'.

A favourite verse which I have often quoted in my ministry, is Psalm 25:14. The *Authorized Version* reads, 'The secret of the Lord is with them that fear him and he will show them his covenant.' The NIV translates it, 'The Lord confides in those who fear him.' This moving truth became intensely real to me in my enforced times of quiet. James exhorts us to 'draw near to God and he will draw near to you' (4:8). We need to cultivate his intimate presence in the quietness, and he is pledged to share his secrets with us. Here is a potential source of endless mutual sharing with a God who is so willing to give from his endless resources. We need such quietness to keep spiritually informed from the highest authority. So often in prayer we begin talking right away, when the Lord might want to take the initiative in speaking to us through his word, the Bible.

Perhaps we are not such good listeners as we should be. Everyone needs a listener and everyone needs to listen. A ready ear, available to receive confidences with patience and loving understanding, is a golden blessing. There are many lonely and at times desperate people, who only need such a listener to make things right again. My deep experience led me by the waters of quietness, which David found so refreshing in his shepherd Psalm 23:2, 'He makes me lie down in green pastures, he leads me beside quiet waters.'

I occasionally see a van in our area marked, 'Clinical Waste Disposal', and it brings to my mind that there was a time when such a van would be carrying on its way to incineration, my larynx with its death-dealing cancer. Again the sense of loss would drive deep. This was very poignantly felt in connection with my involvement with the Festivals of Male Voice Praise. I have never been able to make music seriously, but I love melody, and enjoy harmony and the subtle chords that make music so fascinating. When James McRoberts, the founder of the Festivals, brought seventy Scotsmen to London for a promotional festival, I was impressed and became deeply involved in all the wide developments of that manly witness in different parts of the country. I sang and conducted, and was thrilled to take a lead in great festivals in the Royal Festival Hall and the Royal Albert Hall. It was a privilege to form local church groups of men to sing the good news. To become voiceless in such an environment gave rise to some of my deepest and saddest moments. The Lord who plans nothing but the best for his children, however, wonderfully compensates for losses. I listen to recordings of events, in many of which I have taken part, and mime the words and imagine the melody. In this way I recapture the joy of singing his praise, and the sadness is dealt with in the highest possible way. For sixteen years, from its inception, I was the editor of *Interlink*, the magazine of the Festivals. This gave me a link with choirmen in the UK, Canada and Australia. Writing became a particular joy now that I could not speak.

Our early years

The Sunday before my major surgery I was asked

Above: back from Bible training in 1940, Claud begins his preaching ministry

to give my testimony at Lancing Tabernacle in Sussex, the church to which Dorothy and I belong. We had served in this evangelical church from 1955 to 1966 during a very formative time in the lives of our three children, Gwen, David and Andrew, all of whom it was my special joy to baptize during that time, on their profession of faith in Christ for salvation. Now, with my very limited voice, and when my preaching was about to come to an end, I was able to share the Lord's grace through the years, and prepare the people for a member who would be essentially the same man but without the blessing of a natural voice. There was a special atmosphere that morning, and real prayer support was generated that was part of the explanation of some of the following events. Preparing for that morning brought back many memories. The verse in Hebrews 13:11 reminds us that, 'Jesus Christ is the same, yesterday and today and for ever'; that has always meant to me that he is the Lord of history, experience and eternity. The history part has certainly proved true in our lives.

1938 was the Munich year, when Mr Chamberlain came back from Germany with his piece of paper signed by Adolf Hitler, who promised that he would never go to war with Britain. I woke very early one morning that year in my Bristol home with an unusual sense of the Lord's presence. Before I got out of bed I had faced a clear challenge to prepare for a future of service in the preaching of the gospel. That sense of call has never left me. It led to two war-time years in Glasgow at what was then the Bible Training Institute, now the International Christian College. The college was originally founded by the American evangelist, D.L.Moody. Meanwhile, I had seen an attractive young lady called Dorothy Floyd at Philip Street Baptist Church in Bristol. She was clearly visible to me in the front row of the choir that, in those days, graced the gallery above the pulpit. Our relationship developed and we sensed that the Lord was guiding us. This was especially evident in our sudden and unusual engagement. Being home for the Easter vacation, we were invited to tea with a jeweller friend and, during the meal, he told us of an anonymous letter he had received enclosing a gift to purchase a ring—if the young couple wished to become engaged! The next day we were in our friend's jeweller's shop with the expert selecting a ring, which must have been worth more than the gift. I placed it on Dorothy's finger and we went home with glad and joyful hearts. It was April 1st 1940, and that was one of the wisest things I ever did on All Fools Day! As we look at that ring now, we believe that the Lord gave it to us, and nearly sixty years later we are thankful that he has been in our relationship all the way through. We have always been a team.

In the early part of my involvement with the Floyd family, they passed through a series of traumatic experiences. In the course of one year, Dorothy lost her 25-year-old sister Gwen, who had been frail with heart trouble. Later, the upper floor of their home was gutted by a basket of incendiary bombs, which fell on the roof in a Sunday night air raid, and her father died of cancer shortly afterwards. I was deeply impressed by the way Dorothy, together with her mother and younger sister, drew on spiritual resources to take them through such a concentration of trouble.

I had been back from my Bible training for several months, continuing studies, preaching from time to time, but with no definite indication as to how our Christian work was to begin. However, our marriage seemed to set everything in motion. An evangelist was taken ill, and I was asked to take his place in a week long mission at Shirehampton, on the Avon. Following this, the Bible Training Institute suggested my name for a three-month temporary pastorate to two churches in the Cotswolds. Then came an insistent invitation from Frederick Wood, who, with his brother Arthur, had founded the National Young Life Campaign. John Caiger, one of the evangelistic staff, had been called to become the pastor of Gunnersbury Baptist Church, and the movement needed someone to carry on the witness to young people. With the faultless timing that we have often experienced in later years, these opportunities flowed one after another. For three wartime years we were staff workers with the National Young Life Campaign (now known simply as Young Life). Although based in Bristol and responsible for the West of England, we had opportunities in many parts of the country. Our diary was filled with youth meetings, weekend conferences, tent missions, informal home meetings and Sunday ministry. We were amazed when the Lord worked in the lives of people in spite of our inexperience. There were many during that time who faced the challenge of the gospel positively, and others who came to realise that the reigning Christ demanded complete obedience to his authority. This period laid a gospel foundation for the whole of our future ministry

One of our appointments was on the edge of London at New Park Hall in Barking, Essex. We began to sense that the Lord was going to lead us into what we felt was our original calling—the leadership of a local church. After some uncertainty about leaving youth evangelism, I accepted a call to become Pastor of New Park Hall. It was felt wise to postpone the beginning of the new ministry for a while, as there had been increased enemy air attack in the area. It was hardly a safe place for me to take a young wife and infant daughter. However, I was preaching there on a Sunday in early January 1945, when, towards the end of the morning service, one of Hitler's rockets fell two blocks away and destroyed all the windows of the church. I have always admired that congregation who, without any panic, assured each other that no one had been cut by flying glass, gave thanks for our preservation, and closed the service with dignity and reverence. Later the same year, after V.E. (Victory in Europe) Day, Dorothy and I took up the work there, and enjoyed ten years of fruitful service. We learned many things about church life, sometimes the hard way. Our youth emphasis at the beginning was not accepted easily by some of the older members, but things built up as we went along. We were greatly encouraged by the return of children from evacuation and the demobilization of young service men from the armed forces. The baptistry was regularly used, and we look back on our first pastorate with much thanksgiving to God. He set his seal on our ministry in spite of our lack of experience. We proved that he looks for an acknowledgement of our frailty combined with dependence on him, a lesson I needed to re-learn in hospital in Brighton half a century later. We celebrated the centenary of New Park Hall in 1948 and, by a nice coincidence, on the special cele-bratory weekend with Stephen Olford, Dorothy gave birth to our first son, David.

Full circle

After ten years we accepted the pastorate of Lancing Tabernacle, on the Sussex coast. By then, Andrew, our younger son, had completed our family. The eleven years spent in Sussex proved a formative period for our children. They became deeply involved in the church life and came to a real faith in Christ. There was growth and stability in the church and an eager hearing of the ministry. I had a warm, supportive team of elders, and I continued to enjoy my preparation for preaching the great truths of the Bible.

Through the work of the Festivals of Male Voice Praise, I had been in

Above: In 1976,Claud concluded an eleven year pastorate at the lancing Tabernacle in Sussex

touch with what was then known as the Findlay Memorial Tabernacle in Glasgow. It was here that the Festival was founded, and I had preached at some of the festivals. After eleven years at Lancing we responded to a call to pastor that church in 1966. It was a much bigger building, but with a membership only a little larger than Lancing Tabernacle, and it was a dramatic change of setting. For seven years my voice was able to fill that building. We saw the Lord at work in the lives of many of the people. It was a challenging time spiritually and socially. There were great changes in the city during our time there, with much demolition and rebuilding, including a new bridge over the Clyde. We even learned something of the Scottish tongue! We realized that it was a different country, and we enjoyed the richness of the national character and the hospitality of the people, as well as the beauty of the Scottish scenery. We still receive phone calls with that strong accent as some of our former members keep in touch.

Our final pastorate was a surprise. The Deacons at New Park Hall, Barking seemed convinced that a return to our first Pastorate of eighteen years earlier was the right thing for the church. After much prayer and careful thought, we had the same firm assurance, and in 1973 we moved south to the borough on the edge of London. We had come full circle.

Massive changes had taken place since we were there just after the war. From being a truly local church with most members living within walking distance, it had become a largely commuting fellowship. Cottages and houses immediately round the church had been demolished and replaced by estate type homes and high rise flats. The inroads of unbelief in the nation had taken its toll here, and the membership was about half its former size. However, there was a good team of loyal deacons, and for seven years Dorothy and I served the people here. I always enjoyed the beautiful lofty building with its timbered ceiling and roomy pulpit. With the prayerful support of the membership, some of whom were members in our first pastorate there, we saw the Lord use his word with effect, and we began an outreach to the many homes around us. We felt our time there was strategic for us and for the church.

Having passed the retirement age by some eighteen months, we felt it wise to retire from pastoral ministry and, in another of the Lord's timings, provision was made for us to have our own home in Lancing. It was a moving experience to be received back into the fellowship as members. Yet another full circle! The final period of preaching took us to many churches, conferences and other opportunities of sharing the word of God. For seven years Dorothy and I travelled many miles in the interests of the gospel, and enjoyed the fellowship and hospitality of Christian people.

Voiceless service

All these varied experiences; seeing God's word at work, enjoying a fascinating kaleidoscope of personalities and churches, and preaching the truths that meant so much to us, were abruptly ended. For the remainder of my days, I would never be able to speak in a natural voice, not even in conversation. A working lifetime of public service for the Lord and his people suddenly ended. I had no idea how the future would work out for me. What on earth could a voiceless preacher do that would be useful service for his Lord?

The plans the Lord had for me slowly began to unfold. A few weeks after my major surgery I had a visit from Donald Banks and his secretary. Donald came as the Editor of *Challenge*, described as the Good News Paper. This is a mass distribution broadsheet in a popular tabloid format with testimonies, interesting articles and a simple presentation of the good news of Jesus Christ. Churches, individuals and city missions distribute it all over the country each month. Years earlier we had used it effectively in Glasgow to reach many new people. The *Challenge* directors were looking for someone to take over the task of correspondence counsellor. A response form in each issue offers free literature and also, if requested, the opportunity to be put in contact with a counsellor for help, who would answer questions and give encouragement by letter. I was amazed at God's timing. It so beautifully fitted my situation. It would put me in touch with a wide range of needy people to whom I could speak on paper, without ever meeting them or uttering a word. I had recently entered the computer age by learning to use a word processor. This opening door seemed to be wonderfully oiled!

For five years I was able to engage in this work, during which time more than two hundred people wrote to the paper from all over the country and some from overseas. I came into contact with people who were sad and lonely, disappointed and devastated; some had contemplated, and even attempted, suicide. I met 'sin with the lid off' and became involved in situations I would never have known in normal ministry. My very first letter was from a young woman who had worked as a prostitute for eighteen months and had left it because she could not live with herself and her uncleanness. She purchased a Bible and seemed determined to know a different life in seeking Jesus.

I soon found out how desperate some of our nation's prisoners were for outside links and to know that there was someone out there who was interested and who cared. One letter came from a young man, who we will call Alan. He struggled with a desperate drink problem and was at rock bottom. Through drink he had spent every Christmas in prison for the past eight years. I sent him a personal letter with Christian literature, and this became an ongoing correspondence. I gradually noted a change in his tone as he responded to the instruction from the Bible. One day he wrote an enthusiastic letter with the news that he had been delivered from his alcohol addiction. He began to study seriously, and took up the challenge of studying *Knowing God* by J.I.Packer. Alan had lost his dependence on alcohol and found a dependence on the Lord Jesus. In a letter giving me news of his discharge, the chaplain wrote, 'I found him to be a very sincere young man. He took his Christian faith very seriously and I commended him to a local church where his faith can be nurtured.' This was encouragement in the early days of my work, and there were a few who came to real faith as a result of the ministry of writing.

There is a good work being done in our prisons. I think of Colin, with a similar drink problem to Alan. He responded to the counselling, and began to seek the Lord. He had a deep experience of the Spirit convicting him and giving him forgiveness, peace and deliverance while he was waiting for his sentence in the court. Colin went on to be a true witness, having Bible studies in the prison. When he was released, Colin re-married his wife who had divorced him because of his drunkenness.

Ben was caught on a drug run into which he was enticed in order to try and clear his debts. He had a Christian background but wrote for spiritual help in his deep need. Later transferred to Dartmoor, I saw him respond to instruction, and Ben grew spiritually even in that prison. He developed leadership gifts and an ability to speak with a good clear voice. He was encouraged by the chaplain, and is currently taking courses to help him prepare for a future life outside. Ben's course on communication and preaching enabled me to comment on his sample sermons and offer him advice based on my experience in public ministry. He hopes to use his gift to make known his faith when he is a free man. Again I have had an excellent report from the chaplain, and a good character report has taken him to a more open prison. I was deeply moved to be able to encourage a prisoner not only in his faith, but also in preparing him for a useful ministry in the future. Perhaps my preaching will continue through Ben.

Moses, who came from Nigeria, picked up a *Challenge* newspaper on a London underground station during a visit to the UK. He took it home and later wrote a surprisingly frank letter asking advice regarding his decision to take a second wife! Moses had been connected to an evangelical church, but was backslidden to the extent of seriously setting his mind on a polygamous marriage. My letter took a lot of time and thought, but it set out the biblical standards for marriage, and the consequences of his proposed action. I suggested that he read my letter through with his wife and face the implications together. His reply gave me great joy and encouragement. He had done as I had suggested and the Lord had dealt with him in deep conviction as he read. He and his wife committed themselves afresh to one another and renewed their marriage vows. They subsequently became involved in their church and are now serving in Bauchi Province in evangelistic outreach. A gospel paper left at a London underground station was used by the Spirit and through correspondence, to save a marriage in Africa! Two lives were re-directed into fruitful channels. My files include some very encouraging records and the first and last letters are at times quite a dramatic contrast.

However, this ministry through correspondence has many disappointments. The majority of contacts were just a one-off, with no follow-on links. Each original letter contained literature selected to meet the specific need, so I had to be content to know that I had helped personally, had made the gospel clear, and had sent reading material that could well continue the impact. This happened occasionally when, after a lapse of many months, a former correspondent would write to see if I was still able to help. Some ongoing correspondence with much promise and a growing relationship would suddenly end with no reason given. I may never know what had happened to my friend. Looking back on that period, however, I was so glad that the Lord had opened a door leading to so many fruitful relationships. Some of my correspondents found faith in Christ and had been changed, others were encouraged, and prisoners were preparing for their release with Bible studies and courses to give them purpose in a future life of freedom. I may never personally meet any of my postal friends, but I have a number of prisoners, some in Thailand, to whom I still write regularly. They look on me as the one 'out there' who has come to love them, pray for them and take an interest in their wellbeing. Had I been preaching among the churches, great as that privilege was, I would never have made friends as far apart as Dartmoor and Bangkok! I proved again the power of the written word in communicating truth, and that it can be used by the Spirit in vital spiritual dealings with individuals.

After five years of this rewarding work, I felt it wise to hand over to a younger person, retaining only my ongoing contacts. But just at that point another totally unexpected opportunity gave me access to even more people. The Lancing Tabernacle, where we continue in active membership, appointed a new elder to the leadership. Richard Brunton had a ministry to churches of African believers in the London area, and was in touch with pastors by regular mailings and periodic visits to Kenya, Uganda,

Above: In common with so many children, Claud found, to his surprise and delight, that his grandchildren were fascinated by his 'new' voice

Tanzania and Rwanda. In conversation one day he said he was always glad of Bible studies to send or take to these pastors. They would not only be spiritually helped by such material but would happily preach any scripted sermons they received! I began to look at the many files in my study containing hundreds of full notes of Bible messages that I had preached in the past. Could they become missionary ministry by proxy? I carefully scripted one message on the principles of effective prayer, based on Mark 11:12-26, and gave it to Richard. He made copies and mailed them to individual pastors in Kenya. Later when he was visiting Kenya for a preaching tour, he handed out another Bible script. This was part of a package containing cassettes, Scriptures and literature given to the pastors as they registered for their conference. A man has volunteered to translate my Bible studies into Swahili. What an opportunity!

Although my preaching days are over, I am now ministering the living word of God through African lips. The preparation and prayer of past years of study are bearing new fruit. The voices, gestures and expressions of brothers in a totally different context and culture are being used to share truths that the Lord had given me in past days. I have a deep sense of fulfilment in this ongoing and developing overseas ministry, and have the joy of re-preparing messages that had been part of my ministry in the past.

For some time I have been providing two-minute scripts for a daily phone-in programme called 'Message' going out from Brighton. It is heard by many people, and includes a hot-line number for personal contact. An interesting fact is that many calls are after midnight, suggesting that some folk feel vulnerable in the night, and even a recorded voice can bring hope and comfort. This is just another way that my voicelessness is multiplying in its ministry. Dorothy and I have always had a large place in all our programmes for work among children. It was a major department in the churches we have served. In the early years of evangelism, we usually ran a children's early evening meeting before the main adult outreach. Now I found, to my surprise and delight, that children were fascinated by my voice. We visited the school where two of our grandchildren were pupils. The teacher, in her welcome, explained about my 'special' voice and I responded with a brief electronic sentence. We sat in on a story time, and afterwards I found myself surrounded by eager children, asking questions and inviting me to say their names! My problem had become a valid point of contact. At one autumn conference, a small boy overheard me and spoke to me just to hear me reply. He would come after breakfast, at different times during the day and even for a word just before he went up to bed. His mother told me that he had told her he would like to have a voice like that. However, when she explained how it came about, he had second thoughts!

Profit and loss

At times, I have tried to work out a profit and loss statement in the light of the years since the dramatic change in our way of life. On the loss side was the lack of normality. There are moments when I have a great longing to be normal; especially when I am aware that every word makes me so obviously different. Just to be an average person would make life easier.

Then, on other occasions, I mourn the sad loss of quiet conversation, and the ability to whisper. Even the low setting on my volume control is electronic and distinctive. The relaxed talk in low tones in private is only a memory. Had I been able to learn the oesophageal speech I could have made some attempt to immediate response in conversation but as it is, there is a pause while I fish out my voice from my pocket. One thing that does give momentary annoyance is when folk say 'don't bother to get it out.' That is a comment on their impatience and it condemns me to silence. Dorothy's losses include my sudden departure from the meal table. A casual cough can cause a blockage in the stoma, which needs immediate attention to restore normal breathing. Again, my surgery took away my sense of smell. As one who has grown sweet peas for many years, and distributed scores of bunches of these colourful flowers to neighbours and friends, I miss their delightful fragrance together with the subtle scents that nature provides. These make up the loss side, the debits of the assessment.

However, there are many gains of valuable things on the credit side. The facts that I have survived to live a full life and continue to enjoy the mutual caring of our long-standing marriage are two of the most important. Another is the acceptance of me as I am among family friends and the church. The voice is part of me, and among those who know me no one expects anything different. So many of the original inhibitions have gone. Being different has become an advantage at so many levels. An interest is quickened with complete strangers, giving opportunity for simple witness and possible follow up. A new tradesman called, and hearing my voice commented on its clarity. His neighbour had a similar artificial larynx but was not getting it clear and still had to use writing often. I suggested he might put us in touch so that I could be of help to him. Such links could well be used to lead to personal sharing of the good news.

In public prayer there is a clarity and audibility that brings the 'Amen' because the prayers are heard when so many sincere prayers are mumbled to the floor. Because in society laryngectomees are only a minority, there is an interest and curiosity which, at times, can lead to profitable conversations with perfect strangers. Once the embarrassment and inhibitions are passed and regular friends and church members expect this voice from me, there are many positives that help greatly when the sense of loss, limitation and being different, begin to overwhelm me.

A sense of humour is sometimes described as a saving grace. It has certainly proved often to be the catalyst that brings laughter instead of tears. One cause of merriment is the fact that, with aspirates not having any vibrations for my machine to pick up, I cannot pronounce my 'H's. The confusion of 'P's and 'B's, 'T's and 'D's have often brought a smile. Collecting my photographs I discovered I had become 'Mr Drigger.' I sometimes explain that I have to take off my tie to blow my nose! I have often been asked if the use of my machine is painful or tiring, and I reply that it is neither; since my speech does not involve breathing at all, it is possible for me to continue talking for an extended time. The only things that would tire would be the battery and the listeners! There are many opportunities for fun and it often dissolves any potential embarrassment. Dorothy and I have a communication code for times when my hands are not free. I can click with my tongue, so one click means 'yes', two clicks means 'no' and three means 'help' — which has not been used so far! It is all part of a light-hearted attitude to a limitation. It has been said that the person who can laugh at himself has a constant source of amusement. Fortunately I can, and therefore I have.

During my training programme with the speech therapist, I had opportunities to be a help to other patients. On several occasions I was invited to attend the hospital and spend time with those who had just had a laryngectomy and needed the encouragement that one day they really would be able to speak. A phone call from a speech therapist at a patient's home asked me to speak to her patient who had just acquired a Servox and was finding it frustrating. An electronic conversation seemed to be a great help to him.

A clear gain is the fact that I can still communicate. I have actually preached! At the Autumn Conference of the Fellowship of Independent Evangelical Churches (FIEC) in October 1993 I was asked if I would give the message at the final communion service. I felt I needed some assurance that they were sure they wanted a voiceless man to be involved in such an intimate part of the programme, but they insisted. I spoke on the wounds of Jesus, referring to the occasions when Jesus drew attention to his wounds. I reminded the conference that when the Roman soldiers nailed Jesus to the cross they had no idea they were making marks that would last for all eternity. The fact the Jesus was nailed to the cross for our sins is the focus of heaven's glory. I found a rapt attention, with the audience seemingly forgetting the voice and focussing on the message. Several were helped on that occasion. As it happened, a year later, the speaker booked for the communion message was taken ill on the way to the conference and I was asked to fill in at short notice. So it transpired that, having been the speaker at the first Autumn Conference at Hildenborough at Frinton-on-Sea, Essex, many years before, I found myself the final speaker at the last two. To sense the joy of preaching again is something that remains with me.

I am sure that I have a valid credit balance on my assessment. The gains far outweigh the losses. This naturally brings into focus the mysterious factor of the sovereign purposes of God. At the natural human level, the worst thing that could happen to a preacher and singer is to lose his voice. Most people could hardly imagine a more total and devastating tragedy. It is so final and complete. But believing that the Father has a purpose for his children means that the possibility that it was the best thing that could have happened becomes clear. All the positives of my experience pointed to that fact. The much wider ministry that has come, the use of being different for the gospel, the full life that I am still living, enabled by the Spirit of God, all suggest a divine plan that is the only explanation of our experience.

Facing the future

At times I recall the consultant saying, 'I am sorry that it means major surgery but you must have it done.' In effect, I was trading my voice for my life. An ambulance driver, who should have known better, once informed me, 'My father had your trouble and it killed him'; an example of insensitive and clumsy comments that can make life harder for suffering people. In the darkness of this experience I faced death as a reality. The Lord has seen fit to spare my life, but as older believers, Dorothy and I know that our time is limited. However, heaven is more real and near than it has ever been. Like Bunyan in his *Pilgrim's Progress* the lights of the celestial city seem to shine in the distance. My brush with death has led me to pray that my witness might be effective at the end. John Wesley once said of the early Methodists, 'Our people die well.' I trust that as I move on to the final lap, the heavenly ties will be more real than the earthly ones. Growing old is

very challenging and can either be illuminated by anticipated glory or darkened by things that will pass away.

Every day is golden from the Christian point of view. Yet it is necessary to remind ourselves that the Lord richly provides us with everything for our enjoyment. For the believer, the limited time left is not a morbid concern, it can be an eager anticipation. It is wise to dwell on the promises about the future at times and live in the enjoyment of them. We should give more time to studying what God says about heaven.

I have sometimes wondered how I will be remembered when I am no longer here. It is very likely that, having lived a number of years with my unusual voice, I will be thought of, not as the preacher, the pastor, or a minister of the gospel. It may well be that the last impression I give, my epitaph, will be the man with the electronic voice! I have thought about this, and realise that it doesn't matter. What does matter is that the way I faced up to it will glorify the Lord. It came to me with real force that the whole question of being remembered by posterity is an issue that concerns people of all ages. Eccentrics have lived in specially constructed graves for weeks to get a mention in the *Guinness Book of Records*. Many of the most grotesque and bizarre activities have been prompted in this way. However, all our track records are being devoured by passing time and the failing memories of people. Even if we make the record book it will only be seen by those who buy it and read it! It is amazing how humans seem to long for immortality, from the boy who scrawls his name on wet concrete, to the person planning a huge obelisk for his final

Above: The Triggers today. Dorothy and Claud are eternally grateful that the Lord brought them to faith in Christ while in their teens. Of the trials they have lived through, they witness to the fact that God has had a plan; their longing is that he should be exalted in anything that has been overcome or achieved

resting place. For Dorothy and myself as Christians it doesn't matter. The only record that matters is the one kept by the only person who knows all the facts, the Lord himself. It is a wonderful release to have that conviction.

Several factors in our story are a deep joy to me. One is the loving prayerful support of family and friends throughout the testing times. The quality of friendship has been glorifying to the Lord and a strength to us both. The surrounding love of the church family is a constant proof of the wisdom of God in what Paul calls 'the mystery'—the calling out of a people for himself. This concept, followed biblically, provides all we need in times of joy and sorrow. The Lord and his people provide a shelter in the time of storm.

Another fact that became real to me, especially in the early days of my time of testing, is that there is no need for a voice to speak to the Lord in prayer. The soundless communication in the secret place, the cry from the heart that reaches the throne, is a comfort and strength. Conversation with him is immediate with no wait for me to fumble in my pocket!

Dorothy and I are eternally grateful that the Lord brought us to faith in Christ while in our teens. Having a spiritual family heritage was a large factor, but I tremble to think what the story might have been had we not had that clear experience of conversion. Thinking back to the mistakes I have made, the tendency to take the line of least resistance, the pride factor, and dealing with all the pressures of Christian service, I marvel at the Lord's patience, long-suffering and willingness to forgive. All the time he had a plan and we only want him to be exalted in anything that has been overcome or achieved.

Finally, the Christian faith has always been marked by singing and vocal expression. The poems of the Old Testament enshrined in the book of Psalms are full of expressions of audible praise and prayer. In Psalm 5:3 David seeks the Lord with the words, 'Morning by morning, O LORD, you hear my voice.' In Psalm 18:6 David, 'Cried to God for help. From his temple he heard my voice.' We read phrases like, 'Proclaiming aloud your praise', and Psalm 40:3 shows how God in salvation, 'Put a new song in my mouth.' Having been deprived of such joys for some years, there is a growing interest in what lies ahead. The promise of future glory, being like the Lord Jesus and sharing his life with the singing of a new song, creates a special attraction for me. That expectation has become very personal. The prospect of having bodies like the Lord's on the mount of transfiguration promises an indescribable experience, but it will be wedded for me to the thrill of singing that new song with a brand new resurrection voice!

Them and us?

Peter Williams

When Paul and his friends started attending the church, Peter and Brenda wondered how on earth they could be integrated. But the pastor and his wife were soon to learn that they brought with them their own special values that would teach the church so much about love, friendship and loyalty.

It was a Sunday morning and I was sitting with my wife Brenda in the congregation of a church we were visiting. We were listening to a sermon on the theme of evangelism and witness. At one point the preacher related a story which moved us both deeply, as it illustrated a beautiful lesson we had learned in recent years.

A medical consultant boarded a plane for an inter-state flight in America and he found himself sitting next to a little girl with Down's syndrome. The stewardess explained that the child was a regular passenger and there was always someone to meet her at the other end. After a minute or two the consultant was surprised when the little girl asked, 'Did you eat your breakfast this morning? My mummy says everyone should eat their breakfast.' 'Yes', the consultant responded, 'I eat breakfast every morning.' The little girl was quiet for a moment or two and then she enquired, 'Did you clean your teeth this morning? My mummy says everyone should clean their teeth.' Smilingly he assured her that he had cleaned his teeth. By this time the plane was ready to take off and the last passenger took his seat across the aisle and settled down with his newspaper. Once more the little voice interrupted, 'Do you love the Lord Jesus? My mummy says everyone should love the Lord Jesus.' The consultant replied, 'Yes indeed, I do love the Lord Jesus and I have tried to serve him all my life.' Silence once more and then, motioning with her head to the man opposite, she said, 'Ask him if he ate his breakfast this morning?' He hesitated, but the little girl insisted, 'Go on, ask him.' The consultant leaned over and apologetically explained that the little girl next to him wanted to know if he had eaten his breakfast. 'Yes, I did,' he replied. Another pause—then, 'Ask him if he cleaned his teeth this morning.' The consultant squirmed but, with a weak smile, conveyed the message and passed on the answer that the man across the aisle had cleaned his teeth. After a moment or two came the question he was dreading, 'Ask him if he loves the Lord Jesus.'

The consultant tried to explain to the little girl that that was a very personal thing and not the kind of question to ask a stranger. But she insisted, 'Go on, ask him.' He was forced to look within himself and ask

Left: Peter Williams with Paul, Hughie and Anthony

why he was so reluctant to ask what is the most important question anyone could be faced with in this life. Finally, the consultant leaned over and enquired, 'The little girl wants to know if you love the Lord Jesus.' The man put down his paper and said, 'Do you know, I have heard people talk about their love for Jesus, but no one has ever really explained to me what it means.' For the rest of the flight the consultant had the opportunity to witness to this stranger about the gospel.

As I listened, the words of Jesus came to mind, 'I praise you Father, Lord of heaven and earth, because you have hidden these things from the wise and learned, and revealed them to little children.' And I thought: Yes, even children with Down's syndrome. That story fittingly serves to introduce an experience we shared at our church on the south coast of England, in learning what it means to be a church family.

It was about five years after the commencement of my ministry that Paul began attending the services, and within a very short time he had endeared himself to the whole fellowship. Over the next three years or so, Roger, Hughie, Anthony, Peter and Jane joined him. There was nothing unusual about this, except that for us as a fellowship and for myself in particular, this was to be a new and strange experience because these people were different. Of course, we are all different from each other in many ways: physically we are taller or shorter, fatter or thinner, white or black, as well as being different in culture and customs, temperament and tastes; but these people were different in a special way. Paul and Hughie were born with Down's syndrome, a genetic disorder that, with other things, results in learning disabilities; there are, however, a wide range of abilities among Down's people—just like the rest of us—at least one Down's syndrome person has passed her driving test. The others who came with Paul and Hughie also had various degrees of learning disability, or what used to be described as having a mental handicap.

I had never really encountered this situation before, at least not at such close quarters, and now here I was with a group attending my church on a regular basis. They were all residents of a Christian home situated in the same avenue as our church and established in 1986 by Prospects—formerly known as A Cause for Concern—a Christian organization aimed at focusing help and support for people like Paul and his friends, and for their families. From the beginning of the home, our church was involved by providing people to help in decorating and others to serve on the local committee.

As a pastor, I was confronted with a situation that I was not sure I could handle. How could we integrate into the life and worship of the church a group of people with learning disabilities and character traits that were different and at times difficult? At the same time I knew that they had their own sense of dignity and self worth, their own spiritual needs, and a capacity for spiritual understanding and growth in the Christian faith. Above all I was anxious to avoid a 'them and us' attitude from creeping in among the congregation. I must confess that until this group came to our church my own attitude towards people with learning disabilities left much to be desired. It was not that I was consciously prejudiced or hostile in any way, and I was always ready to give my money to help provide the necessary care for such people. But I had never seriously thought about them in the way that I now had to. If I am really truthful, I had never thought of them as being 'people' like the rest of us, needing fulfilment, work, objectives, the opportunity to make choices, to create relationships, to attend the worship of God's house and to enjoy hobbies and leisure activities.

What kind of people are they?

For my own part as pastor of the church, and it was also true of most of the members, the whole experience of relating to the group was a learning curve, difficult at times, but very rewarding. I had to learn that in spite of their disabilities, they could achieve a great deal with the right kind of help and encouragement, and that in certain areas they were as able and as accomplished as the rest of us. They were all capable of living full and worthwhile lives. In one of their official pamphlets, Prospects makes that abundantly clear. It states that the charity is 'committed to supporting people with learning disabilities so that they can live their lives to the full. People are supported in using diverse social and leisure facilities including adult education classes, art, music and dance; recreational facilities including swimming, horse-riding and rambling; leisure services including libraries, churches, sports centres and social clubs. People are also supported in their choice of work in the local community in offices, a bakery, playgroups, a cafeteria, a garage, a youth hostel and old people's homes.'

Certainly those belonging to our church group lived very full and productive lives and in no way could the quality of that life be described as 'poor.' They enjoyed plenty of social activity with outings to different places, visits to the homes of church members, useful employment and hobbies of all kinds to fill up their leisure time. Paul works in the workshop linked to the home and Hughie has a part-time job working in the kitchen of one of the local hospitals. Hughie was very excited when he told me that he now had a second job as a cleaner in the residential home. In his leisure time he loves messing about with his computer and he attends computer classes to improve his efficiency. Anthony is interested in cookery and is pursuing a catering course at a local further education college with a view to obtaining a qualification that will enable him to hold down a full-time job. Jane works part-time in a local florist and also part-time in one of the local hotels. In her leisure time she attends computer classes, and she loves horse riding. In the light of all this, it is difficult to understand how anyone can think that people with learning disabilities are not capable of living lives of real value and purpose.

Sadly, there is still a strong current of opinion in our society that believes that the only sensible approach to the 'problem' of disability—mental or physical—is to prevent the birth of such babies in the first place. In reality this means abortion. But that is an option not open to Christians. We cannot subscribe to any view that excludes or discriminates against those who do not fit easily into the acceptable categories of society. It may be true that it is not from the ranks of those with an impaired intellectual function that we get our political leaders, TV stars, sports personalities, captains of industry and newspaper editors, but is achievement of this kind the only measure of what makes us truly human? Christians believe that all men and women are the unique creation of God, 'Then God said, "Let us make man in our image, in our likeness..." So God created man in his own image, in the image of God he created him; male and female he created them' (Genesis 1:26,27). This account of the human race stands in direct contradiction to modern evolutionary teaching, which asserts that we are the products of impersonal mechanical forces. In today's world human life is cheap, and personality is devalued and robbed of its dignity. This is seen all too clearly in the brutality of the continual wars that afflict our world, in the violence that is a common feature of our society in the media and therefore in the street, and in the thousands of needless abortions that occur every year. But if we accept that we are made in God's image then this gives us a reverence and respect for all humanity, including those with disabilities.

Looking back, after many years of sharing friendship with Paul and his friends, as a church we are thankful to God that he brought them to us. We certainly receive from them as much as we give, and we have discovered that if they are different from the rest of us, it is not their learning disabilities that sets them apart so much as certain qualities they possess that many of us find very humbling and challenging. At times their lives make us feel ashamed of our own poor Christian discipleship.

Four of the group, Paul, Hughie, Anthony and Jane, were at our home for tea. I had retired from the pastorate of the church, so I hadn't seen them for some months and it was like a great re-union. The warmth of their welcome in the big hugs they gave was so real and uninhibited, not a bit like the polite greeting we generally give each other. Paul and Hughie are especially loving and out-going and often greet folk in the church literally with open arms. Many in the fellowship had to get used to this open display of affection and some never really did manage it and found it all a bit embarrassing.

Paul was especially affectionate towards Brenda and treated her like an older sister. He would discuss seriously with her on various matters, but was always mindful of her position as the pastor's wife. This measure of understanding clearly came from his background as the son of a pastor and therefore he knew something of the problems associated with life in the manse. Both Brenda and I found this loving approach by the whole group to be very moving, and in no way did we ever have cause to feel uneasy about it. Moreover doesn't all this say something to us about the way we relate to each other as believers? Are we perhaps too formal when we meet together in church, in the mistaken idea that anything else would be unbecoming and irreverent? I realize that we have to keep a balance, and that the open display of emotions in a lot of hugging, kissing and easy familiarity, which characterizes some fellowships, can be superficial, off-putting and poten- tially dangerous. On the other hand, if I were pressed to explain the difference in the open affection shown by the group, I would find it hard to offer an adequate answer except to say that their loving attitude is perfectly natural and not forced in any way. Gradually each member of the group became a part of the church and through their individual contributions added a richness and diversity to its life and worship.

In the community at large there is still a lot of fear, prejudice and resentment concerning people with any kind of disability. Much of this attitude is the result of ignorance and misunderstanding. People are especially nervous when they find themselves in the company of those with a learning disability and they may not like being touched or stroked on the face, as might be the case by someone with Down's syndrome. Many find it difficult to communicate with such people or to understand what they are saying. Or they may wonder if there will be a sudden display of strange and odd behaviour. These responses to people with learning disabilities can characterize the attitude of Christians as well. However, the gospel we preach and believe in demands a different attitude. The apostle Paul reminded the Christians at Corinth, 'But God chose the foolish things of the world to shame the wise; God chose the weak things of the world to shame the strong. He chose the lowly things of this world and the despised things ... so that no one may boast before him' (1 Corinthians 1:27-29). I came to realize early on in our experience with our new friends, that if we were to overcome our fears and prejudices as a church then we had to see their existence among us, not as a problem to be solved, but as a challenge to our understanding of the local church as a caring and loving community of God's people.

Although as a group they all shared, to varying degrees, a learning disability, they were nevertheless all totally different from each other in character and temperament. This was something that we as a church came to recognize as time passed. In the early stages we tended to think of them as a homogeneous group. But we got past that, and it was not too long before we were treating them as distinct individuals, each with his or her personality traits. Paul was solemn and serious, Hughie noisy and laughing, Anthony was loud and with strong opinions that he didn't hesitate to make known, Peter was quiet and with little to say, and Jane was just a lovely girl. For my own part as the pastor, the better I got to know them, the more I appreciated their diversity and the life and colour they brought to the fellowship, as well as the contribution they were able to make to its activity and worship.

Paul—dignified and dependable

Paul was the first of the group to start attending the services at our church, and as he was under my pastoral care for the next thirteen years I got to know him well. He is now in his early fifties and comes from a Christian home. His father had been a Baptist pastor whom I knew and who would worship with us on occasions. More than once he told me how glad he was that his son was attached to such a caring church, and how happy Paul was in the fellowship. I could fully understand his feelings because if I were a Christian parent with a son or daughter who had a learning disability it would certainly help my peace of mind to know that they belonged to a loving and caring church.

I first met Paul about two years before he started coming to us when I preached at his father's church. I clearly remember entering the front door of the building that Sunday morning and being graciously welcomed by Paul as he handed me a hymn book. I was deeply moved because it was perfectly evident that Paul had Down's syndrome, and I thought what a wonderful thing it was that he was able to find spiritual fulfilment by sharing in the worship and being involved in the church's activities as a steward. Two years later Paul reminded me of our earlier meeting. We asked him to become a steward, as he had previously been in his father's church. Like the other stewards, he was given an identifying badge, which he wore with a sense of real pride. It has to be said that no church ever had a more gracious and conscientious steward. Paul was always at the church well before time, getting the books ready to hand to people. If first impressions count, then the manner in which one is received at the door of the church is very important when someone is visiting for the first time. Paul was always gracious and warm in his welcome to people, always ready with a smile and, for those he knew well, even a hug!

Paul's outstanding characteristic, which set him apart from the others in the group, was his natural sense of dignity. Physically he is short and on the stout side, but unlike Hughie or Peter he would never come to the service on a Sunday with an open neck shirt or wearing jeans. Always he would be dressed in a dark suit and tie, and with a serious air about him. On the other hand he did have a neat line in fancy waistcoats and bow ties for less formal occasions; he was always very pleased whenever Brenda complimented him on his smart appearance.

Paul is also sober in his personality. He has a gracious manner, but a tendency to speak too quietly and not very clearly, so that it is difficult at times to understand what he is saying. This meant that people would sometimes avoid getting into conversation with him, especially in an after church meeting on a Sunday evening when there would be a lot of background noise and loud conversations. Sometimes I would see him sitting at a table on his own, or else with Jane or Peter or one of the others, but even they would not always be talking with him. This is one of those instances where the rest of us must be prepared to make a real effort to exercise patience and understanding with people who have a learning disability. We need to ask if we would like to be in a church lounge full of people laughing, talking and enjoying informal friendship, but ourselves left sitting alone with no one to talk to.

I used to carry a black brief case to church containing my Bible, sermon notes, and books. One day I realised that, shortly after he became a steward, Paul had also started carrying a black brief case. To this day no one, including myself, has ever discovered what is in that case! I suppose it was all part of his sense of dignity and responsibility as a steward in God's house. Even Hughie got into the act at one time and began carrying a black brief case, but it wasn't the same because he didn't have the right air of seriousness to go with it, or the dark suit and tie. Anyway, with Hughie it was only a passing fad and after a few weeks he left the briefcase at home.

The members of the group certainly had their own ideas about things. I once asked them in a discussion time, to give their opinions on how the pastor should be dressed in the pulpit. They all felt quite strongly that he should definitely be dressed in a suit and tie because, to quote Anthony's words, 'It is setting an example and honouring God.'

As a steward, Paul like the other stewards, had his own special seat on the outside of the aisle with a steward's card placed on it. Although I myself have never seen this happen, I have been told by several church members that when I walked down the aisle at the close of the service, Paul would immediately get up and follow me, with a stately walk and carrying his brief case. This so impressed one visitor that she asked Brenda if he was the assistant Pastor! Another aspect of his quiet dignity was the way in which he would always help me off with my coat when I arrived in the vestibule, and hang it up for me; Paul was always there to help me on with it at the close of the service.

Paul is a lovely man, quiet and gracious, and very happy and contented with life. I wish in that respect that many more of us were like him since, in spite of all the blessings we enjoy, there is an ugly itching covetousness and discontent at the heart of our society today.

Hughie—exasperating but endearing

What a character! About fifty years of age, a bit harum-scarum, exasperating at times, swinging between high spirits and periods of deep quietness when he would hardly say a word—but always loveable. Hughie was a great favourite with everyone in the church fellowship. Everybody knew him because he maintained such a high profile! From the moment he came to us he made his presence felt because he was so active and noisy; he was always laughing, scurrying around doing something or other or else helping out with someone. Hughie was so different from Paul.

Virtually from the moment he joined the church it became clear to me that, just as Paul had his own job of stewarding, Hughie too wanted his own special role and responsibility. I could see this from the way he was always fiddling around with the hymn books in the vestibule before and after the service, arranging and re-arranging them on the shelves, much to Paul's annoyance. Or else he would be running upstairs to the recording room or in and out of the book room; always he was fidgety and restless and wanting to get involved. And why not? After all, people with learning disabilities are no different from many of us in that they may want to be busy doing things and developing their particular gifts and potential as far as possible. They were all integrated in the wider community and the workplace, mixing with non-disabled people and sharing in a whole range of activities. I wanted to see that same kind of involvement carried over into their church life, not simply 'us' doing things for 'them' but allowing them to be themselves, and to share in the life of the church in their own unique way.

But that was easier said than done. For a time I was at a complete loss as to the kind of job I could give Hughie. There is a limit to the sort of special task you can give to someone with a learning disability especially when there are already a lot of workers in the church. However, I eventually made Hughie responsible for putting the hymn numbers on the hymn boards at the beginning of the service, and also for seeing that the water carafe in the pulpit was always full and the drinking glass washed and clean. He was delighted with these responsibilities, and carried them out with great seriousness; in fact, if for any reason he was unable to be at a service he would ring the Secretary or one of the deacons so that arrangements could be made for someone to take over. I found such a conscientious approach to his tasks very encouraging. I only wish that many others in our churches would learn from Hughie and have the same sense of dedication. How often, in common with other Christian leaders, I have been let down at the last minute by members. And what of the failure by so many in our churches to be faithful at the services on a Sunday or at the weekly prayer meeting and Bible study? Neither have I really understood the reason sometimes given for not attending the Sunday services, 'We had the family visiting.' Shouldn't our family be aware that on a Sunday we have a previous appointment with God? Faithfulness, loyalty, commitment, dedication, call it what you will, there is not nearly enough of it among Christians today. Hughie was an example to us all.

On one occasion Hughie's zeal led him to ring the changes by providing me with a green-coloured drinking glass. The result was that at the close of the service an elderly lady asked me what was that 'green stuff' I was drinking in the pulpit. I think she might have been worried that the pastor had suddenly become addicted to some exotic stimulant in readiness for the sermon! If, as happened on a couple of occasions, an unthinking deacon dared to fill the water jug in the pulpit, this would really upset Hughie and he would angrily report it to me expecting, I suppose, that some kind of disciplinary action should be taken. When it came to putting the hymn numbers on the boards this was a job Hughie guarded still more jealously, so that even the organist was not allowed to interfere. Only rarely did he get the numbers mixed up, but when he did, he confounded both the congregation and me. I never fully understood Hughie's reaction when I spoke to him about it afterwards. He would either be very embarrassed and apologetic, or else he would treat the whole thing as a big joke and fall about laughing as if he had done it on purpose.

Hughie's real sense of enjoyment and responsibility in carrying out these tasks was clearly seen when he came to me one day and asked if he could replace some of the old card numbers which had got a bit tatty. He then set to work and made the new cards himself painting the numbers on them very neatly. He also felt we ought to have a smarter pair of hymn boards and he actually arranged to have new ones made by some of the residents in the home who were involved in crafts and woodwork.

For a long time Hughie plagued me with a request that he be allowed to read the Bible from the pulpit. In the end I spent a little time with him in an effort to get him to read a couple of verses from a hymn and then brought him into the pulpit with me one Sunday to repeat the hymn with me as if he were reading it. This pleased him enormously and he never made that request again—although he was always making some suggestion or other. Every so often we would have a soloist taking part in the evening worship and Hughie was obsessed with the notion of making his own contribution in this direction. The only trouble was he couldn't sing! In fact he couldn't pronounce the words properly and there would be a lot of grunting sounds in his singing; there was little I could do to help him with a solo. Another request which he would make from time to time was to become a deacon, and however patiently I explained to him that this was not possible he would always end up by saying, 'Why can't I?'

At a church members' meeting, Hughie would sit directly in my line of vision in the front row, just like a member of the House of Commons trying to catch the Speaker's eye. When it came to an open discussion on some matter Hughie would have his hand up in an instant. I knew that what he would have to say would not be relevant to the matter in hand, but I never ignored him—much to the amusement of some and the annoyance of others. When allowed his contribution, Hughie would get up and make a little speech or ask a question, perhaps about the water in the pulpit or some other matter. If for any reason he felt his opinion was not receiving due consideration he would try a more oblique approach after the meeting, by putting pressure on Brenda, usually with the introduction, 'Tell Pastor.' But the important thing for Hughie was that he was sharing in the proceedings and making his contribution like everyone else. And that is what mattered as far as I was concerned.

The really big occasion for both Paul and Hughie during the church year was the House Party held at Brunel Manor in Torquay. This was something they would talk about for weeks beforehand. We were usually about fifty in number, and the week would be taken up with addresses by a visiting speaker in the mornings and evenings with the afternoons free for people to go out. The highlight for Hughie and Paul was the Thursday evening when I would invite them to serve the bread and wine at the communion service. I would explain to them very carefully beforehand what they had to do, and at what point they were to come forward to take the plates with the bread, followed by each of them taking a cup to serve the wine. I told them how they were to wipe the cup with the napkin before handing it to the next person. It was a deeply humbling and moving experience to see the solemn manner in which they approached this. They considered it a great privilege and their sense of reverence would put many of us to shame. So seriously did they consider it, that they would forego the afternoon outing on the Thursday so that they could prepare themselves for the evening service. They would both be immaculately dressed in a white shirt and red bow tie, which was entirely their own idea. The slow and serious way they walked as they served the congregation, was a very moving experience.

Such unashamed simplicity and a sense of the sacred is a valuable reminder to the rest of us that, in spite of their disabilities, Paul and Hughie possessed another ability which so many of us seem to lack these days when entering into the holy presence of God. Ours is a noisy frenetic age and something of that noisy unholy spirit has entered into the worship of our churches. David Wells has expressed it like this, 'Robbed of such a (holy) God, worship loses its awe, the truth of his word loses its ability to compel, obedience loses its virtue, and the church loses its moral authority' (*In The Wastelands*, Eeardmans 1994 p136).

I once asked Hughie and Paul how they felt about serving the communion and they both explained in their own way that they were nervous and excited because they wanted, as Hughie said, 'To do our best for God.' I was glad to hear them say this, because it assured me that they both had a proper understanding of the meaning of the communion service and the Lord's table, and were not overawed by some superstitious reverence for the elements themselves. It was evident to me, as I served them with the bread and wine, that they knew the significance of the elements as representing the body and blood of Christ, and that it was an awareness of being in God's presence and of serving him that filled them with such a deep sense of the sacredness of the occasion.

Anthony—up front

Anthony is a very serious person but in quite a different way from Paul. He is not solemn and dignified like Paul, but is loud and talkative. Also his degree of learning disability is not as pronounced as Paul and Hughie and he is able to read a little. He manages to sing the hymns quite well from the hymnbook or the overhead screen and he can, with some difficulty, follow a reading from the Bible. Neither Hughie nor Paul is able to read. Anthony was a young man of about twenty when he first came to us some ten years ago. He enjoys conversation and can engage in a good discussion about spiritual matters. He holds very strong opinions about most things, and in his loud voice will blurt them out regardless of who may be present. Anthony tends to pontificate, but is very likeable for all that. He is faithful in attending all the meetings, including the weekly prayer meeting and Bible study, and also the prayer time before the evening service. He will regularly take part in prayer, mentioning the pastor and the other residents in his home. I wish there were a lot more in our churches who, like Anthony, would make the prayer meeting such a priority. He also loves the preaching of God's word and lets it be known that the sermon is the most important part of the service. I was told by a fellow-pastor that Anthony had attended a meeting in another church, when the speaker happened to make reference to the brief attention span of people with a learning disability, and how we should be sensitive to that. Anthony jumped up and said in his loud voice that he disagreed with the speaker and that he should come to his church, because the pastor always preaches for thirty minutes!

It is a great help when trying to integrate a group like ours to have people in the church who are willing to befriend one or two of them and make a real effort to treat them as individuals. This happened in Anthony's case. He became very attached to a couple who took a great interest in him. They invited him into their home, and always remembered his birthday and special events in his life. But what was especially loving and caring about their attitude was that they invited Anthony to sit with them during the services on a Sunday. This was in spite of the fact that he suffers from a particularly disturbing form of behaviour by continuously shaking his head from side to side sometimes in a violent manner. It is not hard to imagine how disruptive this can be for the couple concerned and how difficult it may be for them to concentrate on the preaching. But Sunday by Sunday Anthony sits with them. Given this degree of caring by church members, the task of a pastor to make those with a learning disability feel they really are part of God's family is made so much easier.

Anthony and the others are all sincere in their Christian faith and they know exactly where they stand in relation to the gospel and salvation. On this issue there were more lessons that we had to learn. To begin with, we had to be careful not to underestimate their ability to understand spiritual truths and treat them like children, when in fact they were adult men and women. But equally, we had to avoid talking above their heads and make intellectual demands that exceeded their grasp. This can be quite a challenge and calls for a lot of patient thought, especially when dealing with abstract concepts like 'sin', 'holiness' and 'faith.'

When Paul and Hughie asked to be baptized. I wondered how I was going to handle it, and whether the church members would think that, with their disability, they would not be able to appreciate the seriousness and signif-icance of baptism. All the candidates were expected to attend baptismal classes where the Bible's teaching on baptism would be explained. I could hardly have Paul and Hughie attending the classes with a half dozen non-disabled candidates. In the end I met with them privately and explained carefully and simply the meaning of baptism, and I was perfectly satisfied that they understood all that was involved. The next problem was the baptismal service itself. The candidates were expected to give their personal testimony and explain why they were getting baptized, and this before a packed church of some four hundred people. With Paul and Hughie I asked them a few questions about their faith and Christian experience, which they answered quite adequately, and the whole service proved to be a great blessing to everyone present.

I was discovering as time went on that, given the right kind of support and encouragement, people with a learning disability are able to cope with a whole variety of experiences which the rest of us might have thought were beyond their capabilities. For example, could they handle the issue of death and bereavement? The answer to this came when Roger, one of the earliest members of the group, was taken seriously ill and died. I watched the others carefully to note their reaction. They took it all in their stride. When Roger was dying they would talk to me about it very solemnly and with a great deal of sadness, but after his death they got on with their lives and would talk quite positively about Roger having gone to be with the Lord Jesus. This was yet another lesson for all of us.

Peter—the flag waver

Peter was in his thirties and on the whole a very happy person, rather quiet but always co-operative and friendly. He wanted to share in the life of the church, but not in any special way like the others. On Sunday mornings, when the time came for the children to leave the main service to go to their classes, Peter would go out with the 'Adventurers' and share in whatever activities were going on at the time. This was not a case of treating him as a child since it was something he wanted to do. We had one small problem however. Peter, in a perfectly friendly way, liked to cuddle the children occasionally and some of the younger ones were a little frightened by this. But it was all quite harmless and the teachers were well able to contain it.

At one time Peter started to bring a tambourine to the services. I didn't mind this, except that he couldn't really play the tambourine and would rattle it at the wrong time—after the hymn had finished! Undoubtedly he felt he was contributing to the worship and it was his way of praising God, and that is what mattered. Later he gave up the tambourine and brought a flag along instead. I thought at first that this was an improvement, if only because it was quieter, but I was mistaken. Peter would wave the flag very energetically during the singing, and although it didn't bother me in the pulpit, I felt sorry for those sitting behind him. But this was a trivial inconvenience, and Christians should not get too upset about things like this. Some objected, and thought that Peter should be stopped because they interfered with the dignity and orderliness of worship. Peter was expressing his felt need for God and his sense of exhilaration at being in his presence and with God's people. He had to express himself in his way.

Most of us can express our adoration and praise through the singing of the hymns and choruses, the reading of the scriptures, the prayers and by listening to God's word in the sermon. But Peter and his friends, because of their disability, are limited in the way they can express themselves in worship. Many of them cannot read or write, they cannot understand the message to the same degree as the rest of the congregation, and in addition they may have other disabilities such as blindness, poor speech, lack of body co-ordination, epilepsy and so on. How then are they to worship God except in ways we may find unusual and even unacceptable? After all, we have our own difficulties in worship when it comes to expressing the richer world of the spirit through the poorer medium of the physical frame and emotions. This is evident from what happens in the great fervour and excitement associated with revivals, and in many different patterns of worship to be found in evangelical churches today. C S Lewis in his *Screwtape Letters* writes, 'We have only laughter to express the most ribald revelry and the most godly joy; we have only tears to express the most selfish and worldly grief and the most godly sorrow. Therefore we must not be unduly surprised that spiritual rejoicings are so similar in their manifestations to rejoicings of a more worldly kind.' It may help us in worship to accept the occasionally unusual behaviour of those with a learning disability if we remember this.

Jane—sweet and sensitive

Jane is now in her late twenties and a lovely young woman. When she first came to our church she was just twenty and was lively and attractive, always smiling and very apt to giggle at the slightest thing. She is now more mature and is much quieter, though she still enjoys a laugh. When Brenda and I invited Jane to tea, we found it harder to hold a continuous conversation because of her slow speech and lapses of memory. However, with a little patience and encouragement on our part, she gradually opened up and told us quite a lot about herself, her hobbies, and above all her Christian faith.

Jane enjoys living at the Prospects home and gets on equally well with all the members of the group who seem to treat her almost like a sister. She lives a very full and satisfying life, and when visiting the home a short while ago I found her working on a print of flowers, using a technique that I certainly didn't understand, but the result was very beautiful. Jane goes horse riding every Friday and gets a great deal of pleasure from it. She loves talking about her horse Tom, and she told me recently that she has a certificate of merit for her horse riding. Like Hughie, Jane also likes messing about with the computer.

Jane takes her Christian faith very seriously as was evident from the fact that when she came to our house for tea, she brought her Bible with her. During the conversation we talked about her horse riding and suddenly she broke in with a very perceptive question: 'Is it difficult to convert a person from another religion?' Brenda and I were both taken by surprise until it emerged that at the riding stables there was a Sikh, and Jane wanted so much to talk to him about the Lord Jesus. She was clearly deeply concerned that he should know about the Christian faith. What does that say to the rest of us about our willingness to witness to others about Christ? It reminds me of the little Down's syndrome girl and the medical consultant on the aeroplane. In giving her testimony, Jane will tell you that she came to put her trust in Christ as Saviour when she was about nine or ten and later made her faith known publicly through believer's baptism when she was fifteen. She speaks of it as a very special day when the family were all present; she still has the card with a text written on it, given to her on that occasion.

Jane works at a hotel in our town preparing and clearing tables, and when I asked her if she enjoyed her work she said she did but that she found some of those working with her not nearly as kind and loving as the people in the church! Clearly this says something about the fellowship she enjoys with God's people. Jane is in full membership of the church on profession of her faith. The last time I was with the group, we were looking through some albums containing photographs of various activities that had taken place in the church, and Jane amazed us by knowing the names of all the church members and the various positions they held in the church. For Jane it was a reflection of her sense of belonging to the fellowship and being part of the church family. She gets on very well with the other young people in the church and attends the eighteen plus group. Jane is also faithful at the weekly Bible study evening and is a very happy and contented member of the church.

The church family

In spite of this positive picture, I wouldn't want to give the impression that having people with learning disabilites in the church is always easy. Far from it. They have their own problems and difficulties just like the rest of us, and they can also cause problems in relation to other people. I had some members who were unhappy that a person with a learning disability should be a steward since they felt it might give visitors the 'wrong' impression, whatever that was supposed to mean! I recall that when I first met Paul as a steward in his father's church it gave me distinctly the 'right' impression. It was the impression that here was a very welcoming church, if it included people like Paul. I also remember difficulties arising because of the behavioural problems of a young man with a learning disability, as it happened also named Paul. He was with us for only a short time. Paul would be in a mood of deep depression most of the time and suddenly, for no apparent reason, would become quite violent, grabbing and hitting out. In a former church where I was pastor we had a girl with a disability who suffered from convulsions, and some of the church folk simply couldn't cope with that and found it all acutely embarrassing. There may also be strange and peculiar expressions of behaviour such as laughing out loud during the service, or shouting, or getting up and walking out for no good reason or shaking the head from side to side. Some of the members would get irritated by these disruptive forms of behaviour and would avoid sitting anywhere near them. But shouldn't we in the church attempt, in a loving and gracious way, to understand one another and to see the unfamiliar behaviour of some as a challenge to our belief that the Christian fellowship is all-inclusive, with a place for all sorts and conditions of people?

From time to time tensions would arise even among the members of the group themselves, and just like the rest of us they would then exhibit anger, jealousy or meanness. This simply shows that the differences between those with a learning disability and the rest of us, who consider ourselves normal, are not as great as we think. To exhibit anger, jealousy and meanness is normal human behaviour, but we accept each other nevertheless. If we love God and understand the New Testament concept of the church as the family of God, we must respond to those with learning disabilities with real love and sensitivity and accept them as our brothers and sisters in the Lord Jesus Christ. It must never be a 'them and us' approach.

An enriching experience

Looking back on the privilege of having Paul and his friends worshipping with us over a number of years, we can ask what we learned from that experience and whether it helped us as a church. I have no doubt that we learned a great deal from it both as members and as leaders. We would have been much poorer had we not had Paul and his friends worshipping with us.

For many of us, it created a deeper awareness of the need for love and support for people afflicted by the problems associated with learning disability, ageing, and other physical and sensory handicaps. It has made us much more positive in realizing that they too can live full and enjoyable lives. None of us can feel sorry for Paul and Hughie and the others, because it is so evident that they are not suffering any more than the rest of us. What they do need is our love and understanding. But in many ways they taught us more about love, friendship and loyalty than we could ever teach them. In this respect they have given to all of us a deeper insight into the caring and compassionate aspects of the gospel. We can no longer be content to see the care of people with learning disabilities as the responsibility of government and Social Services alone; it involves the whole of society, and especially the Christian community.

Until quite recently, people like Paul and his friends were confined to large impersonal institutions, but with the implementation of the

Community Care Act in 1993 they are now encouraged either to live in their own homes, in residential care, or in homely settings in the community. This is a tremendous improvement because it meant for such people a much greater degree of independence and a greater sense of personal dignity. But looked at from the Christian perspective this social provision, whilst meeting many of the needs of those with learning disabilities, doesn't cover everything. There is still an important place for Christians and churches to play their part in showing that the Gospel of Jesus Christ can minister to the whole person, not only physically, emotionally and intellectually but also spiritually.

Through our involvement with Paul and his friends within the church fellowship, many of us came to understand in a much deeper way what is the essence of our humanity in the biblical meaning of that term. The Psalmist says, 'For you created my inmost being; you knit me together in my mother's womb. I praise you because I am fearfully and wonderfully made ... My frame was not hidden from you when I was made in the secret place. When I was woven together in the depths of the earth, your eyes saw my unformed body. All the days ordained for me were written in your book before one of them came to be' (Psalm 139:13-16). This is far removed from the language of today's abortionist, who speaks of the embryo as a 'product' of conception, 'womb tissue', 'a collection of cells', or 'just a foetus'.

The Psalmist reminds us that we each have our own special personality and identity as God's handiwork, and that we are not merely an evolutionary product that survives for a little while and then decays and falls to the ground like a leaf on a tree. This is as true of Paul, Hughie, Anthony, Peter and Jane as it is of the rest of us. Like us, they too are created in God's own image and likeness, and they too have an immortal soul which God desires to nourish and care for in order to bring out their full potential for his glory and to fulfil his purpose in the world. It was our privilege as a church to share in that process by having the group within our church family and, through fellowship and worshipping together, to help them nurture their faith in the Lord Jesus Christ.

For my own part, having Paul and his friends under my pastoral care, helped me personally to focus once more on the vexed problem of human fragility and disability in this life—and to straighten out some of my thinking on the matter. There are no easy solutions to some of the problems we encounter as God's children, neither are there any easy answers to some of the questions that arise concerning his dealings with us. This is because there is a mysterious side to the nature of God that we cannot get to grips with.

Among the last words of Moses to God's people was the reminder that 'The secret things belong to the Lord our God' (Deuteronomy 29:29). There are indeed many such secret and hidden things which can cause us deep frustration at the intellectual level, and a good deal of anguish at the emotional and spiritual level. The mystery of disability is one of them. When faced with the hurt and disappointment associated with the birth of a disabled child, the Christian may be tempted to ask, 'Why does God allow it if he is a God of love?' But deep in our heart we know that we should not blame God, and that God is not out to spoil our life. On the contrary, the Bible teaches that we are close to God's heart, and that he wants only what is for our good. Furthermore, God has proved his love for us through his own suffering in the death of his Son on the Cross for our salvation. In the light of this, we must keep in mind that the main purpose of the gospel is not to make us happy, or to provide a featherbed existence and a life free from hard questions. Its chief purpose is to reconcile us to God in Christ, and when we look at what lies ahead for the believer it is surely the case that 'Our present sufferings are not worth comparing with the glory that will be revealed in us' (Romans 8:18).

The cynic may continue to shake his fist at heaven and demand to know why God didn't make a world which is always kind and beautiful, without the ugliness of pain and suffering. But God did make a world like that. The only flaw was introduced by human nature. It was the sin and disobedience of Adam and Eve that tainted and distorted everything from the beginning. So, whether we like it or not we are part of a human system in which sin has entered, and unless we abdicate from the human race we have to learn to accept that that is just how it is. Only when we are willing to accept the ugly fact of sin, can we begin to act constructively towards resolving the tragedies caused by sin—by turning to God's own solution in the cross of the Lord Jesus Christ.

The presence among us of these loving people also helped some of us to gain a deeper understanding of our true selves, and of what life is really all about from the Bible's perspective. This may sound strange, but sometimes when I was in their company, talking and sharing with them, I felt I could almost envy their life-style. They have a serenity or simplicity about them which is far removed from the fast, glitzy lifestyles portrayed on the TV commercials and in the glossy magazines—and which we are all supposed to want desperately for ourselves. The values which underlie our society, and which shape the lives of millions of people, are for the most part cheap and superficial and are directed by greed, pride, ambition and selfishness. Added to this is the frenzied pace of life in our competitive world, with its mad scramble for the material prizes and the desire for success, which creates ever greater tensions and anxieties in people so that they become increasingly unhappy and discontented.

Once, when Jesus talked to the disciples about greatness, he stood a little child in front of them and said, 'I tell you the truth, unless you change and become like little children, you will never enter the kingdom of heaven' (Matthew 18:3). In saying that, our Lord was turning the world's value-system on its head. When I find myself in the company of Paul and his friends, I feel they are saying the same thing in a non-verbal way. What do we mean by greatness? Is it someone who is rich and famous, or who has achieved some renowned success in this life? If that is so, then Paul and his friends are completely out of the running, for in the opinion of many today the quality of life they enjoy is not worth having. But that was not our Lord's estimate of the Pauls and Hughies of this world when he took that little child and spoke to his followers about greatness in the light of eternity; 'Therefore whoever humbles himself like this child is the greatest in the kingdom of heaven' (Matthew 18:4).

I don't want to sentimentalize, but when I am in the group and hear Hughie laughing at his own jokes, Anthony voicing loudly and earnestly his opinions on some matter or other, Jane just sitting there smiling, Peter and Paul quiet and serious, then I have the feeling of being in the company of people who are happy and contented with life in a simple and yet profound way. But these are also the people who our clever, sophisticated, hedonistic society has little time for, and would look down upon pityingly and patronisingly—and even deny them the right to life. What arrogance and conceit that is. It is as if our flashy life-style is so superior to theirs, when in fact we have only to look at the violence, misery and hatred in our world to see the mess that our clever, sophisticated, hedonistic society has made of it all. With a little humility there is a lot we can learn from Paul and his friends which would give a simpler and gentler dimension to our lives and which in turn would bring us a greater sense of peace and contentment.

Entebbe!

Edison and Caroline Sempa

July 4th 1976 is an anniversary date that Edison and
Caroline Sempa would prefer to forget, but the results of
that fateful day will be with them for life. Seriously
wounded in an unequal shoot-out, the young soldier faced
a long struggle for survival, then for mobility and finally as
a refugee in a foreign country. As committed Christians
they are determined to serve Christ in their adopted
country without allowing disability to hinder them.

On June 27th 1976 an Air France civil airliner, en route from Tel Aviv to Paris, was highjacked by Palestinian terrorists. The plane was diverted to Benghazi in Libya, and here the non-Jewish passengers were released. The ninety-eight Jews on board were flown to Entebbe, in Uganda, where they were held as hostages in exchange for the release of Fatah terrorists in Israeli prisons. A week later, on Saturday July 3rd Israel's Cabinet made an unexpected and secret decision that resulted in one of the most incredible operations in military history. An airborne commando unit plucked the hostages from Entebbe airport, four thousand kilometres from Jerusalem. The daring raid, led by Yoni Netanyahu, the brother of the future Prime Minister of Israel, was an amazing success story. Sadly, an elderly Jewish hostage, who had earlier been removed to a local hospital, was murdered as a cruel reprisal, three other hostages were caught in cross fire, and Yoni Netanyahu was killed by a bullet through the heart. Apart from this, everything from an Israeli point of view went according to plan. But for me, First Lieutenant Sempa, an officer in the Ugandan army of Idi 'Big Daddy' Amin, Sunday, July 4th 1976, followed a very different and unexpected plan.

I was born in 1953 in Bushenyi District in the south-west of Uganda. My father was a soldier in the old days of colonialism and as a boy I always admired the way he looked in the smart uniform of the Kings African Rifles. He was tall and handsome—a real man to me—and I determined that when I grew up I would be like him and wear a soldier's uniform. He was away most of the time, but when he came home every four or five months, he always brought presents from the big city for us five boys and our sister. As a family we were nominal Christians, knowing something of the message of Christianity but not taking it very seriously. I loved to go to church every Sunday and sing Christian hymns, and my mother was keen to teach me to read the Bible, especially the Psalms which I loved so much, but I wasn't a true Christian. I attended different schools, both Protestant and Catholic, and when I left school I went straight into work employed by the Ministry of Agriculture, researching on economic data under the supervision of Makerere University, which was the only university in Uganda at the time.

In 1973 I joined the army, and after my basic training I was sent with other junior officers to the Baghdad Military College in Iraq where we were trained as marines and paratroopers. In my heart I knew this was a wrong career for me, but outwardly Idi Amin seemed a good and kind person. It was only much later that I discovered that he was a brutal dictator; anyway, as a soldier I thought I would be able to protect my own tribespeople. I was commissioned as a First Lieutenant, given charge of twenty marines attached to the Air Force, and based at Bugolobi in Kampala. Our base included one of the best equipped hospitals in the city, and civilians were not infrequently referred to it for treatment. Early in 1974 I met Caroline Kisanyu while she was waiting for treatment for malaria. We fell in love, and before the end of the year we were married.

Uganda was an Islamic country, and since most of my fellow officers were Muslims, life was very hard for me. Although I was only a nominal Christian, I was often confined to barracks and not allowed out when the others were free to do so. It also meant that I was frequently ridiculed and given some of the duties that others despised. On the occasions when I was allowed a pass, I went to the only Christian services that I could find; these were often secret meetings in people's homes. My conversion took place in a suburb of Kampala. I was invited to a Christian meeting held in a garage that had been turned into a worship centre. The meeting took place at night because of the fear of persecution by Amin's Islamic anti-Christian regime. During the singing, and even more so during the preaching and praying, God touched me in a special way; he brought me to my knees and I surrendered my life to the only Saviour and Lord. Caroline and I were living in married quarters at the time and when I told her about my decision to follow Christ, she was not only happy but also determined to find out more for herself. Whenever possible, we attended meetings together.

Idi Amin was out of the country when the hostages arrived at Entebbe. As Chairman of the Organization of African Unity he had attended a summit meeting in Mauritius. Whenever the president was due to return, security was very tight at the airport. The added responsibility was that we had to guard the new airport, in which international planes landed, as well as the old airport in which the hostages were being held. The two airports were about a thousand metres apart, but the head of state always used the new airport. General Idi Amin had sent additional soldiers, ostensibly to guard the airport, but in reality to safeguard the Palestinians whilst they threatened the hostages and negotiated with the Israeli Government.

Entebbe shoot-out

July 3rd 1976 was not like any other day. The previous evening, while we were preparing our equipment for duty, I felt distinctly uneasy and something disturbed me that I could not shake off. I was not actually rostered for duty that day, but was covering for a fellow officer who was away. I had been ordered to take my unit to the airport, and when I assessed the situation I knew that something was not right. The men travelled to the airport light-heartedly, chanting our usual army songs and ready for a twenty-four hour duty. The officers' briefing had informed us that security was to be extra tight because a plane containing foreigners was at the old airport. This is all we were told, but an uneasy feeling kept pounding in my heart. I had been a Christian for almost a year but I was not fully committed to Christ and in many ways my life was inconsistent. Perhaps God was speaking to me, but at that time I could not discern his voice. I now realise that he was preparing me for something that would change the whole course of my life.

Once on duty I soon picked up that the 'foreigners' were Jewish hostages, guarded by well-armed Palestinian terrorists. It was wise for us to mind our own business and simply carry out our usual guard duties. As the only Christian soldier on duty that night I felt sorry for the Jewish hostages who were being ill-treated and terrified by their captors. An order had been given for mattresses and food to be sent to the hostages, and although I dared not show my sympathy for them to my superior officers, I was in charge of delivering these provisions to the Israelis. I prayed for them as I went about my duties. But all the time I knew something was going to happen—though I had no idea what it would be. As the light faded, we were looking forward to the end of our shift. We should have been relieved at about 20.00 hours, but the other unit was late in arriving, and even when they did arrive, I knew that I would have to stay late to pass on the orders for the night.

Our President arrived at Entebbe around 23.00 hours and we were told that he was to come and speak with the hijackers. He knew exactly what had been happening because he was the one who had authorized the Palestinians to land. He was welcomed at the old airport by the soldiers and straight away went to speak with the hijackers and hostages. My unit remained outside, being extra vigilant. After finishing his business, he was driven to the State House. It was now approaching midnight and still the relieving unit had not shown up. The building in which the hostages were held had many rooms and the off-duty soldiers had quarters there. My unit was exhausted, we had been on duty for eleven hours and we just wanted to stand down and go to sleep.

. It was now Sunday July 4th and it was very dark. I did not leave my position to go and check why the others were running late, instead, I stayed on guard duty outside the building. As I stood there, alone, I felt in my mind that something was already happening. It was very unusual for a shift change to run this late, especially in the military where punctuality is all-important. I was so desperately tired that I had a struggle to keep my eyes open, but I dared not fall asleep on duty! As I waited, I could hear some sort of commotion. My Captain, Mohammed Yahayah, and I watched as a number of vehicles approached and surrounded us. Due to exhaustion I was absent minded for a moment and did not immediately assess the situation. Suddenly I was jerked into reality by an order from my Captain, 'Edison, go and check who those people are. The Head of State has already left, and that place is out of bounds.' The vehicles kept coming towards us, all the time flashing their headlights furiously. I gripped my gun and was about to obey the order when one of the soldiers said, 'Edison's voice is not strong enough Sir. Let me go.' The lights of the jeeps were so bright that while Gogo charged at the gate to stop them, it looked as if he was under a spotlight. When he reached the gate, he started shouting, 'Ho la po, ho la po', which is Swahili for 'Stop immediately.' He gave the order clearly and repeatedly. In the army, if you ever heard this order by your superior and did not comply at once, specially when entering a barracks or going on guard duty, you would be gunned down. Even if you were in the middle of a sneeze or a sentence that order would make you freeze! But those vehicles did not stop they just kept on drawing closer and closer, totally disregarding the order. Adrenaline started rushing through my body and it was then that I heard the first round of ammunition being fired.

I watched as Gogo slowly fell to the ground. I had no time to recall that that should have been me. I heard the second round, and then all that I could see was fire in the air. Shells and bullets flew everywhere. I saw people unloading from the jeeps, running around us and spreading in all

Above: Edison and Caroline are the proud parents of five boys and an adopted daughter

directions. I took cover, changed my position, and jumped to another position. As fast as I moved to a new position bullets seemed to follow me. There was a deafening blur as bullets whizzed about, hitting the floor, buildings, and sadly, my soldiers. Suddenly I felt the searing pain of a bullet entering my flesh. I fell to the ground and lay still. Two bullets had entered my buttock through the right femur and damaged my right sciatic nerve. I felt them tear through my bones and stop! Another bullet passed so close to the left side of my head that it left a severe burn. If I had moved a fraction to the left, the bullet would have entered my brain. It all seemed so unreal. I could not believe that I had really been hit.

I knew that I must not scream and that somehow I must find cover. There was an area of ground that was in deep shadow and my aim was to get there in order not to be noticed. I was already a target marked for death. I could no longer hear the voice of my Captain or that of any of the other soldiers. I knew that I had to stay down, keep under cover and not make a sound. I had been trained to roll or crawl in a situation like this so that I would not be seen. The Israeli commandos just kept on shelling. I knew that it was useless to return the fire; I was completely surrounded and could not see where to direct my aim. To open fire would simply betray my position. I concluded that when surrounded by an enemy that is well armed, determined, and unseen, a seriously wounded soldier is probably wiser to remain quiet! In fact, the Israeli commandos killed every wounded soldier they found.

I was bleeding very badly, but I found myself extremely calm. The pain was unbearable and that is when I cried out to God. I found myself saying, 'Oh God, I have been shot, please save me. Save me Lord and I will serve you for the rest of my life.' In the history of warfare, how many soldiers have prayed that prayer? But this one meant it, and I kept my word. The bullets stopped and I started to crawl painfully into the darker areas. Airports are mostly open land and it would normally be impossible to find a hiding place. God gave me the strength to crawl until I came across a large box; I never discovered where that box had come from. I prayed for strength to break it open and then to get inside. Unfortunately I didn't quite fit the box, so the lower part of my body had to remain outside! Crawling to that box was the most painful journey I have ever travelled. I lay in my box and listened, helplessly, as the melee continued all around me. The gunfire became more and more sporadic and finally died away. Then I faintly heard the Israelis gathering their people to the planes and the roar of the aircraft as they took off. The Israeli Commandos, with all of the hostages, flew away. I was left alone in my box and surrounded by an eerie silence.

At that time I had no idea what had happened or who the attacking soldiers were. Nor did I know that I was the sole survivor from my entire unit. I just lay in the box in severe pain and trying to stem the flow of blood from my right leg. But it was no use, the blood filled my boots until it felt like thick wet mud. After a while, I couldn't feel any sensation in my body; I was like a block of wood. I felt my breath slowly fading away. I found it hard to breathe, and knowing that any one gasp could be my last I had to breathe aloud to assure myself that I was still alive.

After about an hour, but what seemed like for ever to me, units of the Ugandan Army arrived to take control of the now deserted battle area. I heard tanks and people talking, but I was so weak that I could not even recognise the language that was being spoken. I heard ambulances, but I couldn't call out because I was too weak. Twice I tried to shout, but no sound came out of my mouth. Then I prayed to God for strength. Once again I tried to call out and now a sound came out of my mouth, 'Wajama mimi Edison Sempa ya Marine, Kugye saide mimi!' ('People, it is me, Edison Sempa from the Marine, please help me'). As it happened Wandele, a friend of mine who was an officer from the tank corps, heard my faint cry and came running over with some of his men. I heard them cock their guns and then Wandele called out 'Nani? Nani?' (Who is it? Who is it?). I could only reply 'It's me, Sempa.' That name told them my tribe and the Captain asked in my tribal tongue, 'Sempa, who put you in this box?' It was with great difficulty on their part and a lot of pain on mine that I was pulled from the box. At one point the soldiers pulled at my legs to get me out! The injured leg caused me excruciating pain.

I was rushed to Entebbe General Hospital but by the time I arrived I was unconscious. Only later did I learn that all our soldiers on duty at the airport that night were killed. My wife Caroline came to my bedside and she sat with me during the long days when I was unconscious. After a while I could hear the distant voice of Caroline urging me to eat something, but I could not respond. I felt my leg hanging limply in the bed.

Caroline's story

It was around 6.30 in the morning when I received news of the Entebbe airport incident from the Radio Uganda. There was little detail, simply the announcement that the Israelis had taken back their people who had been hijacked by Palestinians. All the same it was terribly frightening to me, because I knew that Edison was on duty that night. I could do nothing but wait for any further information from the barracks or friends. As it approached 7.00 am there was a knock on the door and with fear and trembling I opened it. A friend of Edison from the barracks brought news that was frightening to listen to. I found myself silently praying to God, 'I need your strength. Amen.' I had no words in my mouth to pray because my mouth was dry and my whole body was shaking. The young officer remained calm, as if there was nothing wrong. I broke the silence and asked him whether he had received the news in the morning. He said 'Yes' and was suddenly quiet again. So I asked him whether he had heard anything about Edison. He bowed his head, and I could see from his face that he had bad news. He told me that Edison had been badly wounded and that they had rushed him to Mulago Hospital, which is our biggest hospital in Uganda. I asked whether Edison was still alive, and he replied that he was not sure because a lot of soldiers that had died were all taken to Mulago Hospital so that their relatives could identify their loved ones. By now we were both in tears.

Within a short while my neighbours arrived to ask me whether I had heard what happened at Entebbe Airport. Edison was a friend to so many and soon the house was full with friends and relatives crying. This only made me feel more and more alone. Some of the friends that came to see me were Christians who we used to have fellowship with on Sundays, and their prayers comforted me and I sensed that God was with me in my time of fear and discomfort. Edison and I were Christians, but we were not very committed; we went to church on Sunday and that was all. I sat down quietly and asked myself, where do I start now? God is so good all the time and he is faithful. Immediately I seemed to hear a small voice saying, 'So do not fear, for I am with you' (Isaiah 41:10).

I knew that I had to go to the army barracks to get more information and to ask how I could get to Mulago Hospital. I desperately needed to confirm whether Edison was alive or dead. In the end I gathered all my courage and made the journey to the barracks. When I arrived, I sensed that many people had died. Everywhere was very quiet—there were no radios turned on and no children playing outside. The whole barracks was in great pain. As I entered the main office, an officer quickly stood and asked me whether I was the wife of Edison. He held his breath for a moment and quietly reported, 'I am very sorry to tell you, your husband was severely shot, and he has lost a lot of blood.' He went on to say that nobody was sure whether Edison was still alive. There was nothing that I could say except to ask if they would provide transport for me to Mulago Hospital. Within no time a Landrover was made available to take me to and from the hospital.

The journey to the hospital was a very miserable one. It seemed as if the vehicle was not moving and the miles had doubled. Thoughts rushed around in my head and I did not even know where to start looking for Edison. We finally reached the hospital around 2.00 pm. The driver came with me to the reception and asked whether we could see Lieutenant Edison Sempa, who was involved in the Israeli raid at Entebbe Airport. The receptionist told us exactly where we would find Edison. Suddenly panic gripped me; doubts flooded my mind and I didn't know whether I could handle this situation. I wondered whether I should go on or turn back and go home. We started walking to the ward, but I walked with great fear. I did not know what to expect. I did not know whether I was going to arrive just too late.

I was not prepared for what I found. I tried to look at Edison's face, but I could not recognize that it was him. His face had changed. He could not lift his head, and when I touched him he did not respond. I sat down and cried. Then I found that in my heart I was thanking God that Edison did not die at the airport. I found faith to believe that since he did not die immediately, God was going to heal him. I knew that it would be a hard time ahead, but the Lord was on my side. People arrived minute by minute, crying, praying and giving thanks to God for the life of Edison.

Edison and I had a baby of four months old who still needed a mother's care, and leaving my baby at home with a young girl of just ten years was another worry. But he also was in the hands of God. The time at the hospital was agonizing. I could hear people crying for their loved ones who had been killed; on my part I kept touching Edison to feel whether his heart was still working. Every day was a miracle because no one expected him to live another day. Even the doctors were convinced that his time was over, but God's time is unpredictable.

For one long month there was no response from Edison. He could neither eat nor drink and I sat hour after hour waiting for his final breath. I worried about the pressure sores he developed because he was lying on one side without any movement. Edison had a lot of friends who came to visit, and they encouraged and comforted me in that hard time. When Edison's parents heard the news about their son, his father rushed to Kampala to see him before his last breath. It was also a shock to him, but he stood as a man and started caring for his son. I felt a change when he came because we encouraged each other.

During this time I was learning that there is no one to trust in this world but only God. Money was not the answer, only God who created heaven and earth. I decided to rededicate myself to God and accept his word in my heart. I asked God to take away all the fears that I had and to help me stand completely in him for everything. I would come each morning to see how Edison was, but it was the same story—no improvement, but his breath was still there.

Exactly one month passed without any response, and then God began his miracle in Edison. When I came in one morning I met my father-in-law in the corridor. My heart started thumping and I thought, 'Edison is dead.' When my father-in-law looked at me he could see that I was afraid and, with my lips and voice trembling, I asked why he was standing in the corridor instead of being near his son in case he needed help. 'I was waiting for you', he answered. Then he laughed and said, 'Guess what, now your husband can see!' I became a doubting Thomas and said that unless I could see for myself I would not believe. I rushed to the ward and when I got to his bed, Edison immediately lifted his head and looked at me. The first words that came out of my mouth were, 'If God is for us who can be against us?' (Romans 8:31). My father-in-law and I joined together and gave thanks. The doctors could not believe that Edison would ever see this world again and all our friends were just waiting for the death announcement. I believe this was really a second chance that we were given to live again, this time for God. Now my faith grew in a way that I had never known in my life before. While reading the word of God, I came across Philippians 1:6, 'Being confident of this, that he who began a good work in you will carry it on to completion until the day of Jesus Christ.' I stood on that powerful Scripture at all times and shared my confidence with others.

From the day Edison began to open his eyes, his face started coming back to normal. The next morning I brought our five-month-old son to see his daddy, and when Edison saw his baby he was able to manage a little smile. I started praying that Edison would begin to talk again, because it had been almost six weeks without me hearing any words from him. The doctors were not giving me any promises at all. Church friends continued coming in and praying every day and giving thanks to God for Edison's life. As time went on, he started sipping some drinks and milk, and now he showed a big improvement. His voice developed slowly, and within two months he could whisper to those who were close to him. What a miracle! Life became just a little more normal. But there was a lot to fit in, as my baby needed more of my attention. I saw the hand of God on Edison and believed God in everything. What is impossible in my eyes, is possible with God (see Luke 1:37). Everyone who visited Edison in the hospital believed that the God we serve is faithful and ready to help in time of need.

West Germany

Caroline's quiet and calm support nursed me back to recovery. Even Idi Amin came to visit this sole survivor among his Ugandan troops at the airport. He held my hand and said that everything would be 'all right', assuring me that if necessary I would be sent to England or West Germany for further treatment. No expense would be spared for the medical care of this young officer. I believe God moved the heart of Amin to make compassionate decisions that were beyond him naturally. He called my clinical professor to arrange specialized treatment for me abroad and promised that the Ugandan government would provide all the necessary expenses. I thought about Psalm 91:14, '"Because he loves me", says the Lord, "I will rescue him; I will protect him, for he acknowledges my name."' During that time the doctors tried to save my right leg but unfortunately too much damage had been done. Meanwhile, every day I woke with pain and slept with pain. The pain was unbearable and each day my life was hanging on a thread. The pain was so great that I could not sleep or even relax for a while. My friends, especially my non-Christian friends, had lost all hope for me. Caroline stayed by my side to give me support with her love and prayers, and this kept me going day by day.

I struggled to regain strength and some little mobility, but I could hardly move, developed pressure sores and lost my appetite completely. It was evident to both Caroline and myself that if I stayed in hospital much longer I would simply waste away. Besides, I was fed up with hospital, and after seven months I persuaded the senior consultant to allow me to go home. I still had to visit the hospital daily, but at least Caroline could help me build up my strength. However, it was clear that my progress was painfully slow, and my consultant recommended that I should be sent to the United Kingdom for urgent treatment. Unfortunately the British

Government refused me permission.

We did not give up hope and my church prayed with us. Eventually I received the news that I was to be taken to Germany for treatment. At the hospital in Bonn the specialists spent three months trying to reconstruct my sciatic nerves and encourage the blood to flow in my leg. After a while I was allowed to stay in a hotel and attend the hospital daily. It was a lonely time, and I missed my family terribly. But I learnt to speak German so that I could talk with those around me, and although I had no Christian fellowship I grew to rely more upon the Lord himself.

In May 1978 I was informed by a surgical consultant that the painful swelling on my right hip was a tumour which, if left untreated, would be fatal within two or three months. A few days previously I had had a lovely vision, and it helped me as I now received this bad news. I had just attended another hospital appointment where I had been told that yet more scans and tests would be needed to find out what was wrong; I was feeling angry that all the previous tests and treatments had turned out to be a waste of time. As I stood in the sunshine, I saw a shadow that formed a cross; suddenly the thought came to me, 'Take your problems to the cross and leave them there.' Was it just a shadow, or a message from God? I needed time to think. Somehow the flowers appeared especially beautiful, their perfume so strong, and the butterflies looked so dainty. I knew that God was in control. In my mind I took to the cross all the pain I had been experiencing and the fear of the diagnosis; I gave it all to Jesus.

Following various scans, I was told the worst possible news, yet I felt incredibly peaceful because of that recent experience. A large abscess was pressing on my bones in the joint where the knee-joint joins the leg. The original suggestion was to try to replace the nerves in order to save my leg. But this was found to be too late. The only alternative was amputation below the knee. This meant my removal to another hospital, this time in Cologne. The consultant there advised me that two surgical teams would be needed to operate to remove the abscess on the femur and to amputate the leg below the knee. I would be in intensive care for a few days and would be in hospital for at least six weeks. As the abscess was on the bone near the main sciatic nerve, the surgery could prove fatal. Other possible complications would be bone infection and damage. I was told to expect temporary, and possibly permanent, paralysis of the right side with no sensibility or movement. If all went well, I could at least be promised a lot of physiotherapy to aid future mobility, but for some weeks I would be limited to a wheel chair.

This was hardly a cheerful prospect, but God enabled me to remain amazingly peaceful on hearing this schedule of treatment. The consultant asked me what I would do until the operation. I replied, 'Pray a bit more and trust a bit harder.' I remember his cynical smile as he said, 'If that is what keeps you happy. Anyway, we can do with all the help we can get with this one.' Surgery was arranged for July 4th, when two of the best surgical teams would be available. My family was naturally very anxious for me, and in my phone calls home I tried to reassure Caroline; but from a few thousand miles distant it was not easy; I honestly did not know whether these next few weeks would be my last. My mother was amazed at my calm faith and at times she felt very angry about the situation. On the other hand, Caroline was a tower of strength and confidence to me. The ministers and members of our church back in Kampala—Makerere Redeemed Society of the Lord—were wonderfully supportive. God kept reminding me of encouraging Bible promises and the song, 'I know who holds the future and he will guide me with his hand.' The minister of my church, Isaac Wilson Balinda, arranged a prayer rota to cover the time of the operation, and the church members experienced the same peace and strength that I enjoyed.

When I came round from the operation I had my first experience of phantom pain. I could feel a dull ache in my leg and concluded that, after all, they had been able to save it. When one of the nurses came to me I commented hopefully, 'Ruth, I think my leg is alright.' She looked at me tearfully and replied, 'No Edison, they took it away.' Then she gave me a big hug, and we cried together. To the amazement of all the doctors and nurses I was immediately able to speak normally and by the next day I was able to eat. My surgeon, Dr Immüser, told me that the operation had gone brilliantly, better than anyone had expected. When he came to me on his ward rounds he would frequently exclaim 'Edison—miracle; Edison— miracle.' After four weeks I was able to walk on my own with the aid of a frame on wheels. Caroline and my family back at home, together with my fellow Christians, were all jubilant at the way God was answering their prayers. However many of my relatives who did not share my Christian faith were confused, and were sure that something was bound to go wrong soon.

My progress was so good that some of the follow-up treatment that had been planned was cancelled and the second expected operation was not needed at all. I began to take walking lessons again and the exercise proved to be at times amusing and interesting and at other times very difficult. But I was determined to walk again. Soon, I was able to return to my hotel in Badgodsburg and for the next two months I made regular trips to the hospital's outpatients department.

Return home to danger

At the end of 1978 I was fit enough to return to Uganda. I looked forward to going back to my family in order to comfort them and to rebuild my life again. But if I thought that my troubles were over, I was mistaken. The following year Idi Amin was toppled from power and the whole world learned just how brutal his regime had been. Amin fled to Saudi Arabia, and terrible fighting followed as the Tanzanian army aided the Ugandan rebels to take control of the country. All those known to have been in Amin's army were hunted down and imprisoned; many were massacred. I found myself in a military prison for one night and it was only by a miracle that I was released the next morning.

Knowing that my life was in danger I fled to our family farm in the country, some two hundred miles from Kampala. As the troops entered the city they looted everything; we lost our house and all our possessions, and the only thing that I could do was to rely entirely upon God. Caroline fled to the bush with the children and I was so anxious for them that I decided to risk returning to the city. I reported to the local military commander in order to obtain a permit for travel. This time I took the precaution of removing my leg to prove that I would be useless to an enemy! He apparently was convinced when confronted by this broken man on crutches, and I received my permit. Many of my friends were either killed or imprisoned. Eventually I found my family and took them back to the country with me.

For two years we managed, though there was little enough to eat. Gradually, as people drifted back from the city to take refuge in the villages, the countryside was no longer a safe place to live. At least in the city we could be lost in the crowd, so we cautiously returned to Kampala. We shared a house with a friend and his family, and Caroline started a small business selling clothes. We were also back at our church and among the Christian family where we could feel the warmth of love and the security of friendship. For my part, I started a non-profit organization for the disabled. It was called Disabled Progressive Self-help Project (DISPROCO). A few disabled people like myself decided to help ourselves and others by earning our own living. We held weekly meetings for planning and encouragement and I was soon appointed as the Public Relations Officer. My job was to encourage companies to either employ disabled people or to provide ways in which they could help themselves. With the help of Oxfam we started making trays out of old newspapers; a Japanese company even gave us a Toyota pick-up truck. By 1984 we had one hundred members and employed over thirty people in our factory.

Sadly, by 1985 the country was once more in turmoil, with guerrilla bush warfare, horrible rumours everywhere, and many deaths. When a new government was installed in 1986 our hope for peace never materialised. Things only got worse. However, I was by now very actively engaged in Christian work. I preached in the streets of Kampala and was invited abroad to attend Christian conferences and to give my testimony of God's grace in my life. I visited Amsterdam, Singapore and even America, where I spent four months speaking at churches and to the military. I had no idea that this would cause me so much trouble!

On my return to Uganda everyone was suspicious of everyone. My passport was promptly taken away from me and I was called in for interrogation. My passport showed that I had travelled widely, and since there is no way that I could afford such extravagance I was thought to be an agent for a foreign country. It was with great difficulty that I persuaded the authorities that I was simply a Christian attending Christian conferences and churches, and that it was those churches that had been paying my fare. I was allowed to return to my village, but the suspicion and fear continued. By 1989 I was warned that someone was looking for me, and I knew instinctively what this meant. It was time to leave.

Escape to England

Caroline left the country first and alone. She arrived in Britain with no contact and no address, the cold of an English winter, and the loneliness of an unknown refugee. These were frightening prospects for a girl who had never been outside Uganda before. The London Borough of Merton had a place available in Mitcham for Ugandan asylum seekers and Caroline's first prayer was that God would lead her to a Christian church where she could worship and find friendship. It was all very confusing as there were many churches in Mitcham. However, someone recommended Mitcham Baptist Church and it was just what she had hoped for. Caroline commented, 'The first day I visited was very exciting; the pastor welcomed me warmly and the whole congregation was so happy to meet me. The love of God in the church has continued to this day.' The church joined in prayer for the rest of the family who were still in Uganda. Caroline had no idea where her children were, or whether I was dead or alive.

In November 1990 Caroline received a call to say that her five boys were at the airport! She had received no prior information that they had got out of Uganda or how, but it was a wonderful reunion. I arrived in England on March 19th 1991 with my only two remaining possessions: my nine-year-old adopted daughter Barbara and a walking stick. Five years after my escape, my younger brother, a fine Christian man who worked in the office of the Minister of Education, was murdered in Kampala. He left a wife and three small children. I know that I would have died also if I had still been there.

By the time I managed to escape from Uganda I had lost touch with Caroline. I had been in prison and then in hiding and all our contact had been broken. Eventually the immigration authorities located the rest of the family and I made my way to Mitcham on Sunday April 7th 1991, just one week after Easter Sunday. But nobody was in—all the family was at church—so I sat on the doorstep and waited! That afternoon Caroline sent a note to Roger Watkins, the pastor of Mitcham Baptist Church; it was a beautiful understatement of our happy reunion and my utter exhaustion, 'Dear beloved pastor, Praise the Lord so much. I thank the Lord for you and the whole church for the prayers you offered for my husband. I found him at home after the service. I would have liked him to come and greet the church but he was a bit tired. We shall meet you on Sunday. God bless you. Caroline Sempa.' The following Sunday the whole church gathered in a circle around us to praise God for the remarkable deliverance of our whole family, and our five boys sang to the congregation.

My first shock was the weather! After escaping from a hot country, it was so cold in England. Our second shock was the adjustment to a culture that we thought would be Christian. Instead, we found that there were so many nominal Christians without any commitment to the Saviour; people were careless about the teaching of the Bible, and Sunday was treated as just another working day. I was not prepared for all this. But the first day I entered the doors of Mitcham Baptist Church is one that I will treasure all my life. Smiling and happy faces welcomed me. There have always been people who have opened their doors and hearts to us. The welcome was real and full of the love and joy of Jesus Christ. That joy and love has kept us there to the present time.

With the encouragement of my family and Roger Watkins, I was able to spend three years at Spurgeon's Baptist College to be trained for Christian service. I later attended the two-year *Prepare for Service* course at Reading which is organised by the Fellowship of Independent Evangelical Churches. At the end of this course I was invited to serve as an honorary staff member at Mitcham Baptist Church. At long last I felt that I had fulfilled the promise I made to God as I lay dying on the battlefield at Entebbe airport twenty-two years earlier. I am now so happy to be a Christian worker in the pastoral team of the church that took me in, befriended my family and me, and helped to pay my student fees. Living in an area populated by people from many nationalities gives me a wonderful opportunity to share with them the life of hope and purpose that I began on the battlefield at Entebbe. Every life touched by the power of God is a story we will hear in heaven.

God's ability in my disability

Caroline and I have six children. Emmanuel is the youngest, Moses is studying at the University of Sussex in Brighton, Barbara lives away from home and works as a trainee solicitor, Geoffrey and Arnold are currently on placement, midway through their university course, and Ronald works as a chef. All our children are following the Saviour as their Lord. I certainly miss not being able to play football or cycle, but at least I can drive a car. I still suffer from severe phantom pains in my absentee leg, and often in the summer months I am grounded by sores that force me to leave off my prosthesis for two weeks at a time. But God takes my disabilities and replaces them with his abilities. Proverbs 3:5-7 has often come to me powerfully from the Lord, 'Trust in the LORD with all your heart and lean not on your own understanding; in all your ways acknowledge him, and he will make your paths straight. Do not be wise in your own eyes; fear the LORD and shun evil. This will bring health to your body and nourishment to your bones.'

I certainly know the truth of God's promise in 1 Corinthians 1:27-29, 'God chose the foolish things of the world to shame the wise; God chose the weak things of the world to shame the strong. He chose the lowly things of this world and the despised things... so that no one may boast before him.' Through my family and me God can show how kind and how powerful he is. I have a strong belief that all that has happened to me was God's plan before I was born. We serve the God who knows the end from the beginning.

Horizons

Graham and Tessa Pole

Between them, Graham and Tessa can log over one hundred years of experience of life from a wheelchair! In that time they have overcome most of the obstacles to living a meaningful life: they are married, they have travelled, and they run their own home. Their dogged determination and their keen sense of humour have turned what could have been disaster into a story of the triumph of faith over adversity. Brian Edwards, who was their pastor for fifteen years, tells their story.

Saturday 26 May 1973 was a perfect day for a wedding. The sun ruled in a cloudless late spring sky over the church of St Francis in Selsdon, Surrey. The bridegroom and his best man were early in their place, well before the two hundred guests had arrived. The groom boasted a pale purple shirt and a smart brown and blue flecked suit; his shoes were polished until they reflected the brilliance of the day. The congregation settled into their seats and, in the usual barely subdued whispers, discussed and guessed at the bride's outfit. When she arrived, thirty minutes late and in a white Mercedes, she wore an attractive lilac dress made of crimplene, with long sleeves and a short skirt; her hair was decorated with flowers. The two young bridesmaids completed the scene in their neat blue dresses with floral yokes. The day and setting were just right, and everyone was excited and happy. It would have been like any other wedding except for the fact that the bride and groom were severely disabled and confined to wheelchairs.

Between them, Graham and Tessa had spent a total of sixty years in hospital and residential care. These two wartime babies suffered from cerebral palsy that left them with little or no muscular use in their legs, and with Tessa's speech so seriously affected that it took her many years to learn to articulate normal sounds. Life, for both of them, had been a long and uphill struggle against loneliness, the indifference of society, the usual frustrations of the disabled, and finally the over-protectiveness of well-intentioned carers who could not imagine the possibility of Graham and Tessa living together as husband and wife.

Graham was born in Harrow, North London, a few months before the outbreak of World War II. He was an only child and his mother tried hard to care for him. But there was little support at a time when the nation had seemingly more important issues and greater tragedies to occupy its attention. A grand outing for the toddler with callipers to the waist, was an exhausting walk to the nearby cake shop which was owned by his grandmother. His reward for the journey was one of her special home-baked cookies.

Pictured overleaf: Wedding day 26 May 1973 marked a turning point in an uphill struggle against the over-protectiveness of a society that could not imagine how Graham and Tessa could possibly live together independently as husband and wife

During the early years of his life, Graham had no friends, few people visited, and for most of the time he simply stayed at home. He occupied his time by starting a stamp collection, which he still enjoys half a century later, and by listening to his records. The old 78s were played again and again. Rock was his favourite, but he could enjoy most music and his feet and legs longed to roll with Lonnie Donnegan and Acker Bilk, but whenever he tried it, he always ended up as an untidy heap on the floor! Tapestry also caught his imagination, and when he was not peeling potatoes for his grandmother—a childhood occupation ingrained in his memory because he hated it—he could be found at his tapestry frame while listening to Lonnie. In spite of having no friends and no visitors, Graham was reasonably happy, if only because few demands were placed on him and besides, never associating with able children meant that he had little knowledge of any alternative to his own lonely way of life.

When his mother was weakened by glandular fever and the onset of a heart condition, Graham was shunted between relatives until, at the age of twelve, he began his long experience of residential homes; first in Croydon and then in Broadstairs. Finally, at the age of eighteen he arrived back in Croydon and settled into a new home. Here, at Coombe Farm, he was to stay for the next seventeen years of his life.

Coombe Farm was an old Victorian farmhouse that had been purchased by the Spastics Society (renamed Scope in 1994). It boasted a grand reception area with an impressive staircase and a huge panelled dining room. The servants' rooms had been converted into bedrooms to house the forty or so residents, each of whom suffered from cerebral palsy in one of its varied forms. They arrived at the age of sixteen and were supposed to move on at twenty-five, but since there was nowhere for them to go, most stayed on longer. The old farmhouse was situated in acres of woodlands, gardens, and even a golf course for the public. An added swimming pool was especially popular. The Spastics Society was breaking new ground in their attempt to care for these disabled young people, about whom most of the nation cared little.

The daily routine at Coombe Farm meant that the residents were up at seven in the morning in order to breakfast by eight. They settled to contract work and craftwork from nine until midday and the afternoon 'shift' ran from one o'clock to five. The contract work was boringly tedious for many of the residents who were capable of much more than gluing plastic buttons for hours on end. In those days Coombe Farm was enlightened in encouraging the residents to dress themselves, and they were even able to try their hand at cooking cakes from time to time. However, they never had to think for themselves, and all decisions that affected their lives were made for them. Some parents assumed that their children would never grow up and would always remain child-like; consequently some were treated like this well into young adulthood. Most activities, even the entertainment offered on Saturday evening, was compulsory; you attended whether you wanted to or not. An assembly was held each morning and several churches took turns to conduct services on Sunday. Bible classes were available as an option.

Graham made the best of his new surroundings. His quick mind and keen sense of humour helped him through most disappointments, but not even Lonnie Donnegan could get Graham's legs moving and the callipers were replaced by a wheelchair.

Tessa was born in Bungay, Suffolk in 1940, when Britain appeared to be losing the war. She was the youngest of four children, though a brother tragically died under anaesthetic whilst having his tonsils and adenoids removed; he was just eight years old. It was six months before Tessa's condition was diagnosed and eventually she was accepted by a hospital in Norwich 'to see what they could do for her', but after a year she caught measles and was sent home. A short stay in Great Ormond Street Hospital for Sick Children did not help her much. After two operations, and experiments with every available type of walking aid, Tessa left hospital still unable to walk.

Tessa was an oddity in a small village unused to disability, and wherever she went people stared at her. She played with her cousins and her sister to relieve her mother a little, but by the age of five Tessa's mother, with the best of intentions, was unable to cope with her young daughter's severe problems any longer. Tessa found herself in a hospital in Hampshire and for the next six years she never went home. Her only contact was with the children around her—all of whom suffered from a wide range of disabilities. They were given two hours for lessons each morning, and spent the rest of the day in bed. Tessa played endlessly with her few dolls. The most exciting activity of the day was the arrival of the physiotherapist, when at least the children could escape from their bed for a short time of exercise. A full programme of education, physiotherapy, occupational therapy and speech training was yet to be developed for children like Graham and Tessa. The Spastics Society had not yet been formed, and looking back Tessa concludes, 'We were somewhere between the deaf and the blind; no one knew quite what to do with us.'

No one thought to explain her disability to Tessa, but she picked up the drift of her condition along the way. This was confirmed when, at the age of eight, Tessa overhead a doctor and nurse discussing her case, 'She's got cerebral palsy', commented the nurse, 'but she doesn't understand.' 'Oh, but I do', thought the sharp eight-year old. Bright she may have been, but it wasn't obvious. Without the challenge of normal children around her, and with no serious attempt to teach her to talk properly, Tessa appeared to be simple and awkward. At the age of ten and a half, Tessa was sent to a boarding school in Wiltshire, but it proved to be a short stay; she was experiencing trouble with her bladder, and because she was thought to be incontinent, she was sent home.

For a while Tessa and her mother struggled on together at home. It was a hard and lonely experience. Although her mother tried to do the very best for her, she could barely cope with a young teenage daughter who was severely disabled, could not speak properly, and was becoming rebellious in spirit. There were no social workers, no one to help, and nobody called. Tessa's mother despairingly commented once that she could bury Tessa in the garden and no one would know. A clergyman called to see if Tessa wanted to be confirmed, and she said yes because it was at least something to do. The ritual was duly performed, and Tessa and her mother occasionally attended church.

In 1957 there was a new move, this time to Coombe Farm where Graham had arrived eighteen months earlier. Tessa and her mother hoped that one day she would get better, but the reality was slowly dawning. The careless pessimism of doctors only served to reinforce the fact that she had little hope of improvement and a bleak future. Tessa's speech was unintelligible and consequently people avoided her; she was treated as though she was simple. She had no friends and nothing to look forward to. Her horizon had closed in. In a simple understatement Tessa recalls, 'I was pretty fed up.' Although she enjoyed knitting and craftwork, she was often depressed and wished she had never been born. She admits that, had she known how, there were times when she would certainly have taken her own life.

Tense and frustrated, Tessa embarked on a policy of non-cooperation by refusing to do what was wanted of her. It was her way of getting her own back on a society that, to Tessa's thinking at least, didn't seem to understand her and didn't appear to care very much either. The Society that ran the home was caring, but Tessa couldn't see that, or didn't want to, and with all her non-cooperation she felt no better; she began to realise that she was the only one who was really hurt by it. This new resident at Coombe Farm had so much potential stored behind the façade of her inarticulate speech and wasted muscles, but she was a prisoner of her own circumstances and could never win. Inside, she seethed with frustrated anger, and because she could not express herself in words, she would work herself into a paddy until the staff had to sedate her to calm her down. That strong will that would later serve her so well, had yet to be positively channelled.

Slowly, the teenager grew into womanhood and the rebellion was abandoned for a more mature and measured assertiveness. She was offered speech therapy at last and this opened a new dimension to life. Her sharp mind could now communicate intelligently with others; for the first time people would actually sit and talk with her. Tessa felt she was being treated as a human being, and an adult one at that. She rode her first bicycle here at Coombe Farm, an achievement she can still reflect on with pride. For his part, Graham could do no more than perfect the skill of negotiating his own wheelchair.

Here in Croydon, so much was done for the residents. They were cared for well enough, but to Tessa's thinking, too well. Their whole lives were planned and provided for, and Tessa's longing to be independent left her continually frustrated. She was convinced that, if given the chance, she could make many of her own decisions and do things for herself. Just how much she would one day achieve was still a dream away.

Although Graham often felt deeply sad and longed to be fit and well, his keen sense of humour and accommodating nature helped him accept his new home fairly readily. At least it was better than being moved from one place to another; and now, at last, he had his own wheelchair. His horizons were opening a little. Graham hardly noticed the new arrival to the home,

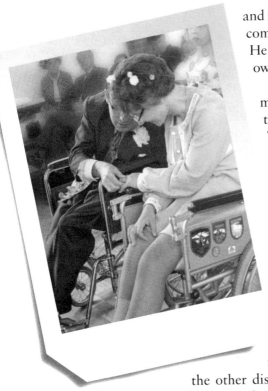

and if he had, since Tessa could not communicate well, why bother? He had enough problems of his own.

Both Graham and Tessa were making as much progress as their disabilities would allow. They could both propel their own wheelchair and this gave them a measure of that longed-for independence. With a positive approach, the step down into a wheelchair—whether self-propelled or powered—can open up a whole new way of life. Having learned to speak properly, Tessa could now join a Girl Guide company and even go to camp along with some of the other disabled girls; but better still she could camp with 'normal' girls as well. Graham joined the Scouts and camped with them. Horizons were certainly opening. But they were about to open even more widely!

New horizons

Each year the residents of Coombe Farm were taken on holiday, and in 1963 they went to Westcliffe on Sea, near Southend. It was here that Graham took notice of Tessa for the first time. For a while he watched her, sitting in the sun and busy with her knitting. His opportunity came when a needle slipped from her hand and dropped onto the promenade. Graham seized his chance, negotiated his chair alongside Tessa's and, with

Above: When they took their vows, it would have been like any other wedding except for the fact that the bride and groom were severely disabled and confined to wheelchairs

probably even more difficulty than Tessa herself would have had, retrieved the knitting needle and handed it triumphantly to its owner. For the rest of the holiday Graham enjoyed cruising alongside Tessa, retrieving lost items, and engaging her in conversation. Tessa was unaware that when she dropped a stitch she was embarking on a course that would eventually tie a knot! But that knot was a long way ahead.

Back in Croydon there was little privacy for the couple in their new-found friendship. The best they could do was to wheel off into the large grounds of the home where they could be alone in order to talk together and, once the chairs had been parked close enough, even hold hands. Holding hands meant instant immobility! For the first time they began to understand what real friendship was. They shared endlessly how they felt about life and their disability. They had each found someone who understood and who would talk personally about it. It was an experience to be cherished as often as they could escape from the watchful eye of the staff.

Unfortunately their relationship did not meet with enthusiastic approval from those in charge at the home. They may have been young adults in their mid-twenties, with clear minds, an independent spirit, and a deep love for each other, but relationships like this didn't quite fit in with the authorities' expectations for severely physically handicapped people. When they helped each other, even in such a small matter of fixing a watchstrap, it was frowned on—they were getting too close! The rebellious spirit of Tessa surfaced once again. Inwardly she screamed, 'Why can't we be friends?' They both set out consciously to outwit the establishment; so, whenever they could, the two wheelchairs would rendezvous under a small group of trees in a secluded part of the golf course as far from the home as possible!

Tessa had just received bad news! A visit to the optician confirmed that her eyesight would deteriorate; stronger lenses would help for a while, but the 'outlook' was not encouraging. Another blow to her pent-up emotions. It was about this time that an Occupational Therapist offered to take her to church. Tessa grasped at the opportunity; it was at least an excuse to get away from the home for a while and she could meet other people. So, each Sunday, Tessa went along to East Croydon Baptist Church. She invited Graham to join her. He had first heard the message of

Christ at the age of fifteen when he was in another home in Croydon. Slowly he realised that Christ loved him and cared enough to die for him. For the first time in his life, Graham started to read his Bible.

Not long after beginning her regular attendance at the Baptist Church, Tessa spent one very sleepless night. God had been challenging her to accept Christ as Saviour and Lord, but it was a hard struggle for this independent spirit. She spent much of the night praying. At last, not knowing what to expect, she gave her allegiance to Jesus Christ. Tessa was just twenty-four. Some changes were immediate. She realised that she had to live more contentedly and work at enjoying life; she found that she could now keep her tensions and frustrations under control, and her times of sadness became less frequent. Life at last had meaning and purpose. In obedience to her Lord's command Tessa was baptised by immersion at the Baptist Church. The matron of the home was not too happy because Tessa was supposed to join the Church of England!

Graham and Tessa hardly rushed their relationship and it was three years before Graham decided on his next move. In 1966 the home was unable to arrange for a holiday for the residents, so Graham went to stay with his aunt in Harrow for a short break. Whilst he was here he bought an engagement ring: three diamonds and three red garnets. He guessed the size, and it was a perfect fit. His aunt was inquisitive about these trips to the jewellers, but Graham kept his counsel, and no one knew of his scheme until he returned to Coombe Farm. Here, in the reception hall, he lost no time in proposing, and Tessa immediately said 'Yes.'

Tessa may have been decisive in her response to Graham's proposal, but it was another seven years before they were married! Gradually their relationship was accepted, and the way was prepared for them when Anne and Vic, two friends in the home who were more severely disabled than Tessa and Graham, were married. When Tessa eventually shared with her social worker that she and Graham planned to marry, she was met with a very supportive response. Everyone seemed to recognise that inevitably love will find a way, and now the clandestine meetings on the golf course could come to an end.

Graham and Tessa were sent on a marriage preparation course with a difference. They were taught how to safely boil water in a kettle, how to make a bed, how to get in and out of their wheelchairs, order a taxi, go out for the day, book tickets and go shopping. Tessa recalls, 'Until this point, I had only ever seen meals on a plate, now I had to learn how to make them get there!' They were wisely taught how to face the challenges of the physical side of marriage. Everyone was very helpful and understanding. Friends from the church and in the home all rallied to make their wedding a very special day, and this was followed by a two-week honeymoon in Southampton.

A shattered dream

Graham and Tessa moved to a new residential home in East London, where they settled into a large and adequately furnished room. Almost the first words of the warden to them both were at once encouraging and frightening, 'I think you are both too independent for here', he confided, 'you should have a flat of your own.' For all her longing to be independent, Tessa had never really expected a place of her own. She had always assumed that she would spend her whole life in residential care. Anything else was just a fanciful dream. The fact that someone recognised the possibility of this newly married couple living independently was a great morale boost, but at the same time it was a shocking challenge. What if they really couldn't manage?

All the excitement of planning for the wedding, and those glorious two weeks together in Southampton, soon became happy memories of a rapidly fading past. They found themselves in a home among people with a whole range of disabilities including Multiple Sclerosis, Parkinson's disease, strokes, and many others—it was a real culture shock for them both. What was worse was that there was nothing to do all day. Everything was still provided for them, meals were prepared and served, laundry was washed and ironed, cleaning was done. Most of the residents just watched television until it was time for the next meal, or bed. But this was not Graham and Tessa's style. They had driven their four wheels through a host of bureaucratic and social barriers to get married, and now they seemed to have come to the end of the road once again. Life became empty and disappointing. They felt devastated by what was happening. Their ambitions and expectations seemed totally unattainable. Their dreams were being shattered.

For months on end they never went to church, in fact they never went anywhere. They prayed together and cried together, 'Lord, what are you doing with us?' At times they doubted his love. Graham even began to wonder if it had all been a terrible mistake to get married. Everything was so hard, so disappointing. Boldly, they had taken the hard decision not have children, although it nearly broke Tessa's heart to do so, because they appreciated the risks involved, the high chance of a disabled child and their inability to adequately care for a young family. But now they were losing everything. They still had no independence and little privacy. More than twenty-five years on, Graham and Tessa still can't talk about those distressing months without tears.

Tessa remembered that the night before her wedding Tom Brown, the chief swimming instructor at Coombe Farm, had said to her, 'Wherever you go, be sure you get in contact with a church, because you won't ever regret that.' She called him. Tom made contact with Holy Trinity Church at Mile End and, true to his promise, they never regretted it. Each Sunday, members came and escorted them to church. For the first time they began to join in activities with able people; it was all very exciting. But still there were the stark, occasionally amusing, reminders that they were residents being cared for in a local authority home. One Sunday, no one arrived to escort them to church. Determined not to be 'grounded', Graham and Tessa set off on their own. Unknown to them, a well-meaning member of the public rang the home to report that two residents had escaped in wheelchairs! When eventually they returned after church with their escort, they felt like a pair of monkeys who had broken out of the local zoo!

The time spent in this home was not the happiest of their lives, but with their usual determination and the mutual support of each other, they set out to change things! They made it possible for other residents to go to church, arranged for a minister to regularly visit, encouraged better activities in the home, and organized a Residents' Committee to lobby for greater privacy and more independence. This meant that staff could no longer wander in and out of residents' rooms without an invitation. They were hard years, but they were not wasted years either.

After two years struggling with this situation, a flat was found for them in Surbiton, Surrey. Perhaps, by now, they were considered safer out of the way! The flat was on the first floor, but was served by a lift. They now had a kitchen, bathroom, bedroom and lounge, all adapted for wheelchairs—

and all to themselves. They were delighted. However, Tessa now discovered that it was no easy task to live normally in the world outside an institution. Organising their own lives without constant oversight, arranging for their own doctor and even shopping together, were all new and constantly challenging experiences.

Five years on, in 1980, a bungalow, complete with its own small garden, became available, and here Graham and Tessa were to be as fully independent as they could be. They were soon provided with power chairs suitable for outdoors, and this gave even more independence.

Wider horizons

Tessa at last had the independence she dreamt of for so long. She is now mistress in her own home and, under the new Care in the Community arrangements, she is expected to arrange and pay for her own home cleaning. Today, when a visitor calls at the front door of their neat bungalow in a quiet suburban cul-de-sac, they are answered first by an intercom and then by an automatic latch-opener. Inside, their home is much like any other. The doors are wider than normal of course, though Graham still manages occasionally to jam himself in a doorway; but then, his chair is around four feet long. Paint is a bit chipped here and there, and in the kitchen, workbenches are set at a low level. When you call, you have to hunt for a chair because extraneous furniture only clutters up the 'freeway', but the budgerigar sings from the lounge and the rack of CDs indicate that Graham has still not lost his love of music.

Tessa is an organised housewife, as Graham has learned over the years, sometimes to his annoyance. What aggravates her more than most things are, 'When people let me down, fail to turn up, and disarrange my day.' They have their own duties and Graham is responsible for setting up the Teasmade for the morning cuppa. Tessa cooks a meal twice a week, washes up afterwards, looks after the family laundry, and can still generally tidy round; Graham keeps up with his craftwork and out of Tessa's way when she is in 'tidy-up' mode. One of their joint pleasures is swimming. Once a week they spend an hour in the pool where Graham finds that he can move his legs a bit and uses his arms to propel himself along; for her part Tessa swims on her back, 'Because that's the way I've been taught.' Horse riding is a special treat for Tessa; it is the only time that she gets a higher view of life around her, and that makes her feel good.

Each morning Graham goes to the local centre where he occupies himself with various craftwork. Tapestry is still his favourite, and he confidently asserts, 'I love it; nobody is going to take the needle out of my fingers.' But it is becoming more difficult for him, and the tables are turned when it's Graham who drops the needle. Tessa joins him at the centre for three days but, like most housewives, she jealously guards her weekly shopping expedition; an assistant helps her with the items that are beyond wheelchair height.

Having set up home in their new bungalow, they were not content simply to explore a few roads around them. People travel abroad for holidays these days, so why not Graham and Tessa? Over a few years they visited Israel, Canada, USA, Belgium, Holland and Switzerland. They have been up mountains in a cable car and have floated in the Dead Sea. They love flying, and as far as Graham is concerned it is easily the best way to travel. Airlines are generally well able to handle wheelchair-bound passengers. It is not always easy to find escorts who are free and able to accompany them on holiday, and such holidays don't come cheaply either, but the achievement and enjoyment makes it all worthwhile.

Attitudes to life

With more than twenty-five years of marriage behind them and a steady erosion of the use of their muscles, little by little their independence drains away. Carers now come in each evening and morning to prepare them for bed and get them up. They can still do part of the work themselves but it is, as they express it, 'a big struggle.' They have both experienced periods in hospital. Tessa spent eight weeks in hospital after a Girdlestone operation for the removal of her hip joint. To a limited extent she could fend for herself and call for help when she needed it. But for Graham, placed in a side ward where he had no contact and could easily be overlooked, life in hospital was especially hard, 'They can't really cope with someone like me', he reflects, 'and it is so tedious in a room on your own.' Graham has two dislocated hips and only with painful effort can he ease himself up in his chair from time to time. Pressure sores are a constant threat. It is this constant battle against ill health that is yet another burden to be added to the routine of people like Graham and Tessa. Although both of them have reasonable strength in their hands and arms, their legs are useless and both suffer from arthritis.

When asked about their hopes and fears for the future, Graham just hopes he can carry on going to the day centre for as long as possible. Tessa, 'like everybody else', fears getting old and not being able to do things. She is not afraid of dying, but because she is a little more able than Graham, Tessa knows how much he depends upon her and she knows that he could not cope alone. For Graham, one of his biggest struggles in life is 'speaking loud enough so that people can hear me.' For Tessa it is often 'just keeping life going.'

Occasionally Tessa will let you inside her personal life. They both pray and read the Bible together, but Tessa has learnt to pray alone, constantly. It is then that she finds she can see God's hand in her life and this gives her great peace. But often when she is alone, she feels very discouraged and convinces herself that 'no one in the world really wants to be bothered with us.' Carers come and go and they do their job, but do they really care? People have their own lives to live and their own problems to face, Tessa reasons, 'And they can't be expected to bother about us.' She is very sensitive to people's responses to her; their smile or frown affects her significantly.

It's not just the loss of independence that is hard for the disabled person; after all, Graham and Tessa have never known full independence. What is often worse is the assumption by people that they, and not the disabled, know what is best. Tessa finds life hardest when decisions are made on her behalf, as if she is incapable of having an opinion, or if she has, that it is not really important. On the other hand, and paradoxically, she finds it equally annoying that people always have to be asked and never see that a need is obvious. This Catch-22 means neither Tessa nor those who want to help can always win. For all her longing to be independent, Tessa admits to being the world's worst when it comes to decisions; she gets confused and flustered, and finally has to force herself to make a decision before she makes herself ill with worry.

In a moment of introspective honesty Tessa admitted 'I suppose I'm a bit aggressive at times; in fact, I do get ratty.' A chuckle from Graham confirms the point! Having known them both for twenty years, I think Tessa might be a little hard on herself here and I suggested that I would prefer to use the word 'affirmative.' She has learnt by the long, hard way, that the disabled sometimes have to assert themselves in order to gain a hearing or to be taken seriously. There is a patronising and condescending attitude by many able people, including, sometimes, those in a caring role; it shows itself in the unspoken impression that, 'We are doing you a favour, and you should be grateful that you get all this help.' Tessa has even endured the suggestion that it must be nice getting large disability pensions.

On the other hand, what is so impressive about these two is their positive outlook on life. Tessa and Graham are the first to laugh at themselves. It may seem a daft question, even unkind perhaps, to ask them whether they enjoy life, but they have no hesitation in replying. 'Yes', says Tessa, 'but like everybody else, at times things happen to upset the applecart.' That phrase 'like everybody else' actually reveals a lot about Tessa's philosophy. Whilst she is not at all sensitive to the label 'disabled', she does see herself as more able than most would allow. 'Is there any such thing as an able-bodied person?' she questions, 'Everybody has some disability. Not everyone can climb a mountain, even though they may like to.' It is this confidence that she is achieving what she can, and that no one can achieve all they would like to, that enables Tessa to cope with each disappointment that comes along. In response to the same question, 'Do you enjoy life?' Graham is less philosophical and more direct, 'Yes, thank you', he replies with a mischievous grin. And when you press the point with, 'But life is tough isn't it', he responds simply, 'Oh yes. I'm so slow.'

Slow he certainly is, but not undetermined. Some years ago when he decided that it was time for him to follow his wife's good example and be baptised as an evidence of his Christian faith and commitment, I offered him an alternative to full immersion. I had in mind the extent of his disability, but did not say so. Graham is always economic with words so his unhesitating response was, 'Why?' When I offered my reasons, he just pretended not to understand. In the event two strong men lowered him into the water and a third assisted me in believer's baptism by immersion—but not before I had made it clear to any critics in the congregation that this was the way Graham demanded it!

Holidays abroad are not the only pleasures for this pair of jet-setting four-wheelers. They are equally content with the more simple experiences

Above: Despite their enormous disabilities, Graham and Tessa try to live to the full, 'We have each other, and we've had a lot of happiness'

of life. In reply to my question, 'What is your biggest enjoyment in life?' Graham's unlikely response was, 'Getting up in the morning, because it brings life back and gives you a new day.' Before Tessa could reply to the same question he cut in with a laugh, 'Her first cup of tea in the morning.' Tessa's own response was more measured, 'To live life to the full', she replied seriously, 'we have each other, and we've had a lot of happiness.' That seemed to say it all.

When I touched on the subject of euthanasia, Tessa was visibly moved, 'If it ever becomes legal' she responded thoughtfully, 'what concerns me is people's minds; I mean, whether it becomes our choice or theirs. Already a lot of decisions are made on our behalf.' She genuinely fears that this could be the final decision taken out of her hands. Even at their lowest points in life, when death would have appeared to be a comfortable release, both

Graham and Tessa knew that such a course was both wrong and unnecessary. Whilst their Christian faith means that they have no fear of death, it equally supports their determination to live life to the full and leave God to determine the day of their departure to a new and better life.

Their relationship with the local Christian church has always been a lifeline for Graham and Tessa. For two decades a rota of members have cooked Sunday lunch for them, prepared vegetables, regularly provided escorts to accompany them safely to church, invited them to social evenings with their pastoral group, and have been available to advise on finance and help with repairs and emergencies. There is less need now for some of the help that was required years ago before Care in the Community became a legal obligation on local authorities. But they both value most of all the friendship and 'lots of love' that they receive from their Christian friends. Graham and Tessa are never absent from church on Sunday evening, whatever the weather, unless ill health prevents them—or their escorts forget to call for them! They enjoy meeting their friends at church and learning from the Bible.

At his baptism service Graham bore witness to the love of God through Christ in his life. However, when asked what was the greatest thing Christ had done for him, Graham dispensed with theological accuracy and declared, 'He gave me Tessa'—at which the congregation thoroughly enjoyed the unorthodox reply and Tessa exploded with emotion!

Their Christian faith has been challenged but not cowed by their experience of life. I threw a few strategic questions at them and here are their unedited responses:

Question   Does suffering and disability draw you closer to God?

Tessa   Perhaps for some people, but most are driven away because of bitterness. It's hard to be a Christian, but I must say that I couldn't cope if I wasn't. You have to be very strong with the Lord because you could fall away from your faith easily.

Question   Are there any advantages being disabled and confined to a wheelchair?

Tessa   (After a pause as she stares thoughtfully for a few seconds), No, not really.

Graham   (Ever ready with the neat response), You can get around quicker.

Question	How do you answer someone who might say, 'If there is a God, why are you in a wheelchair and so disabled?'
Graham	Because this is how God wanted me to be.
Question	But surely that makes God unkind?
Graham	No, it shows people what you can do from a wheelchair.
Tessa	It also shows people that there is real life, however poor your body is.
Graham	But you must keep at it.
Question	Why?
Graham	Just to prove that you can.
Tessa	I must admit I sometimes feel right under. In fact quite often. But when I have time to think it through, I can go forward again.
Question	What would you say to someone who wants to end it all because life is too hard?
Tessa	I would persuade them to share their real problems. We would share our story and say, 'If we can do it, so can you.'
Question	Have you ever been approached by people asking if they can pray for you so that you could be healed?
Tessa	No, never.
Question	Why do you think that is?
Tessa	Because people are realistic! And they can see in us that we know the Lord, and he didn't heal everybody.
Graham	Because they think we're doing all right.

And that about sums up Graham and Tessa. They are doing 'all right.' If Tessa gets 'a bit ratty' at times, and Graham is so infuriatingly laid back about things that you expect his chair to tip up, that just proves how human they both are. They have battled through bureaucracy, asserted their right to live as independently as possible, demonstrated that severe disability and faith in Jesus Christ are beautiful companions, and have proved that life on four wheels can have wide horizons. Their positive joy, confident hope and determined spirit are an incredible challenge to all who know them. That makes it 'all right.'

Four-wheel drive

To live successfully in a wheelchair demands courage and determination. Life is a constant battle against the disability that put you there and the stereotypical thinking of society. For some, the disability is obvious and no one questions your right to be on four wheels, others may look very well and the unspoken (and sometimes spoken) question is, 'What's wrong with him then?' But whether the four-wheeler looks well or not, you can be sure that they are constantly battling against ill health. By its very nature, commitment to a wheelchair brings is own dangers like atrophied muscles, bladder infections, and pressure sores (which are not the innocent inconveniences that many suppose—they can have fatal consequences).

The first outing with a walking stick is never easy, especially if you are a mother with a young family in tow. But the progression to a wheelchair is much harder. Life changes radically. It's not just the way you view life, but the way life views you. Life on four wheels has its amusing side, it has to or you could not cope, but it is never an attractive alternative to two legs. However, in her usual determined way, Barbara early came to the conclusion that if the choice was to keep actively mobile in a wheelchair, or stay at home, then the decision was already made. For many years we could manage with a pushchair, but the disadvantage of this is that I could not walk beside Barbara and our conversation was always over the shoulder. Barbara was unable to use a self-propelled chair because her arms and hands were too weak. This meant that she had no independence; she just had to go where I pushed her and face the way I left her. Not infrequently I would start chatting with a friend only to be interrupted after ten minutes with the rebuke, 'Do you think I could join in this conversation?'

I can't recall when it happened, but I know that before long Barbara and a wheelchair were so inseparable in my mind that it became just part of normal life. It may sound strange and unreal, but I almost forgot the wheelchair. Barbara didn't! She told me that she often dreamt of walking and running, but as she woke up she fell over and found herself struggling to stand up. But she drove herself on to live as normal a life as possible.

It is all too easy to fall into the trap of thinking and talking about being 'limited' or 'confined' to a wheelchair. That kind of language assumes the negative side must always dominate. I am not unrealistic enough to suggest we cannot use those words, but they focus on what you can't do rather than what you can. In fact, the whole point of a wheelchair is that it opens a new life-style and new horizons. On one occasion when I asked Graham why he thought God had allowed him to be in a wheelchair, his reply was simple and convincing, 'To show what can be done on four wheels instead of two legs.'

Perhaps the contrast of attitudes was illustrated best in the responses of Tessa and Graham to my question, 'Are there any advantages being disabled and confined to a wheelchair?' Tessa paused thoughtfully for a few seconds and replied, 'No, not really.' Graham, with a grin, wrapped his answer succinctly, 'You can get around quicker.' I know Barbara would have responded in the same way as Tessa—practical and no pretending. Tessa and Barbara compared themselves with those who are able and fit. But Graham clearly thought of what he would be without his chair. The first approach sees the chair as a limitation, the second as liberation. Both are right of course, but Graham's mind-set is more positive. The alternative is to be confined indoors, so, a wheelchair, scooter or buggy is an open door to the great outside. They provide a significant degree of freedom and independence.

On the move

Twice Barbara and I visited South Africa and spent altogether two months in that beautiful country. On both occasions I was there by invitation to preach, and Barbara had a strong ministry among the ladies. On the second visit we decided to take some holiday as well. We only had Barbara's pushchair with us, but any wheelchair in South Africa is an uncommon sight; that made us appreciate how privileged we were. I have four favourite cameos of Barbara there.

The first photograph was taken in the township of Alexandra where we visited the Baptist pastor and his family and the school that they ran. We had an armed policeman to accompany us and he insisted on pushing Barbara. The kids crowded round her, fascinated by an adult in a wheelchair and poking at anything on the chair that could be poked. In the picture Barbara is surrounded by a sea of small black and inquisitive faces; but what that photograph cannot convey is the chatter between Barbara and the children—even though neither side had much idea what the other was saying!

The second picture is very different. It was taken outside Emmanuel Baptist Church in Florida Park, Johannesburg. Barbara was never eager to speak at meetings, believing that she could not say anything that others would not say far better. For this reason she sometimes turned down opportunities, and this later made her feel guilty at having failed to serve the Lord. However, one thing she was insistent on was that she did not want to talk about herself and her suffering. Instead she would speak on the Bible and what the Lord meant to her. Here in South Africa Barbara was persuaded to do this, and I have a picture of her surrounded by thirty or so ladies from a Bible class. Her ministry was always straightforward and simple. That was the kind of person Barbara was, and that, I believe, was precisely why her ministry was so valuable. She never spoke over people's heads.

The third picture is of Barbara on top of Table Mountain in Cape Town. We had gone up in the cable car and it was so windy that I could only push her outside for a few minutes. Her face is screwed up against the wind and her hair is blowing about wildly, hardly a flattering picture, but one of my favourites. She was determined not to visit Cape Town without getting to the top of that mountain.

My fourth picture was taken in the Kruger National Park. Our friends, John and Elaine Joubert, had taken us to spend three days in the game reserve, including two nights living in a 'rondawel'—in the style of a traditional African round house, albeit with mod cons and air-conditioning! At Oliphants we sat on a veranda and scanned a 180° panorama of bushveld with the river winding lazily below us and the animals settling down for the night. Barbara is sitting in her chair scanning the wildlife through her telescope. We basked in the African sunset and listened to the sounds of an African evening. As the sun disappeared, a silent electrical storm lit up the whole sky with a constant display of sheet lightning. These were magic moments, and we both relished every one of them. It was a privilege never to be forgotten.

Our relatively short experience of foreign travel at least provided us with some interesting stories to re-tell. Generally, airlines are well used to handling disabled passengers. But it can be a different story when things go wrong! It once took us twenty-two hours to return from South Africa because the generator packed up on our BA flight and we had to turn back to Nairobi for repairs. Two hours later they gave up the attempt and decided to transfer us to another aircraft. Disabled passengers were left to last and when all three hundred passengers were settled on the new plane, the cabin staff tried to work out how best to transfer Barbara. It was our first and only experience of trundling across the tarmac, weaving in and out between the wheels of a Boeing 747 and finally being offered a ride on the flat bed lift that normally conveyed the catering trolleys into the cabin. Our anxious airhostess at first protested, 'My passenger is not going up on that', but the grinning airport attendant indicated that the choice was either that or stay grounded. So, I jumped up alongside Barbara and we were raised in style into the 'galley'—much to the amusement of the watching passengers.

Barbara enjoyed it all. She loved flying and everything about the airports. In flight she was too nosy to sleep, afraid that she might miss something interesting. I found it all tedious and wanted to sleep but rarely could. I recall being woken by her at 3.00 am high over somewhere or other because Barbara thought I would like to see the beautiful sunrise!

In 1995 we took a party of fifteen young people and leaders from Hook Evangelical Church across Europe to the Czech Republic. It was a friendship visit to the Czech evangelical youth choir that we had entertained here in England the year before. We covered 2,500 miles and camped in our van, whilst the rest of the party stayed in hostels. This time we took Barbara's power chair, and fortunately we had many strong guys with us who were happy to lift Barbara into the churches. The evangelical church in Vsetin had three flights of steps amounting to about three dozen in all. Barbara always found such 'rides' scary to say the least.

We stayed with the same powered wheelchair for many years because, once we had adapted it for her, it suited her well. At conferences and in the large stores she could at last be independent. Every manager should be made to negotiate the aisles of his store in a wheelchair; then he would know just how difficult it is for wheelchairs to avoid scattering his display stands. I made sure that we were insured for accidents because I always had a fear that one day Barbara would crash into someone or something and we would find ourselves caught up in a civil action. I should have had more confidence in her. I never recall her doing any more damage than occasionally chipping a little paint from a doorframe.

Barbara's ability to go off on her own when we were shopping was at times embarrassing. I recall arriving at a checkout only to find that Barbara had gone missing—with the money. I traded on the patience of the assistant and the short queue behind me whilst I went on a hunt. I wandered the store enquiring, 'Have you seen my wife, she's in a wheelchair', and when I found her I threatened that if it happened again I would 'ground' her by pulling the plug!

However, there were more amusing occasions. We had a tail-lift fitted to our motor home and Barbara would drive onto the platform before being lifted and delivered into the van. This meant that when she came off, she was driving backwards. I would let the lift down, whisper directions as to whether she needed to move left or right to avoid an obstacle, and Barbara would drive off. More than once bystanders rushed forward to stop this 'runaway' chair as it ran backwards off the platform.

We were always so grateful for that wheelchair. Now, I could at least walk beside Barbara and even put my hand on the arm of her chair—our equivalent of holding hands. It opened a new horizon for Barbara, and her determination to be as normal as possible meant that with her drive and the four wheels, we went almost anywhere we wanted. The chair could cope with a 1:4 gradient, cover twenty miles on one charge and was certainly capable of negotiating rougher terrain than Barbara could endure. Her only complaint was its speed. Our model was limited to 4 mph and she hated to be overtaken by other wheelchairs. It was one of her greatest annoyances when, on the way to church, Graham and Tessa would speed past and leave Barbara grumbling yards behind.

It was more of a challenge to Graham and Tessa than to most four-wheelers when they decided to holiday abroad. They were certainly more adventurous than we ever dreamt of being. Over a few years they visited Israel, Canada, USA, Belgium, Holland and Switzerland. They have been up mountains in a cable car and have floated in the Dead Sea. They love flying, and as far as Graham is concerned it is easily the best way to travel. Although airlines are generally well able to handle wheelchair passengers, it is not always easy to find escorts who are free and able to accompany them on holiday, and such holidays don't come cheaply either. However, the achievement and enjoyment makes it all worthwhile. Paul and Helle have travelled most of Europe, and whether it is the way he drives or the places he goes, Paul has been through four wheel chairs in his life so far.

Please wipe your wheels

Paul has always been a watchdog for fellow four-wheelers. Fortunately he came from a family where he was treated much the same as his brothers and sister. He shared their games, their holidays and their hidings. So, as he grew into adulthood, he could see no reason why society should not share its facilities with him also. Unfortunately society did not always have the same mind. He was often made to feel that he should apologise for being disabled and ought not to inconvenience others in order to live a normal life. It was as if he was being asked to wipe his wheels before coming indoors. In fact, that actually happens to them. They have a friend who occasionally invites them over but only on sunny days, and then they sit and have a drink in the garden because she worries that the tyres of Paul's chair will spoil her lovely pale carpet!

Paul and Helle have often turned to Hebrews 12:13 as an example of God's understanding of the failure of society to help the disabled, 'Make level paths for your feet, so that the lame may not be disabled, but rather healed.' Perhaps the apostle had a different application in mind, but his illustration makes the point that society often disables the disabled. Paul and Helle write of some of their experiences of society's expectations.

'Soon after we moved into our new bungalow, the local authority wanted an official support group for The International Year of Disabled People. A number of us teamed up with interested parties to form a group. Our aim was to look at different ways in which facilities within our town could be made easier. One project included the Mayor going around in a wheelchair to carry out everyday tasks! We visited all public buildings in the area and conducted a survey of their accessibility for disabled people. Not only were most of the buildings totally inaccessible for someone in a wheelchair, but the comments we received proved that there is a barrier which exists within people's attitudes.

'At our local sub post office Helle was told, "You can't bring that in here", pointing at me! At the main Post Office we were asked, "Tell us how many of you want to come in and then we can organise a lifting party one day." At yet another sub Post Office we were met by a rather perplexed and indignant manager who asked, "What do you want to come in here for? This is a Post Office." He seemed unaware that disabled people might need to cash their own pensions, pay bills, buy stamps or send a parcel. At the railway station we were assured that the inability of a wheelchair to access one side of the platform was not a problem: all we had to do was to get off the train one station earlier in the neighbouring village and walk the rest of the way. That this would incur a 'stroll' of a mile and a half seemed of little consequence. But if that did present a problem, then we could continue to the station beyond ours, cross the station in this village and catch the next train in the opposite direction; we would now be on the correct side of the platform for a whelchair to leave the station!

'At that time even the churches did not seem to consider it a particularly high priority to provide access for any disabled members of the community who wished to join them in worship. Most responded, "Oh yes, we must get round to that some time, perhaps in our next building programme." As far as I can recall, only one of the churches at that time was accessible. At last, one church we visited responded positively. When we first arrived at Binscombe Evangelical Church we caused a bit of a stir, but eventually they assured us, "If you come back next week, we will have a ramp for you". They were as good as their word, and when we returned after a couple of weeks, there was the ramp. Granted it was a little makeshift, but it was there. And they didn't leave it at that. Soon a new concrete ramp was built. We were so impressed, not only by this practical ministry but also by the sermon, that we continued to attend and eventually became members.

'But it is not all negative. There are also some unorthodox ways of tackling the obstacles of life, as for example, when Helle's parents celebrated a very important Jubilee. It was to be held on the first floor of the firm's premises and of course there was no lift, but my brother-in-law was determined that I was not going to be left out of the proceedings. He owns a lorry company and so he brought into the yard one of his trucks with a tail lift. I drove onto the lift and was unceremoniously raised to the level of the next floor where there was a delivery entrance. I was really impressed!'

Perhaps all four-wheelers need their own truck with a tail lift. It would be a great asset when confronted by those thoughtless car drivers who insist on parking across the pavement. Not only is it illegal but it often means a wheelchair user has to move into the road just to get past. It is even more of a hazard for the blind person who has carefully identified the inside wall or fence and hardly expects to walk into a parked car. Drivers would gradually learn, if every member of the public who discovers a car parked in this way would slip a note on the windscreen reminding them of the danger to the disabled.

Wheel advice

Between them Graham and Tessa, Paul and Barbara could muster over one hundred and fifty years in a wheelchair. From their experience, here is a summary of advice when you meet someone wheelchair:

1. Don't stare at them—talk to them

A disability may be obvious or it may not. The disabled person may ride an electric buggy that is so well equipped it looks ready to explore the surface of the moon, or they may be trundling along in a vintage NHS model; they may handle the chair expertly or clumsily. Whatever draws your attention, resist the temptation to gawp. If you really want to know more, go and ask.

On the other hand, only a very sensitive disabled person will be offended by the incredulous gaze of a toddler who then runs off with an excited, 'Look mummy, that chair goes along on its own.' When Barbara wore a cape there was no sign of hands or controls, and the chair really did appear to glide silently on autopilot. Paul loves children and is loved by them; so much so that they would knock on his door to see if he could come out and play! It's therefore not hard to understand that one thing that annoys him intensely is an embarrassed parent who orders their enquiring child to 'be quiet and come away.' Junior will gain a far more positive attitude to disabled people if mum would bring him over to talk. Not many wheelchair users will be offended by a polite, 'Excuse me, I hope you don't think it an intrusion, but Tommy would like to know how your wheelchair works.' Paul would be delighted to show Tommy the controls—and probably give him a ride as well.

When I asked Graham and Tessa what was hardest about a life-long relationship with a wheelchair, they both put at the top of their list, 'people staring at us.' Graham has his own way of dealing with this intrusion; when they come within range he innocently asks, 'Haven't you seen me before?' I've still not worked out the best answer to that, which I suppose shows how effective the question is. When she was a girl, Tessa found that people would ask her mother, 'Can she talk?'; to which the wise mother would respond, 'Speak to her and see.'

Barbara and I often re-told the experience we had when visiting a small village church many years ago. At that time she was in a pushchair and, once I stood her up, she could walk with difficulty to a seat. We arrived late for the service, and advertised our presence by scuttling all the milk bottles in the church porch. As we entered the building, a group of elderly ladies turned round to stare at the 'intruders.' They watched our every move as I parked the chair, engaged the brakes, and stood Barbara up. As she took her first, faltering step, one of the onlookers loudly informed the small congregation, 'Oh, she walks!' Fortunately she was probably too deaf to hear my ungracious response in Barbara's ear.

2. Don't ignore them—they're only people

Graham and Tessa admit that it is easy to be hidden in a crowd, and people are slow to come and talk. Embarrassment or a feeling of helplessness may lead some to act as if the wheelchair and its occupant simply don't exist. They don't know how to respond, or what to say. They may fear that the disabled driver is all that they think they are—old, deaf and a little simple!

The, 'Does he take sugar?' syndrome, is sadly rooted firmly in reality. I recall the occasion when Barbara was suffering from an annoying cough and the man to her right lent across in front of her and asked me whether my wife would like a glass of water! Tessa complains, 'It's as if we're not there. People talk about us, over us, even in front of us, but not to us.' Paul and Helle advise, 'Don't lean on a person's wheelchair; the chair is part of their body space. Talk directly to them, rather than through a companion. Be relaxed and make eye contact; in fact, greet them in whatever way would be appropriate for anyone else.'

3. Don't presume and assume—listen

Most four-wheelers have learnt to be as independent as their disability allows. They actually don't need help from every well-meaning member of the public, and generally will not be afraid to ask when they do. However, an escort to cross the road, someone to hold open a door, or a quiet offer of help to lift something down from a high shelf is always welcome.

But never presume to move a disabled person unless you first inquire whether they wish to be moved. A whispered, 'Are you okay here, or can I move you into the shade?' is thoughtful and courteous. By all means offer assistance, but always wait until your offer is accepted before taking action, and listen carefully to instructions. They may be enjoying this opportunity to soak up the sun and the last thing they want is that patronising, 'Oh you poor thing, you must be so hot, let's get you out of the sun' as they are shoved into the gloom.

Powered wheelchairs are heavy, robust, and some come apart easily— they are meant to. So please don't offer to help lift one unless you know that your back can stand it. A chair with two batteries and two motors always requires four people to lift it safely, however light the occupant may be. When you are ready to assist, listen carefully to instructions. The owner of the wheelchair always knows best. Helle and Paul arrived at a church that was celebrating its 150th anniversary. There was wheelchair access through a side door but unfortunately no one could find the key to the door. The welcoming vicar met them and, in his zeal to help, grabbed at the armrest of Paul's chair. It promptly came off in his hand and he sheepishly enquired, 'Oh, what shall I do with it?' Helle's response was not calculated to cover his embarrassment, 'Well, for a start you could try putting it back on again, then I will tell you how you can help us.' Paul freely admits that this sort of approach robs him of any sense of dignity and makes him feel more like a sack of potatoes than a person. Don't rush to help: Enquire, listen, and only then respond. Remember, if you manhandle a wheelchair someone can mend it, but if you damage its owner...

In one of those churches where pews fill every available space, Barbara had no alternative but to drive to the end of the row and half block the aisle. Being a new church to us, we had no idea who rented this pew each week. We soon found out! When the occupant arrived and found his way barred, he simply grabbed the handles of the wheelchair and tried to push Barbara out of his way. Unfortunately he had met his match in our Everest and Jennings Elite Whisper. The automatic brakes were on and the chair would not budge. But his determination gave Barbara a nasty jolt before he wandered off to find another pew. Barbara was silently furious—until we were alone in the privacy of our van. I wonder if he shouldered his way to the front of the tea queue after the service?

Don't presume that you know what is wrong with a disabled person, or for that matter that you have a right to know. At one church we visited, a nurse approached Barbara with the question, 'Have you ever been in the Royal Free?' On receiving Barbara's response to the negative, she followed up with, 'Oh, only, I've nursed many patients with MS in the Royal Free.' Her assumption about Barbara's disability was wholly misjudged and Barbara longed to respond, 'Good, when I get MS I'll know where to come.' This approach to the disabled is perhaps only marginally less insensitive than the more common, 'What's wrong with you then?' Remember that no one has the right to inquire into the medical history of anyone else. You have to earn the privilege to such information. After a while in conversation, when you have gained each other's confidence, or when you have shared your own situation, it may be appropriate to enquire. Some people have hidden disabilities and may look perfectly healthy, but you can take it that there are not too many people driving wheelchairs just for the fun of it.

Many assume that the only conversation for the disabled is their disability. Some, of course, love to tell you all about their trials and limitations, but not many. They live with that all day and every day, and they just long to talk about something normal. The man who sat down beside Barbara, nodded to her wheelchair, and opened the conversation with, 'How long have you been in that then?' drew attention to the very thing Barbara was trying to forget. On the way home in the van we planned her response to that question the next time it came up. However, never able to put people down when they meant no harm, Barbara could not bring herself to reply, 'Since nine o'clock this morning', or better still, 'How long have you been in those brown shoes?' Barbara was never personally upset by people's clumsiness; and it's a good job she wasn't. Her sense of humour served her well, otherwise she might have been a little worried by one man's opening gambit, 'My wife was in a wheelchair for twelve years. She died last year.'

4. We've heard it all before

You may take it as given that all the jokes about driving licences, L-plates, and taking tests, have been made—ad nauseam. I'm not suggesting that disabled people never enjoy humour. Frankly, if they didn't laugh at their situation they would never survive. The only mechanical failure of her wheelchair that Barbara ever experienced happened at a conference. The drive shaft to one wheel broke, which meant that she could only drive in circles. In my next sermon I appealed for the help of a mechanic, and compared Barbara's limited travel with too many Christians who spend their lives simply going round and round but never making progress. Years later people still remind me of my preacher's point at Barbara's expense.

Of course, the better you know a four-wheeler, the more you can take liberties. Only occasionally did Barbara object to our fun at her expense. When we were out for the day or on holiday, our friends would banter. But they had the right to, and Barbara enjoyed it. The chair became the packhorse for unwanted bags, jumpers, coats and even umbrellas. As a family we were not always kind to her. In the pushchair days, I can recall us leaving Barbara in the middle of a small stream and walking off. One evening when we were out for a walk, Andrew stopped at a new hole in the footpath, parked his mother beside it, placed the workmen's warning light beside her chair, and walked on. On the other hand, although she accepted with good grace the unflattering metal-framed halo jacket that accompanied her from Frimley Park Hospital, she refused to allow Andrew to hang a notice on the back of her chair which read simply, 'hard-hat area.' It certainly looked like a piece of builder's scaffolding, but for Barbara that was a joke too far. Even the family didn't always get it right. Sometimes my own tomfoolery embarrassed her. I would sneak a lift by standing on the rear stabilisers, and only her repeated and firm command, 'Brian, get off', reduced me to eventual obedience. When friends jammed a couple of rolled umbrellas behind the handle bars and pretended to drive her chair like a go-kart, I half expected to watch a miracle of Barbara getting out and walking away in disgust.

There are few disabled people who cannot laugh with others at themselves. They have to. Their situation is not amusing, but it's often very funny. When Graham turned his chair over because he misjudged the curb, he ended up in hospital. It was hardly amusing, but it has provided a lot of teasing ever since—especially as Tessa has never been so careless!

5. Mind your language!

I have always been tempted to write underneath the label 'Disabled Toilet' a little note that says simply, 'Then fix it'! Perhaps they really mean to say 'Wheelchair accessible toilet.' But then someone might suggest that wheelchairs don't need toilets. All of which demonstrates that we must not be over sensitive about language. For our part, Barbara and I were never squeamish about the word 'disabled.' After all, 'physically challenged' hardly seemed to be an intelligent alternative because, as Tessa would quickly point out, everyone is. No one can do everything. But there are some things and some occasions when a little thoughtfulness would help.

The first twenty-four hours of Barbara being in a new ward were normally a nightmare for me—and more so for her. First I had to communicate to the staff that Barbara, with the strongest will in the world, could do nothing for herself; she could not even press the call button, and anyway, she would suffer rather than bother them. Then I had to establish politely what most nursing staff were unwilling to admit, that when it came to nursing care, I knew far more about Barbara's needs than they ever would. So would they please listen to me. And thirdly, I had to convince them that it would be in everyone's best interests if they let me help as much as possible. And no, I would not take legal action if I ricked my back. Once we had established these three points we got along fine. But sooner or later I would be asked, 'Are you Barbara's chief carer?' I knew what they meant and I knew why they had to ask it, but everything in me wanted to shout, 'No, I'm her husband.' However, I never corrected them, and as occasion demanded I used the expression about myself, but it was just another way by which our relationship was unintentionally challenged by the language used.

The words we use and how we use them do matter. In their counselling service, Paul and Helle offer some advice from their own experience. They suggest that it never hurts to ask people how they wish to be described. Generally 'people with disabilities' or 'disabled people' are acceptable, but the collective noun 'the disabled' is impersonal and defines a group that is separate from society. They suggest that there are some words and phrases that should never be used, even if we are not directly referring to people with a disability, and certainly never as a joke or insult. These include: cripple, spastic, retarded, defective, deaf and dumb, deaf as a post, blind as a bat, mentally deficient. And never use the designation 'the handicapped.'

Similarly, there is a way of speaking that can be condescending and patronising. Some people think that they must always be light-hearted when talking to those in wheelchairs; they make constant jokes and try to keep the conversation as superficial as possible. Even some professionals think that incessant 'jolly talk' is the antidote to depression—but it isn't. Many seriously disabled patients want calm honesty rather than bubbly pretence. Long-term disabled people mostly know as much about their condition, and in some areas more so, than the medical staff. And the more senior professionals readily acknowledge this. Of course some people just don't know what to say and either sit in embarrassed silence, refusing to make any eye contact, or they address the escort or companion instead.

When Graham and Tessa were invited to a meal and Tessa came home with the comment, 'I really enjoyed today, they made me feel so normal', she gave the best compliment possible to her host family. There is no reason why conversation with disabled people should not be exactly the same as with anyone else—that usual mixture of casual quips, serious talk, passing comments on the latest news, and an enquiry into their views on this or that subject. Society often considers that 'the disabled' have few views worth listening to. Whatever their impediment or disability, be patient and wait for an answer. Paul and Helle encourage us never to be embarrassed to use common phrases that may relate to their disability like, 'See you later', or 'I'll be running along now.' That simply implies that you are not over-aware of their difference.

Those who are confined to four-wheel drive only ever see life from the perspective of an eight-year-old. And that is often just how they are treated. Generously, Tessa suggests that when people talk to her she would like them to be comfortable, so she would prefer them to sit down. What she really means, is that it is both intimidating and very uncomfortable to hold a conversation with someone who is towering four feet something above her. Barbara often confided in me, 'That person must have thought I was very rude, I didn't look at him once.' But how could she? It was physically impossible for her to look up to someone close by. Unless yours is just a brief greeting, pull up a chair and sit down; if there isn't a chair nearby, squat or kneel instead.

A few years ago, Paul was the main speaker at a club for senior citizens. He was there to introduce DisCASS, the Disabled Citizen's Advice and Support Service that he and Helle had founded. At the close of the meeting a lady came up to Helle and, totally ignoring Paul commented, 'I don't know what he said because I couldn't hear a thing. But hasn't he got lovely curly hair'—and with this she patted Paul benignly on the head. Paul was forty-three years of age! Treat adults like adults. Only call them by their first name if that familiarity is extended to everyone else present. And never by gestures or language communicate 'down' to them.

6. Canines are cowards

Dogs can sense those who are vulnerable and they go for them. And those who are vulnerable are children and people in wheelchairs. The free roaming dog will always wander over to investigate this strange human who has been cut down to their own approximate level. I frequently had to block their path and dare them to approach closer. The supposed reassurance from the owner that, 'He only wants to say "hello", he won't hurt you', was no reassurance at all. Dog-owners are often as thoughtless as their animals; they seem oblivious to the fact that when you are confined to a wheelchair you have no defence and you are very vulnerable to an inquisitive canine. By definition not too many people in a wheelchair can kick out! In Barbara's case it was hard to make owners believe that merely a swipe from a friendly tail could cause a leg ulcer that would take months to heal.

And whilst on the subject of dogs! Perhaps dog owners, like store managers, should be forced to do a spell in a wheelchair—but for a different reason. All four-wheelers will have had the disgusting experience of driving through what the dog left behind; often it is completely unavoidable, and it is particularly unpleasant for those who have to power their own chair. We all know the experience of sitting in a freezing driveway while our escort washes our wheels. On one occasion Helle had to virtually take the whole chair apart to get it clean. Perhaps worse even than this was the story of their friend who owns a guide dog. He placed the harness on the pavement whilst talking with a friend and when he picked it up...! If only dog-owners would think and clean up after their pet.

7. The lepers' corner at church

I have been surprised at how many churches in the United Kingdom still have a 'lepers' corner. It's that area designated for the wheelchairs. Usually it is right at the front of the church, sometimes side-on to the pulpit, and often, especially in larger buildings, separated from the healthy congregation by a good five metres. But at least these churches have somewhere to park their disabled. We have been to churches that have been taken completely by surprise when someone arrives on four wheels. Apologetic mumbling about, 'We must get a ramp built' or 'One day we'll get round to removing a pew', did little to reassure us of a welcome.

We were even instructed by one helpful steward at a church we visited on holiday, 'You'll find a place at the front for wheelchairs if you go round the back.' Fortunately, we were sufficiently knowledgeable of ecclesiastical jargon to understand what was the back and front of a church. For those who may not be sure, the rule generally is that you enter at the front and immediately find yourself at the back; however, the quickest way to get to the front is usually to enter at the back. Eventually we did find a place at the front, once we had negotiated the labyrinth of corridors at the back. In fact we found plenty of 'place' because the rest of the congregation were so far removed that they stood no danger of catching whatever we had. My family giggled their way irreverently through the service!

Among our own constituency we were more forthright. At one church, Barbara was led to the front, side on to the pulpit of course, and left there alone. I normally saw that she was settled before I went to pray with the church leaders, but on this occasion I had omitted to. From the pulpit I felt for her in her splendid isolation. However, there were times when Barbara considered it in everybody's best interest to hear the truth, and this was one of those times! She informed a deacon and his wife after the service, 'If I was looking for a church to attend in this area, I would never return to this one.' The chastened leaders ensured that in the evening service Barbara would be dutifully chaperoned in the lepers' corner.

Some churches can do nothing to give wheelchair users a choice of seating, and it may not be their fault. The building may be too small or the layout too fixed, and no disabled person should be so unreasonable as to expect to have as wide a choice as those with only two legs. However, churches should never assume that disabled people prefer to sit at the back, or the front. Like everyone else, they have preferences, and some may need to be close by an easy exit.

Every church, even if they have never had a wheelchair visitor in two decades, should ask what they would do if just such a person arrived next Sunday. Could they get into the building? Where would they be seated? What if they needed the toilet facilities? And remember that even a small wheelchair, with foot rests and stabilisers, can be at least four feet long and two feet wide. They are admittedly greedy for room, and they have to have space to manoeuvre. Not every building can cope adequately, but every steward or welcomer, should be able to cope calmly and efficiently. Occasionally we have felt a real nuisance and sometimes Barbara wished that she had stayed home.

Churches ought to be aware that the Disability Discrimination Act imposes upon all public buildings, including churches, the responsibility to have 'taken reasonable steps' by October 1999 to provide services and facilities for the disabled that do not involve structural changes to the premises. Those that do involve structural changes must be implemented by 2004. The Government has provided a Disability Discrimination Act helpline: 0345 622 633.

Finally

Most of this chapter is simply common sense, and it is not intended to make anyone over-sensitive to the needs of those on four wheels. Fortunately our society is becoming more and more aware of disabled people and of their special requirements. Although by no means all those with disabilities are elderly; by the end of the first decade of the new millennium, 5% of the population in the United Kingdom will be over eighty years of age. Certainly as medical skill advances and the percentage of elderly in the population increases, wheelchairs and scooters become a growth industry.

Perhaps we are slowly becoming aware of the fact that those in wheelchairs have exactly the same rights as all other members of the community. We provide nappy-changing facilities for the very young (not 'baby-changing' please—few mothers are really interested in that!), extra help for the elderly, laws to protect vulnerable children, cycle lanes for the greener members of the community, and lifts for us all. The systematic extension of help to enable those using a wheelchair to integrate fully into society should be seen as obvious. On the other hand, four-wheelers have their own significant part to play. To be over-demanding does nobody any favours, and those who insist on driving their small machine at six miles an hour down a busy road are hardly encouraging others to give them credit for common sense.

However, with all the physical changes to the infrastructure of society, a far more important change must be in our mind-set. It is the way we think of, look at and speak about those who are disabled that really matters. If we change here, the rest will follow. We must abandon for ever the ingrained concepts of contemporary society that measure value by economics, quality by activity and meaning by production. All who are disabled on four wheels, two legs, or are simply immobile, together with those who share with and care for their disability, can find purpose and worth in this life. John Wesley, the eighteenth century evangelist and founder of Methodism, offered his own prescription for old age, and he might equally have offered it to those who were disabled, 'Take tar-water every morning and evening... or a decoction of nettles... or be electrified... But remember, the only radical cure is wrought by death.' Although the ultimate has not changed, there are now vastly better options in the meantime!

For those who have a Christian faith, which is all of us recorded in this book, we have the confidence of knowing that God is with us now, and in addition we enjoy the assurance of a future of perfect healing beyond this life. Until then, we all firmly believe that there is real meaning and value for every life. Those who work to overcome disabilities contribute more to society than is generally appreciated. If society would take more notice of them, they will help it to re-assess its priorities, re-align its concerns, and re-evaluate its estimate of people. We hope that our stories have shown this, and we are confident that the ultimate cure really is a cure. Until then, although it may at times be difficult, it is never impossible to discover the value of meanwhile as we extend our horizons of hope.

Also from Day One

The Lord's Prayer for today

Derek Prime

A5 paperback
163 pages   £5.95

The Lord's Prayer is the only pattern prayer that the Lord Jesus provided and is absolutely timeless in its purpose and function. Many readers of this book tell us that it provides an essential reminder of The Lord's Prayer's truths which are unchanging. At its very beginning, The Lord's Prayer reminds us that true worship of God arises from a living relationship with Him as our Father through our Lord Jesus Christ. If you have overlooked the value of this timeless prayer *The Lord's Prayer for today* may be exactly what you need.

REFERENCE: LP
ISBN 0 902548 68 9

"Many have undervalued this prayer...this book will help to redress the balance. "

Evangelical Times

The Ten Commandments for today

Brian H. Edwards

A5 paperback
288 pages   £8.99

At a time when the nation's morality is in alarming decline, it is surprising that so little has been written on the Ten Commandments. Brian Edwards gives us a modern commentary, carefully uncovering their true meaning, and applying them incisively to our contemporary society.

REFERENCE: 10T
ISBN 0 902548 69 7

"Brian Edwards' book finds a well deserved place at the cutting edge of application of this important theme."

The Banner of Truth Magazine

For further information about these and other Day One titles, call or write to us:

01372 728 300

www.dayone.co.uk

Day One 3 Epsom Business Park Kiln Lane Epsom Surrey KT17 1JF England

E–Mail: sales@dayone.co.uk

The Beatitudes for today

John Blanchard

A5 paperback

263 pages   £7.95

There are many excellent volumes on the Sermon on the Mount, but few which provide a full-length treatment of the Beatitudes. This excellent book by evangelist John Blanchard helps to fill that gap.

REFERENCE: BEAT

ISBN 0 902548 98 0

"The quality of the doctrinal and practical content is of the highest order.

A stimulating, humbling, encouraging, practical treatment of the Beatitudes in a very readable style"

Christopher Bennett, Evangelicals Now

No Longer Two

Brian and Barbara Edwards

Large format paperback

144 pages   £6.99

With over half of all marriages in the United Kingdom ending in the tragedy of divorce, it is more necessary than ever that every marriage should begin on a firm foundation. No Longer Two is the fruit of the authors' thirty years experience in counselling couples both before and during marriage. Whilst the book begins with engagement and includes two chapters on planning the wedding day, it will also prove valuable for those already married. *No Longer Two* offers an exciting way of working together at building a strong marriage based upon the clear teaching and common sense of the Bible. Whether or not you are familiar with the Bible, you will find *No Longer Two* easy to work through

ISBN 1 903087 00 7

REFERENCE: NL2

For further information about these and other Day One titles, call or write to us:

01372 728 300

www.dayone.co.uk

Day One   3 Epsom Business Park   Kiln Lane   Epsom   Surrey   KT17 1JF England

E–Mail: sales@dayone.co.uk

Hallmarks of Design
Evidence of design in the natural world

Stuart Burgess

A5 paperback
200 pages   £6.99

"Dr Stuart Burgess writes in plain, easy-to-understand terms of the complexity and beauty of living creatures all around us. God has placed His hallmark on creation, and it is this argument that Dr Stuart Burgess brilliantly expounds. Readers of this book will be intrigued by the delightful summary of example after example, showing hallmarks of design in the natural world. Armed with this material, many scientists and non-scientists alike will by God's grace, have their eyes opened as to the shallowness of evolutionary philosophy."

From the Preface by Dr Andy McIntosh, DSc, FIMA, CMath, FInstE, CEng Reader in Combustion Theory, Department of Fuel & Energy, The University of Leeds

"In this excellent book, Dr Stuart Burgess uses his expert knowledge of design in engineering to present compelling evidence of design in the complex systems of the natural world."

Alan Linton, Emeritus Professor of Bacteriology
Formerly Head of Department of Microbiology, Bristol University

REFERENCE: HAL
ISBN 1 903087 013

For further information about these and other Day One titles, call or write to us:

01372 728 300
www.dayone.co.uk

Day One 3 Epsom Business Park Kiln Lane Epsom Surrey KT17 1JF England

E–Mail: sales@dayone.co.uk